ANIMAL RIGHTS

D1826461

Animal Rights

The Changing Debate

Edited by

Robert Garner
Lecturer in Politics
University of Leicester

First published 1996 by
MACMILLAN PRESS LTD
Houndmills, Basingstoke, Hampshire RG21 6XS
and London
Companies and representatives
throughout the world

ISBN 0-333-61582-4 hardcover
ISBN 0-333-67484-7 paperback

A catalogue record for this book is available
from the British Library.

10 9   8   7   6   5   4   3   2   1
05 04 03 02 01 00 99 98 97 96

Printed in Great Britain by J.W. Arrowsmith, Bristol

Contents

Preface   vii

Notes on the Contributors   viii

Introduction: The Forward March of Animals Halted?   xi

Part I   Animal Rights, Moral Theory and Political Strategy   1

1   Animal Liberation
Peter Singer   7

2   Animal Rights: An Eco-Socialist View
Ted Benton   19

3   Animal Rights: An Incremental Approach
Gary L. Francione   42

Part II   Medical Science, Agriculture and Animal Welfare   61

4   Partial Protection: Animal Welfare and the Law
Mike Radford   67

5   To Farm Without Harm and Choosing a Humane Diet:
The Bioethics of Humane Sustainable Agriculture
Michael W. Fox   92

6   The Use of Animals in Experimentation: An Examination of
the 'Technical' Arguments Used to Criticize the Practice
Andrew N. Rowan   104

Part III   Animal Rights and the Political Process   123

7   The American Animal Rights Movement
James M. Jasper   129

8   Animal Welfare and the European Union
Rosemary Goddard Svendsen   143

9   Putting Animals Into Politics
Richard D. Ryder   166

10 Utopian Visions and Pragmatic Politics: Challenging the
    Foundations of Speciesism and Misothery
    Kim Stallwood   194

Bibliography   209
Index   214

Preface

This volume of articles was conceived as a result of the recognition that it had been over ten years since a similar volume (*In Defence of Animals*, edited by Peter Singer) had been published and that since the mid-1980s there had been significant developments which required mulling over. Not least, I think, is the growing acceptance that animal welfare (if not quite animal rights) has become a mainstream issue worthy of pressure group action and considered government response. It seemed appropriate, therefore, to ask a number of leading scholars and activists to consider the past, present and future of animal protection.

I wish to thank the contributors for producing their chapters efficiently and speedily, and Richard Ryder in particular who has very generously given me much support and encouragement over the past couple of years or so. I also owe a debt of gratitude to Clare Andrews who, when working as a commissioning editor for Macmillan, encouraged me to submit the book proposal in the first place. I hope she enjoys the final product.

Robert Garner
Leicester, March 1996

Notes on Contributors

Ted Benton is Professor of Sociology at the University of Essex, UK. He is the author of a number of books including *The Rise and Fall of Structural Marxism* and *Natural Relations*, the latter being an attempt to apply Marxist thought to animal rights and eco-philosophy.

Michael Fox is Vice President of the Farm Animals and Bioethics section of the Humane Society of the United States. He studied veterinary medicine in Britain and the United States and also taught psychology at Washington University between 1969 and 1976. Dr Fox has written numerous books including *Returning to Eden: Animal Rights and Human Responsibility*, published in 1986.

Gary Francione is Professor of Law and Nicholas de B. Katzenbach Scholar of Law at Rutgers University, Newark. Francione has been active in the American animal rights movement for many years and is co-director of the Rutgers Animal Rights Law Center. In 1995 he published *Animals, Property and the Law*, a damning indictment of the failure of the legal system to protect animals.

Rosemary Goddard Svendsen is a freelance writer specialising in European legislation on animal welfare and conservation. She contributes a regular section on this subject to *Dyrevennen*, the bimonthly magazine of the Danish animal welfare society.

James Jasper teaches sociology at New York University and is the author of numerous articles and books on social movements including *The Animal Rights Crusade* written with Dorothy Nelkin.

Mike Radford is lecturer in law at the University of East Anglia, UK. His course on animal welfare law, which has been running since 1993, was the first of its kind in a British university.

Andrew Rowan is a Professor in Tufts University School of Veterinary Medicine and is also Director of the Tufts Center for Animals and Public Policy. He received a DPhil in biochemistry from Oxford University and worked for several animal societies on the issue of animal research and alternatives. He is the author of *Of Mice Models and Men*.

Richard Ryder is one of the best known figures in the animal rights movement. He is currently Political Consultant to the Political Animal Lobby. He was an experimental psychologist at Cambridge, a social psychologist in New York, a clinical psychologist in Oxford and was Chairman of the RSPCA Council between 1977 and 1979. He has campaigned for animal rights in Britain and abroad since 1969 and has published on the issue widely, inventing the term *speciesism* in 1970.

Peter Singer, currently Professor of Philosophy and Director of the Centre for Human Bioethics at Monash University in Melbourne, is one of the best known figures in the animal protection movement. He is best known for *Animal Liberation*, originally published in 1975 and credited by many as a key influence in the development of the modern animal protection movement. He is also author of *Practical Ethics*, now a classic introduction to applied ethics.

Kim Stallwood is currently Editor in Chief of the American animal rights journal *The Animals' Agenda*. Before taking on this role, he occupied a senior position with People for the Ethical Treatment of Animals which he took on after emigrating from the UK. In the 1970s and 1980s, Stallwood was active in the British animal rights movement being particularly involved with the British Union for the Abolition of Vivisection and the co-ordination of the animal rights response to the legislation on animal experimentation introduced in the 1980s.

Introduction: The Forward March of Animals Halted?

It is over twenty years now since the publication of Peter Singer's *Animal Liberation* (1975), a work which has been widely regarded as the pivotal intellectual contribution aiding the revitalisation and radicalisation of the animal protection movement. Much has happened in those 20 years and, as we approach the end of the century, it is an appropriate juncture to stand back from what has been a dynamic period in order to consider how the – now mature – movement to protect animals has developed, what it has been able to achieve for animals and what future challenges it faces. This is the remit for the collection of articles presented in this volume. Written by leading scholars and activists on both sides of the Atlantic, the contributions are divided into three sections. The first concerns the relationship between the moral status of animals and the type of strategies that the animal protection movement ought to pursue. The second focuses on the ways in which animals are treated, and ought to be treated, in specific contexts and the third considers, broadly defined, the nature of animal protection politics.

The revitalisation of the animal protection movement over the past 20 years or so has been accompanied – and is, at least partly, explained – by the development of a greater radicalism (Garner, 1993a; Finsen & Finsen, 1994; Jasper & Nelkin, 1992). Central here is that the claims made on behalf of animals have been increasingly couched in the language of rights, thereby relegating the previously dominant notions of welfare, kindness and charity. A number of thinkers and activists – such as Peter Singer, Tom Regan, Richard Ryder and Andrew Linzey, to name but a few – were responsible for providing intellectual justifications for granting a higher moral status to animals, and their ideas helped to legitimise an already emerging movement concerned with righting what were perceived as fundamental injustices. As a consequence of this greater radicalism, the preoccupation within the animal protection movement, and to some extent beyond, has been transformed from a concern about individual aberrant acts of cruelty to animals, to an emphasis on what are seen as the fundamental injustices of the institutional exploitation of literally billions of animals in laboratories and on factory farms.

This revitalisation and radicalisation has led to the arrival of animal protection on the political agenda. The multi-faceted challenges to the use of animals in agriculture and science strike at the heart of major government responsibilities and represent a serious threat to the legitimacy of powerful economic interests. Greater public awareness of animal abuse, resulting – at least in part – from high-profile campaigns, has forced decision-makers to consider reform, and those whose interests are served by continuing to exploit animals without interference have had to mobilise to defend themselves. Intermittently, the politics of animal protection has – particularly in Britain – become a high-profile issue, although most of the time it simmers below the surface failing to emerge as a crucial vote decider at election times, regularly being ambushed by anthropocentric concerns usually of an economic nature.

Whatever the frustrations animal protectionists feel about this situation, though, it needs to be said that significant strides have been made. Until the 1970s, animal welfare – let alone rights – was only rarely a subject of political discourse and the fate of animals was in the hands of cosy policy communities consisting of government officials and representatives from those industries and organisations with a vested interest in continuing to exploit animals (Garner, 1995b). Since then, some concrete achievements can be pointed to. Some of these – the decline of the fur industry, the increasing popularity of 'cruelty-free' products and a vegetarian diet – have occurred, in Britain and the United States, as a result of direct appeals to consumers thereby bypassing the political arena. Some legislative dents, too, have been made in the structure of factory farming and animal experimentation. As Mike Radford's article in this volume shows, animals are at least partially protected in Britain and, in the United States, whilst less progress has been made, Congress has shown increasing interest in animal protection and a series of measures have at least secured some protection for laboratory animals in addition to asserting the general principle that the treatment of animals should be subject to regulatory control.

THE FUTURE OF ANIMAL RIGHTS

These successes – of radicalisation, recognition and limited reform – raise the question of where the animal protection movement goes from here. For whilst the movement has grown and matured and the issue of animal protection is now taken much more seriously, governments and the movement's opponents have also had time to develop a coherent response of their own. As a consequence, the novelty value of animal rights campaigns has diminished, the propaganda field is no longer left open to animal advocates (see Finsen & Finsen, 1994, ch.5), and governments have attempted to take the heat out of the debate by making limited concessions

(Garner, 1995b). In the area of animal experimentation, to take one example, it is clear that the Animal Welfare Acts in the United States and the 1986 Animals (Scientific Procedures) Act in Britain have blunted the campaign for further reform and yet, for animal advocates, these measures are clearly inadequate and not just from an animal rights perspective.

The articles in this volume do not offer any panaceas. However, insofar as a pattern does emerge from the widely divergent perspectives represented, the contributions do, explicitly or implicitly, explore the relationship between moral theory and political practice.

There are a number of related dimensions to this emerging debate. In the first place, the promotion of animal rights has been the source of some division within the animal protection movement. Clearly, the *objectives* of rightists and welfarists differ, advocates of the former denying that it is morally permissible to exploit animals for the benefit of humans (or other animals) whilst proponents of the latter seek to ensure that animals are exploited only when the human benefits of so doing are reasonably substantial. This distinction only becomes problematic when it causes divisions over strategy. Unfortunately, this has happened. During the passage of the Animals (Scientific Procedures) Bill, for instance, the British animal protection movement was seriously split. Whilst a coalition of moderates (including the Committee to Reform Animal Experimentation, the Fund for the Replacement of Animals in Scientific Experiments and the British Veterinary Association) supported the Bill and were prepared to enter into negotiations with government, a substantial number of animal rights groups (including the British Union for the Abolition of Vivisection, the National Anti-Vivisection Society and Animal Aid) mobilised against the measure because, amongst other things, it did not prohibit any particular kind of procedure (Garner, 1993a, pp. 205–11).

The suspicions of animal rightists over welfarist measures has been articulated by Tom Regan and Gary Francione (1992. See also Francione, 1995). In this volume, Francione provides an exposition of this view arguing that animal welfare does not work, even in terms of the limited objectives it sets itself, and that only a strategy based upon animal rights norms has any long-term chance of achieving effective protection for animals. Francione's advocacy of what he calls 'incremental abolitionism' does, to some extent, answer the charge that animal rights is an all-or-nothing position with no realistic practical application. By furnishing criteria by which animal rightists can support incremental change it also provides some grounds on which rights and welfare advocates can unite. Conversely, it may be argued that – since there are many types of reformist measures (reducing, for instance, the number of animals used in scientific experiments) which, if

Professor Francione's arguments are adopted, rights advocates ought not to support – his approach is a source of division within the animal protection movement. Moreover, as the articles in this book by Mike Radford, Rosemary Goddard Svendsen and Richard Ryder demonstrate, it is difficult enough to persuade decision-makers to take on board moderate animal welfare proposals without introducing additional constraints, limiting what animal rights groups ought to be focusing on.

Another dimension of this debate relates to the ability of rights theory (whether applied to animals or humans) to achieve the purpose it is designed for. In this context, Ted Benton, in an innovative approach summarised in chapter 2 of this book, draws upon radical socialist and feminist critiques of rights to point out a potential conflict between the formal distribution of rights and the ability of rights-holders to exercise them in practice (see Benton, 1993). This has enormous implications for the adequate protection of those numerous nonhuman animals who are exploited in institutionalised settings – in factory farms and laboratories. Clearly, the traditional liberal-individualist notion of rights – the approach adopted by Regan – which emphasises not interfering with a being's pursuit of her own welfare, is inadequate when seen in the context of the positive responsibilities required to achieve the well-being of such animals.

Even if such a positive conception of rights was to be adopted, however, it is not clear to whom responsibility for factory farmed or laboratory animals is to be assigned. Is it, for instance, the wage worker on the farm, the retailer or consumer of the resulting product, or indeed, the owners of the farm? This, of course, is unanswerable since all are wheels in the cog of a *system* of exploitation. As a consequence, since it might be argued that the 'requirement for rights is ... only a symptom of social pathology and moral disintegration' Benton suggests that one response, relevant to both humans and animals, is to abandon rights theory completely and seek a radical transformation of society whereby values (of benevolence and co-operation) would replace the conflict and competition which make rights necessary in the first place. As Benton points out in his contribution, 'transformed social relations between humans and animals in the direction of eliminating the kinds of institution-alised "reification" and "commodification" ... might be expected to facilitate more benign and compassionate moral sentiments'. In other words, according to this view, it is not the successful application of rights to animals that will lead to their emancipation. On the contrary, the purpose for which rights theory was utilised in the first place (that is the securing of the well-being of animals) will only be achieved, or at the very least, made easier, through a social transformation which leads to a change in human attitudes towards animals.

Some problems with Benton's approach are outlined in the introduction to Part I. There is a third, related, dimension however, which builds upon Benton's central linkage between concern for humans and animals. It has been noted how those involved in the early Victorian days of the animal protection movement were also involved with other social issues – slavery, child labour, women's suffrage and so forth (see Ryder, 1989). Despite this, what is striking about the modern ideology of animal rights is the extent to which its practical expression excludes alliances with other human-based or anthropocentric social movements. In particular, the relationship between animal rights and environmentalism (causes which would seem to have a great deal in common) is strained. The reason for this, as Jim Jasper points out in chapter 7, is that environmentalism is predominantly concerned with protecting nature for human benefits, therefore precluding the perception that animals should be protected for their own sake because they have inherent value, irrespective of the human benefits accruing (Garner, 1994). Likewise, the focus on animal rights divorces the case for the better treatment of animals from other human-centred concerns for, for example, public health, consumer protection and women's issues.

It might be argued that this failure to build alliances with other groups is unfortunate. This is particularly the case when it is seen in the light of the claims that there are important human interests (economic, medical and so forth) that are served by the institutional exploitation of animals. Given this, the fact that there are also considerable human interests – related to the reliability of using animals in the laboratory, and the environmental and public health implications of factory farming (as emphasised in the chapter by Michael Fox in this book) – served by reforms to these processes becomes even more pertinent. These human benefits, secured in tandem with the more compassionate treatment of animals, are explored in the chapters by Andrew Rowan and Michael Fox. Thus, Rowan assesses the technical merits of the practical anti-vivisection case which suggests that the experimental use of animals is not only morally illegitimate but also does not produce the human benefits claimed for it. In a more polemical fashion, Fox calls for an approach to factory farming which recognises the interdependence between animal and human suffering.

The purpose of the above discussion is not to deny the contribution animal rights has made to the modern development of animal protection, the moral validity of the case for granting animals a higher moral status or, necessarily, the future viability of animal rights. What it and the proceeding chapters seek to do is to open up the debate on the utility of animal rights with a view to aiding the further development of the animal protection movement throughout the rest of this decade and beyond.

Part I: Animal Rights, Moral Theory and Political Strategy

In the last two decades or so, the discipline of applied ethics has become a significant growth area in academic circles (see Singer, 1993). Within this broad discipline, an increasing number of professional philosophers have shown a particular interest in the moral status of nonhuman animals. Given this, and more importantly, the additional fact already noted that the writings of some of these philosophers have coincided with a movement which seeks to put their principles into action, it is appropriate to begin this collection of articles with a section which focuses on the theoretical attempts to justify for animals a higher moral status than has traditionally, in theory and practice, been allowed.

This philosophical project, of course, is not new. Indeed, modern proponents of an elevated moral status for animals often draw inspiration from thinkers as diverse as Jeremy Bentham (as Singer does), Albert Schweitzer and the little known Henry Salt (see, for instance, Clarke & Linzey, 1990). What marks the period since the 1970s out, however, is the sheer scale of the battering handed out to the moral orthodoxy about animals (see Garner, 1993a, ch.1). Such is the volume of material that has been produced, in learned papers and popular books, that it would be inaccurate to claim that there is only one radical approach to which all others are either imitators or footnotes (see Finsen & Finsen, 1994, ch.6 for an accessible discussion of the differences between the major contributors). Without doubt, though, for whatever reasons, the two major intellectual figures in the contemporary animal rights movement are Peter Singer and Tom Regan and it is appropriate, therefore, that the three chapters in this section are concerned above all with their arguments.

The Moral Case For Animal Rights

The opening chapter is an edited extract of Singer's review of the ground-breaking collection of articles *Animals, Men and Morals* edited by three Oxford philosophers (Godlovitch, Godlovitch & Harris, 1973) and represents his first published work on animal ethics. As Singer himself remarked in the preface to *Animal Liberation* in 1975: 'five years ago I myself would have laughed at the statements (about animal liberation) I have now written in complete seriousness'. The review article presented here provided an important step in the development of Singer's thought and the positive

1

response generated from the piece encouraged him to set about the task of writing *Animal Liberation.*

It is not the purpose of this book to enter into a detailed philosophical exploration of the strengths and weaknesses of the case for granting a higher moral status to animals (a general account can be found in Garner, 1993a. A useful set of articles is in Hospers, 1987. Book-length studies opposing the idea of animal rights are Frey, 1980; Frey, 1983; Caruthers, 1992; Leahy, 1991). This is not to claim that such an exercise is unnecessary. As Benton asserts, whether or not we accept Singer or Regan's position, the attempt to link the suffering of animals with oppressed human groups only works if one assumes that nonhuman animals are 'sentient beings, with ends, preferences, and a capacity to suffer harm and experience well-being' (the same applies to the attempt to link animal suffering with the position of ethnic minorities, women – see Adams, 1990 – and, in the past, slaves – see Spiegal, 1988). The difference between Singer's utilitarian defence of animals and Regan's rights-based approach is clearly crucial from a philosophical perspective and, in recognition of this, Benton spends some time examining the pros and cons of each position, eventually plumping to focus on the rights position after recognising the 'powerful arguments' against utilitarianism. Francione comes to a similar conclusion. In practical terms, Singer has felt comfortable to be labelled as a rights advocate although he does not think the use of rights discourse is necessary to secure adequate protection for animals, a view disputed by Regan and, as intimated above, by Benton and Francione also (see Singer, 1985 and Regan, 1985).

Benton himself largely accepts Regan's claim that animals have rights as beings with an interest in respectful treatment. He also suggests, however, that one can distinguish between two different kinds of rights-holders. It is a common criticism of the animal rights position that what distinguishes humans from animals morally is the ability of the former to understand what it is to behave morally and the ability to reciprocate by upholding the moral entitlements of others. This is linked to the greater mental capacities of humans which means, it is argued, that we can be harmed in ways which animals cannot. In order to sidestep this problem, Regan (as does Singer) invokes the so-called 'argument from marginal cases' whereby it is suggested that moral equity demands that those humans – such as infants and the mentally defective – whose mental capacities are closer to those of normal adult mammals than to normal human adults, should be granted a moral status closer to the former than the latter. As Singer indicates in chapter 1, failure to do so is to be guilty of what Richard Ryder has termed 'speciesism' – discriminating on the basis of species alone and not due to morally relevant criteria (Ryder, 1989). Since we do not intuitively think it is right to eat and experiment on infants or the mentally defective, the argument goes, it is inconsistent to be prepared to do these things to animals.

Benton accepts much of this argument but still insists that it is possible to distinguish morally between infants, human defectives and animals (so-called 'moral patients'), on the one hand, and normal adult humans (or 'moral agents') on the other. Thus, he argues that the rights that can be properly assigned to moral patients are 'passive' whilst the rights assigned to moral agents are 'active' rights of self-determination. The difference here is that only those with 'active' rights are entitled, and able, to contribute to deciding what the content of their rights should be and, consequently, the obligations which others are to be expected to obey. Those with 'passive' rights, on the other hand, do not determine the nature of their rights and obligations and therefore other moral agents are responsible for ensuring their well-being. This, Benton alleges, means we have to take into account the species-specific requirements of moral patients which, in turn, allows us to recognise that animals and humans may be differentially treated without denying that animals do have rights (of a passive nature) which ought to be protected.

Animal Rights and Political Reality

Singer's and Regan's work on the moral status of animals has been available now for over two decades. Although his major book-length study *The Case for Animal Rights* was not published until 1983, Regan had been developing his position in journal articles dating back to 1975 (the early articles can be found in Regan, 1982). The debate now has become somewhat stale, not least because of the intractability of moral theory. Moreover, by definition, those involved in the animal rights movement accept that serious wrongs are being done to animals and, for them, of greater import is the way in which theory can inform practice – in the sense of strategy rather than objectives. To this end, the contributions by Benton and Francione do move the debate on in interesting directions.

We have already outlined Benton's powerful challenge to the utility of rights language in the absence of significant social reform. In the case of animals, he raises the challenging proposition that the removal of human indifference to, and participation in, animal suffering is to a large extent independent of the rational application of reasoned moral theory. The problem with this conclusion, it might be argued, is that it is derived from a theory which, although having a long and honourable history when related to human society, does not work so well when applied to relationships across the species divide. Thus, the argument – (i) that human rights are worthless without the ability of the holders to exercise them, (ii) that in order to make this a reality significant social reform may be necessary, and (iii) that significant social reform may alter the way that humans behave towards each other – is persuasive. When this is applied to animals, however, it loses a great deal of its force. On one reading it amounts to saying that only when the institutionalised exploitation of animals is abolished will humans develop more benevolent ways of thinking about their relationship with animals. This is clearly absurd and not, I take it, what Benton is arguing. Even a more generous interpretation, however, along the lines that more benevolent ways of thinking about our relationship with other animals can derive from sources other than the rational espousal of rights theory, is, whilst possible, still inadequate. This is so because it does not provide a more plausible alternative approach which can hope to engender such a change in values and, indeed, animal rights theory has been important precisely because it has provided a means by which present methods of treating animals can be declared as unacceptable.

Gary Francione, in direct contrast to Ted Benton, seeks to claim that animal rights is not only effective as a philosophical position but ought also to inform the strategy of the animal rights movement. This is so, he argues, because reformist welfare-based strategies – whereby animal suffering is to be balanced against the benefits likely to accrue to humans – do not provide even the most basic protection for animals let alone providing a means to the abolitionist animal rights objective. This conclusion is partly based on empirical observation which shows that the institutional exploitation of animals carries on apace despite numerous welfare measures designed to alleviate suffering. Indeed, the effect of welfare measures may well, according to this view, be to prolong the existence of animal exploitation since it makes it seem more respectable. More importantly, Francione suggests in addition that welfarism will *always* fail to alleviate animal suffering because it coexists with, and fails to challenge, the structural reality that animals remain in law as mere objects of property (a point also emphasised by Radford in chapter 4). Thus, in societies where property rights are predominant, they will more often than not override animal welfare by 'determining the ambit of protection accorded to animals by law' (this thesis is worked out in full in Francione, 1995).

By contrast to the poverty of welfarism, Francione suggests that animal rights can provide the necessary framework for effective incremental advances in animal protection. Thus, only changes that are themselves abolitionist are likely to be effective since they avoid the need to engage in the trading of human and animal interests (which always works to the advantage of the former) and the replacement of one exploitative regime by another (that is, larger battery cages rather than no cages at all), both characteristic weaknesses of the welfarist position.

Professor Francione provides an important corrective to the simplistic view that animal rights is always politically unrealistic. As a number of people have pointed out, however, his analysis does have its problems, a selection of which can be briefly stated here. (See also Finsen & Finsen, 1994, ch.8; Garner, 1993a, pp. 246–9; Newkirk, 1992.) In the first place, as Francione himself admits, the interdependency of animal exploitation means in practice that the distinction between abolitionist and reformist measures is not always clear-cut. Thus, the abolition of product testing does not mean that the animals designated for it will not be exploited in other procedures. Likewise, a seemingly abolitionist campaign to prohibit the production of veal would still mean that farmers would have to deal with (kill at birth?) those male calves destined to be raised for veal, unless, of course, the dairy trade was also prohibited so that the surplus male calves were not produced in the first place. Moreover, such abolitionist objectives are also open to the criticism (levelled by animal rightists at welfarist reforms) that they hinder further progress by making remaining practices look more respectable.

A further objection is that attempts to distinguish between welfare and rights strategies are likely to be a source of conflict with welfare organisations resentful at the refusal of rights groups to participate in winnable reformist campaigns. Of course, Francione would deny that such welfarist campaigns are worthwhile so we would also need to show that this was not the case. Here, it can be argued that, whilst Francione is right to point to weaknesses in existing animal welfare measures, we need to distinguish between adequate and inadequate reforms. Thus, one can criticise, for instance, the Animal Welfare Act in the United States but not necessarily on the grounds that it is a reformist (non-abolitionist) measure but on the grounds that it is an *inadequate* reformist measure. By itself, though, this does not mean that there are no effective reforms that can be made short of abolishing a particular practice. Put simply, is it not the case that fewer animals used in scientific experimentation is better than more and, similarly, more room for battery hens is better than less?

Francione would still claim, however, that such reformist measures – involving the weighting of human and animal interests – will rarely, because of the property status of the latter, result in the alleviation of animal suffering. This, I think, is a powerful objection. However, it might be suggested in response that deference to property ownership varies from country to country (greater, for instance, in the United States than in the United Kingdom) and from one period of time to another (depending on prevailing governmental ideologies and historical circumstances). Likewise, what constitutes *unnecessary* suffering will depend upon the social climate and, as Benton argues, is not necessarily dependent upon the application of rights theory to animals. It can be agreed that without a major value shift, the pursuit of welfare goals is unlikely to produce major advances for animals. The point is that legislative success tends to be the final stage of a long process whereby a particular goal has become socially acceptable. Here, the philosophy of animal rights can play an important, although by no means indispensable, role.

1 Animal Liberation[1]

Peter Singer

We are familiar with Black Liberation, Gay Liberation, and a variety of other movements. With Women's Liberation some thought we had come to the end of the road. Discrimination on the basis of sex, it has been said, is the last form of discrimination that is universally accepted and practised without pretence, even in those liberal circles which have long prided themselves on their freedom from racial discrimination. But one should always be wary of talking of 'the last remaining form of discrimination'. If we have learned anything from the liberation movements, we should have learned how difficult it is to be aware of the ways in which we discriminate until they are forcefully pointed out to us. A liberation movement demands an expansion of our moral horizons, so that practices that were previously regarded as natural and inevitable are now seen as intolerable.

Animals, Men and Morals (Godlovitch, Godlovitch and Harris, 1973) is a manifesto for an Animal Liberation movement. The contributors to the book may not all see the issue this way. They are a varied group. Philosophers, ranging from professors to graduate students, make up the largest contingent. There are five of them, including the three editors, and there is also an extract from the unjustly neglected German philosopher with an English name, Leonard Nelson, who died in 1927. There are essays by two novelists/critics, Brigid Brophy and Maureen Duffy, and another by Muriel the Lady Dowding, widow of Dowding of Battle of Britain fame and the founder of 'Beauty Without Cruelty', a movement that campaigns against the use of animals for furs and cosmetics. The other pieces are by a psychologist, a botanist, a sociologist, and Ruth Harrison, who is probably best described as a professional campaigner for animal welfare.

Whether or not these people, as individuals, would all agree that they are launching a liberation movement for animals, the book as a whole amounts to no less. It is a demand for a complete change in our attitudes to nonhumans. It is a demand that we cease to regard the exploitation of other species as natural and inevitable, and that, instead, we see it as a continuing moral outrage. Patrick Corbett, Professor of Philosophy at Sussex University, captures the spirit of the book in his closing words:

> ... we require now to extend the great principles of liberty, equality and fraternity over the lives of animals. Let animal slavery join human slavery in the graveyard of the past.

7

The reader is likely to be sceptical. 'Animal Liberation' sounds more like a parody of liberation movements than a serious objective. The reader may think: We support the claims of blacks and women for equality because blacks and women really are equal to whites and males – equal in intelligence and in abilities, capacity for leadership, rationality, and so on. Humans and nonhumans obviously are not equal in these respects. Since justice demands only that we treat equals equally, unequal treatment of humans and nonhumans cannot be an injustice.

This is a tempting reply, but a dangerous one. It commits the non-racist and non-sexist to a dogmatic belief that blacks and women really are just as intelligent, able and so on, as whites and males – and no more. Quite possibly this happens to be the case. Certainly attempts to prove that racial or sexual differences in these respects have a genetic origin have not been conclusive. But do we really want to stake our demand for equality on the assumption that there are no genetic differences of this kind between the different races or sexes? Surely the appropriate response to those who claim to have found evidence for such genetic differences is not to stick to the belief that there are no differences, whatever the evidence to the contrary; rather one should be clear that the claim to equality does not depend on IQ. Moral equality is distinct from factual equality. Otherwise it would be nonsense to talk of the equality of human beings, since humans, as individuals, obviously differ in intelligence and almost any ability one cares to name. If possessing greater intelligence does not entitle one human to exploit another, why should it entitle humans to exploit nonhumans?

Jeremy Bentham expressed the essential basis of equality in his famous formula: 'Each to count for one and none for more than one.' In other words, the interests of every being that has interests are to be taken into account and treated equally with the like interests of any other being. Other moral philosophers, before and after Bentham, have made the same point in different ways. Our concern for others must not depend on whether they possess certain characteristics, though just what that concern involves may, of course, vary according to such characteristics.

Bentham, incidentally, was well aware that the logic of the demand for racial equality did not stop at the equality of humans. He wrote:

The day *may* come when the rest of the animal creation may acquire those rights which never could have been withholden from them but by the hand of tyranny. The French have already discovered that the blackness of the skin is no reason why a human being should be abandoned without redress to the caprice of a tormentor. It may one day come to be recognized that the number of legs, the villosity of the skin, or the termination of the *os sacrum*, are reasons equally insufficient for abandoning a sensitive being to the same fate. What else is it that should trace the insuperable line? Is it the faculty of reason, or perhaps the faculty of discourse? But a full-grown horse or dog is beyond comparison a more rational as well as a more conversable animal, than an infant of a day, or a week, or even a month, old. But suppose they were otherwise, what would it avail? The question is not, Can they *reason*? nor Can they *talk*? but, Can they *suffer*? (Bentham, 1948, p. 311.)

Surely Bentham was right. If a being suffers, there can be no moral justification for refusing to take that suffering into consideration, and, indeed, to count it equally with the like suffering (if rough comparisons can be made) of any other being.

So the only question is: do animals other than man suffer? Most people agree unhesitatingly that animals like cats and dogs can and do suffer, and this seems also to be assumed by those laws that prohibit wanton cruelty to such animals. Personally, I have no doubt at all about this and find it hard to take seriously the doubts that a few people apparently do have ... Nevertheless, because this is such a fundamental point, it is worth asking what grounds we have for attributing suffering to other animals.

It is best to begin by asking what grounds any individual human has for supposing that other humans feel pain. Since pain is a state of consciousness, a 'mental event', it can never be directly observed. No observations, whether behavioural signs such as writing or screaming or physiological or neurological recordings, are observations of pain itself. Pain is something one feels, and one can only infer that others are feeling it from various external indications. The fact that only philosophers are ever sceptical about whether other humans feel pain shows that we regard such inference as justifiable in the case of humans.

Is there any reason why the same inference should be unjustifiable for other animals? Nearly all the external signs which lead us to infer pain in other humans can be seen in other species, especially 'higher' animals such as mammals and birds. Behavioural signs – writhing, yelping, or other forms of calling, attempts to avoid the source of pain, and many others – are present. We know, too, that these animals are biologically similar in the relevant respects, having nervous systems like ours which can be observed to function as ours do.

So the grounds for inferring that these animals can feel pain are nearly as good as the grounds for inferring other humans do. Only nearly, for there is one behavioural sign that humans have but nonhumans, with the exception of one or two specially raised chimpanzees, do not have. This, of course, is a developed language. As the quotation from Bentham indicates, this has long been regarded as an important distinction between man and other animals. Other animals may communicate with each other, but not in the way we do. Following Chomsky, many people now mark this distinction by saying that only humans communicate in a form that is governed by rules of syntax. (For the purposes of this argument, linguists allow those chimpanzees who have learned a syntactic sign language to rank as honorary humans.) Nevertheless, as Bentham pointed out, this distinction is not relevant to the question of how animals ought to be treated, unless it can be linked to the issue of whether animals suffer.

The link may be attempted in two ways. First, there is a hazy line of philosophical thought, stemming perhaps from some doctrines associated with Wittgenstein, which maintains that we cannot meaningfully attribute states of consciousness to beings without language. I have not seen this argument made explicit in print, though I have come across it in conversation.[2] This position seems to me very implausible, and I doubt that it would be held at all if it were not thought to be a consequence of a broader ˙view of the significance of language. It may be that the use of a public, rule-governed language is a pre-condition of conceptual thought. It may even be, although personally I doubt it, that we cannot meaningfully speak of a creature having an intention unless that creature can use a language. But states like pain, surely, are more primitive than either of these, and seem to have nothing to do with language.

Indeed, as Jane Goodall points out in her study of chimpanzees, when it comes to the expression of feelings and emotions, humans tend to fall back on non-linguistic modes of communication which are often found among apes, such as a cheering pat on the back, an exuberant embrace, a clasp of hands, and so on (Lawick-Goodall, 1971) ... So there seems to be no reason at all to believe that a creature without language cannot suffer.

The second, and more easily appreciated way of linking language and the existence of pain is to say that the best evidence that we can have that another creature is in pain is when he tells us that he is. This is a distinct line of argument, for it is not being denied that a non-language-user conceivably could suffer, but only that we could know that he is suffering. Still, this line of argument seems to me to fail, and for reasons similar to those just given. 'I am in pain' is not the best possible evidence that the speaker is in pain (he might be lying) and it is certainly not the only possible evidence. Behavioural signs and knowledge of the animal's biological similarity to ourselves together provide adequate evidence that animals do suffer. After all, we would not accept linguistic evidence if it contradicted the rest of the evidence. If a man was severely burned, and behaved as if he were in pain, writhing, groaning, being very careful not to let his burned skin touch anything, and so on, but later said he had not been in pain at all, we would be more likely to conclude that he was lying or suffering from amnesia than that he had not been in pain.

Even if there were stronger grounds for refusing to attribute pain to those who do not have a language, the consequences of this refusal might lead us to examine these grounds unusually critically. Human infants, as well as some adults, are unable to use language. Are we to deny that a year-old infant can suffer? If not, how can language be crucial? Of course, most parents can understand the responses of even very young infants better than they understand the responses of other animals, and sometimes infant responses can be understood in the light of later developments.

This, however, is just a fact about the relative knowledge we have of our own species, and most of this knowledge is simply derived from closer contact. Those who have studied the behaviour of other animals soon learn to understand their responses at least as well as we understand those of an infant … Just as we can understand infant human behaviour in the light of adult human behaviour, so we can understand the behaviour of other species in the light of our own behaviour (and sometimes we can understand our own behaviour better in the light of the behaviour of other species).

The grounds we have for believing that other mammals and birds suffer are, then, closely analogous to the grounds we have for believing that other humans suffer. It remains to consider how far down the evolutionary scale this analogy holds. Obviously it becomes poorer when we get further away from man. To be more precise would require a detailed examination of all that we know about other forms of life. With fish, reptiles, and other vertebrates the analogy still seems strong; with molluscs like oysters it is much weaker. Insects are more difficult, and it may be that in our present state of knowledge we must be agnostic about whether they are capable of suffering.

If there is no moral justification for ignoring suffering when it occurs, and it does occur in other species, what are we to say of our attitudes toward these other species? Richard Ryder, one of the contributors to *Animals, Men and Morals*, uses the term 'speciesism' to describe the belief that we are entitled to treat members of other species in a way in which it would be wrong to treat members of our own species. The term is not euphonious, but it neatly makes the analogy with racism. The non-racist would do well to bear the analogy in mind when he is inclined to defend human behaviour towards nonhumans. 'Shouldn't we worry about improving the lot of our own species before we concern ourselves with other species?' he may ask. If we substitute 'race' for 'species' we shall see that the question is better not asked. 'Is a vegetarian diet nutritionally adequate?' resembles the slave-owner's claim that he and the whole economy of the South would be ruined without slave labour. There is even a parallel with sceptical doubts about whether animals suffer, for some defenders of slavery professed to doubt whether blacks really suffer in the way that whites do.

I do not want to give the impression, however, that the case for Animal Liberation is based on the analogy with racism and no more. On the contrary, *Animals, Men and Morals* describes the various ways in which humans exploit nonhumans, and several contributors consider the defences that have been offered, including the defence of meat-eating mentioned in the last paragraph. Sometimes the rebuttals are scornfully dismissive, rather than carefully designed to convince the detached critic. This may be a fault, but it is a fault that is inevitable, given the kind of book this is. The issue is not one on which one can remain detached. As the editors state in their introduction:

> Once the full force of moral assessment has been made explicit there can be no rational excuse left for killing animals, be they killed for food, science, or sheer personal indulgence. We have not assembled this book to provide the reader with yet another manual on how to make brutalities less brutal. Compromise, in the traditional sense of the term, is simple unthinking weakness when one considers the actual reasons for our crude relationships with the other animals.

The point is that on this issue there are few critics who are genuinely detached. People who eat pieces of slaughtered nonhumans every day find it hard to believe that they are doing wrong; and they also find it hard to imagine what else they could eat. So for those who do not place nonhumans beyond the pale of morality, there comes a stage when further argument seems pointless, a stage at which one can only accuse one's opponents of hypocrisy ...

The logic of speciesism is most apparent in the practice of experimenting on nonhumans in order to benefit humans. This is because the issue is rarely obscured by allegations that nonhumans are so different from humans that we cannot know anything about whether they suffer. The defender of vivisection cannot use this argument because he needs to stress the similarities between man and other animals in order to justify the usefulness to the former of experiments on the latter. The researcher who makes rats choose between starvation and electric shocks to see if they develop ulcers (they do) do so because he knows that the rat has a nervous system very similar to man's, and presumably feels an electric shock in a similar way.

Richard Ryder's restrained account of experiments on animals made me angrier with my fellow man than anything else in this book ... Experimenting on animals is now a large industry, both academic and commercial. In 1969, more than five million experiments were performed in Britain ... There are no accurate US figures ... Estimates vary from 20 million to 200 million. Ryder suggests that 80 million may be the best guess. We tend to think that this is all for medical research, but of course it is not. Huge numbers of animals are used in university departments from Forestry to Psychology, and even more are used for commercial purposes, to test whether cosmetics can cause skin damage, or shampoos eye damage, or to test food additives or laxatives or sleeping pills or anything else.

A standard test for foodstuffs is the 'LD50'. The object of this test is to find the dosage level at which 50 per cent of the test animals will die. This means that nearly all of them will become very sick before finally succumbing or surviving. When the substance is a harmless one, it may be necessary to force huge doses down the animals, until in some cases sheer volume or concentration causes death.

Ryder gives a selection of experiments, taken from the recent scientific journals. I will quote two, not for the sake of indulging in gory details, but in order to give an idea of what normal researchers think they may legitimately do to other species. The point is not that the individual researchers are cruel men, but that they are behaving in a way that is allowed by our speciesist attitudes. As Ryder points out, even if only one per cent of the experiments involve severe pain, that is 50000 experiments in Britain every year, or nearly 150 every day (and about 15 times as many in the United States, if Ryder's guess is right). Here then are two experiments:

O.S. Ray and R.J. Barrett of Pittsburg gave electric shocks to the feet of 1042 mice. They then caused convulsions by giving more intense shocks through cup-shaped electrodes applied to the animals' eyes or through pressure spring clips attached to their ears. Unfortunately, some of the mice who 'successfully completed Day One training were found sick or dead prior to testing on Day Two' ...

At the National Institute for Medical Research, Mill Hill, London, W. Feldberg[3] and S.L. Sherwood injected chemicals into the brains of cats – 'with a number of widely different substances, recurrent patterns of reaction were obtained. Retching, vomiting, defecation, increased salivation and greatly accelerated respiration leading to panting were common features' ...

The injection into the brain of a large dose of Tobocuraine caused the cat to jump 'from the table to the floor and then straight into its cage, where it started calling more and more noisily whilst moving about restlessly and jerkily ... finally the cat fell with legs and neck flexed, jerking in rapid clonic movements, the condition being that of a major (epileptic) convulsion ... within a few seconds the cat got up, ran for a few yards at high speed and fell in another fit. The whole process was repeated several times within the next ten minutes, during which the cat lost faeces and foamed at the mouth.'

This animal finally died 35 minutes after the brain injection ...

There is nothing secret about these experiments. One has only to open any recent volume of a learned journal ... to find full descriptions of experiments of this sort, together with results obtained – results that are frequently trivial and obvious. The experiments are often supported by public funds.

It is a significant indication of the level of acceptability of these practices that, although these experiments are taking place at this moment on university campuses throughout the country, there has, so far as I know, not been the slightest protest from the student movement. Students have been rightly concerned that their universities should not discriminate on grounds of race or sex, and that they should not serve the purposes of the military or big business. Speciesism continues undisturbed, and many students participate in it. There may be a few qualms at first, but since everyone regards it as normal, and it may even be a required part of a course, the student soon becomes hardened and dismissing his earlier feelings as 'mere sentiment', comes to regard animals as statistics rather than sentient beings with interests that warrant consideration.

Argument about vivisection has often missed the point because it has been put in absolutist terms: would the abolitionist be prepared to let thousands die if they could be saved by experimenting on a single animal? The way to reply to this purely hypothetical question is to pose another: would the experimenter be prepared to experiment on a human orphan under six months old, if it were the only way to save many lives? (I say 'orphan' to avoid the complication of parental feelings, although in doing so I am being overfair to the experimenter, since the nonhuman subjects of experiments are not orphans.) A negative answer to this question indicates that the experimenter's readiness to use nonhumans is simple discrimination, for adult apes, cats, mice, and other mammals are more conscious of what is happening to them, more self-directing, and, so far as we can tell, just as sensitive to pain as a human infant. There is no characteristic that human infants possess that adult mammals do not have to the same or a higher degree.

(It might be possible to hold that what makes it wrong to experiment on a human infant is that the infant will in time develop into more than the nonhuman, but one would then, to be consistent, have to oppose abortion, and perhaps contraception too, for the foetus and the egg and sperm have the same potential as the infant. Moreover, one would still have no reason for experimenting on a nonhuman rather than a human with brain damage severe enough to make it impossible for him to rise above infant level.)

The experimenter, then, shows a bias for his own species whenever he carries out an experiment on a nonhuman for a purpose that he would not think justified him in using a human being at an equal or of lower sentience, awareness, ability to be self-directing, and so on. No one familiar with the kind of results yielded by these experiments can have the slightest doubt that if this bias were eliminated the number of experiments performed would be zero or very close to it.

If it is vivisection that shows the logic of speciesism most clearly, it is the use of other species for food that is at the heart of our attitudes towards them. Most of *Animals, Men and Morals* is an attack on meat eating – an attack which is based solely on concern for nonhumans, without reference to arguments derived from the considerations of ecology, macrobiotics, health or religion.

The idea that nonhumans are utilities, means to our ends, pervades our thought. Even conservationists who are concerned about the slaughter of wild fowl but not about the vastly greater slaughter of chickens for our tables are thinking in this way – they are worried about what we would lose if there were less wildlife ...

Man may always have killed other species for food, but he has never exploited them so ruthlessly as he does today. Farming has succumbed to business methods, the objective being to get the highest possible ratio of output (meat, eggs, milk) to input (fodder, labour costs and so on). Ruth Harrison's essay 'On Factory Farming' gives an account of some aspects of modern methods, and of the unsuccessful British campaign for effective controls, a campaign which was sparked off by her *Animal Machines* (1964).

Her article is in no way a substitute for her earlier book. This is a pity since, as she says, 'farm produce is still associated with mental pictures of animals browsing in the fields ... of hens having a last forage before going to roost'. Yet neither in her article nor elsewhere in *Animals, Men and Morals* is this false image replaced by a clear idea of the nature and extent of factory farming. We learn of this only indirectly, when we hear of the code of reform proposed by an advisory committee set up by the British government.

Among the proposals, which the government refused to implement on the grounds that they were too idealistic, were: '*Any animal should at least have room to turn around freely.*' Factory farm animals need liberation in the most literal sense. Veal calves are kept in stalls five feet by two feet. They are usually slaughtered when about four months old, and have been too big to turn in their stalls for at least a month. Intensive beef herds, kept in stalls only proportionately larger for much longer periods, account for a growing percentage of beef production. Sows are only similarly confined when pregnant, which, because of artificial methods of increasing fertility, can be most of the time. Animals confined in this way do not waste food by exercising, nor do they develop unpalatable muscle.

'A dry bedded area should be provided for all stock.'
Intensively kept animals usually have to stand and sleep on slatted floors without straw, because this makes cleaning easier.

'Palatable roughage must be readily available to all calves after one week of age.'
In order to produce the pale veal housewives are said to prefer, calves are fed on an all-liquid diet until slaughter, even though they are long past the age at which they would normally eat grass. They develop a craving for roughage, evidenced by attempts to gnaw wood from their stalls (for the same reason, their diet is deficient in iron).

'Battery cages for poultry should be large enough for a bird to be able to stretch one wing at a time.'
Under current British practice, a cage for four or five laying hens has a floor area of 20 inches by 18 inches ... In this space, on a sloping wire floor (sloping so the eggs roll down, wire so the dung drops through) the birds live for a year or 18 months while artificial lighting and temperature conditions combine with drugs in their food to squeeze the maximum number of eggs out of them. Table birds are also often kept in cages. More often they are reared in sheds, no less crowded. Under these conditions all the birds' natural activities are frustrated, and they develop 'vices' such as pecking each other to death. To prevent this, beaks are often cut off, and the sheds kept dark.

How many of those who support factory farming by buying its produce know anything about the way it is produced? How many have heard something about it, but are reluctant to check up for fear that it will make them uncomfortable? To non-speciesists, the typical consumer's mixture of ignorance, reluctance to find out the truth, and vague belief that nothing really bad could be allowed seems analogous to the attitude of 'decent Germans' to the death camps ...

There will be many readers of this book who will agree that factory farming involves an unjustifiable degree of exploitation of sentient creatures, and yet will want to say that there is nothing wrong with rearing animals for food, provided it is done 'humanely'. These people are saying, in effect, that although we should not cause animals to suffer, there is nothing wrong with killing them.

There are two possible replies to this view. One is the attempt to show that this combination of attitudes is absurd. Roslind Godlovitch (in her contribution to *Animals, Men and Morals*) argues that from the combination of 'animal suffering is to be avoided' and 'there is nothing wrong with killing animals' it follows that all animal life ought to be exterminated (since all sentient creatures will suffer to some degree at some point in their lives). Euthanasia is a contentious issue only because we place some value on living. If we did not, the least amount of suffering would justify it. Accordingly, if we deny that we have a duty to exterminate all animal life, we must concede that we are placing some value on animal life.

This argument seems to me valid, although one could still reply that the value of animal life is to be derived from the pleasures that life can have for them, so that, provided their lives have a balance of pleasure over pain, we are justified in rearing them. But this would imply that we ought to produce animals and let them live as pleasantly as possible, without suffering.

At this point, one can make the second of the two possible replies to the view that rearing and killing animals for food is all right so long as it is done humanely. This second reply is that so long as we think that a nonhuman may be killed simply so that a human can satisfy his taste for meat, we are still thinking of nonhumans as means rather than as ends in themselves. The factory farm is nothing more than the application of technology to this concept. Even traditional methods involve castration, the separation of mothers and their young, the breaking up of herds, branding or ear-punching, and of course transportation to the abattoirs and the final moments of terror when the animal smells blood and senses danger. If we were to try rearing animals so that they lived and died without suffering, we should find that to do so on anything like the scale of today's meat industry would be a sheer impossibility. Meat would become the prerogative of the rich.

I have been able to discuss only some of the contributions to this book, saying nothing about, for instance, the essays on killing for furs and for sport. Nor have I considered all the detailed questions that need to be asked once we start thinking about other species in the radically different way presented by this book. What, for instance, are we to do about genuine conflicts of interests like rats biting slum children? I am not sure of the answer, but the essential point is just that *we do* see this as a conflict of interests, that we recognise that rats have interests too. Then we may begin to think about other ways of resolving the conflict – perhaps by leaving out rat baits that sterilise the rats instead of killing them.

I have not discussed such problems because they are side issues compared with the exploitation of other species for food and for experimental purposes. On these central matters, I hope that I have said enough to show that this book, despite its flaws, is a challenge to every human to recognise his attitudes to nonhumans as a form of prejudice no less objectionable than racism or sexism. It is a challenge that demands not just a change of attitudes, but a change in our way of life, for it requires us to become vegetarians.

Can a purely moral demand of this kind succeed? The odds are certainly against it. The book holds out no inducements. It does not tell us that we will become healthier, or enjoy life more, if we cease exploiting animals. Animal Liberation will require greater altruism on the part of mankind than any other liberation movement, since animals are incapable of demanding it for themselves, or of protesting against their exploitation by votes, demonstrations or bombs. Is man capable of such genuine altruism? Who knows? If this book does have a significant effect, however, it will be a vindication of all those who have believed that man has within himself the potential for more than cruelty and selfishness.

NOTES

1. A slightly longer version of this chapter appeared initially in the *New York Review of Books* as a review of Godlovitch, Godlovitch & Harris (1973). The editor of this present volume would like to thank Peter Singer for allowing it to be reproduced here.
2. Since Singer wrote this article, Michael Leahy (1991) has produced a book which attempts to oppose animal rights by making particular reference to the writings of Wittgenstein.
3. In 1985, an investigation by animal rights activists revealed that Feldberg (still vivisecting at the age of 89) had carried out painful procedures on rabbits without applying anaesthetic effectively as his project licence required (see Garner, 1993a, pp. 132–3).

2 Animal Rights: An Eco-Socialist View
Ted Benton

At the beginning of 1995, amidst unprecedented government unpopularity, accusations of widespread corruption, high levels of unemployment, commercialisation of health care, and threats to valued public services, the UK political system was suddenly rocked by an explosion of protest action – over the export of calves. The *Financial Times* took the threat so seriously that it devoted an editorial to a careful consideration of the philosophy of animal rights before concluding that protesters 'should not be allowed to prevent others from pursuing a legal trade' (30 January 1995). Why should this be happening now? Why should people seem to care more about *animal* than human suffering? One recent philosophical critic of animal rights, Peter Carruthers, would take an unequivocal view on this: 'I regard the present popular concern with animal rights in our culture as a reflection of moral decadence' (Carruthers, 1992, p. xi).

However, one of the key themes in the approach I hope to outline in what follows, is that the politics of animal rights and welfare is much more indissolubly intertwined with other issues than this simple human/animal opposition supposes. The subjection of animals to intensive production regimes, and their extensive use as experimental subjects for commercial purposes are both forms of social practice in which the needs of living beings are systematically overridden. What I have elsewhere called the 'intentional structure' (Benton, 1993) of such practices as these is one in which animals are treated as means to socially established ends, not as 'ends in themselves', nor as beings whose own ends or preferences need be taken into account. There is a clear parallel, here, with a fairly standard socialist moral critique of the treatment of wage-workers in capitalist industry, according to which workers are estranged from their *own* life-activity, and reduced to the status of a mere commodity. Of course, the analogy is not complete, since the commodity-status of the worker lasts as long as the working day, and leaves open the possibility of a more autonomous period of 'free time' for reproduction, recreation and consumption. Many socialists and feminists would, of course, question the character of these activities, too. However, the formal distinction remains. The commodification of the lives of nonhuman animals in these regimes *is* more fully realised, though, arguably, qualitatively comparable with that imposed on human wage-workers.

The intertwining of human and animal politics has other dimensions than this, of course. The emergence of large-scale concentrations of power in transnational companies in agribusiness and food production and processing (see for example Goodman and Redclift, 1991) has implications for global justice in food distribution, environmental degradation, and human health. The new biotechnologies, especially 'genetic engineering' give cause for a number of legitimate concerns in addition to their implications for animal welfare. Finally, it cannot be inferred from the upsurge of public outage at the mistreatment of animals, that the protesters do not care about human suffering. It is significant that all but a very small and isolated fragment of the current protest movement is committed to non-violent direct action: most would see a contradiction between their aim of reducing animal suffering and causing suffering to humans as a means. More centrally, the 'moral sentiments' from which the protest flows are best regarded as extensions beyond the species-boundary of common human compassion, rather than a morally perverted displacement of it.

Some of these linkages might be accepted by a sceptic such as Carruthers. Insofar as it can be shown that specifically human well-being is at stake in attempts to improve the condition of farm or experimental animals, then so far might the action be well-grounded. However, there is no mistaking the motivation that pervades these newly emergent social movements. The action springs directly from compassion for the suffering of fellow sentient beings. The parallel I drew above between the (partial) commodification of human wage-workers and the exploitation of animals in intensive livestock regimes, can only work as a moral critique if it is first acknowledged that the nonhuman animals involved are, indeed, sentient beings, with ends, preferences, and a capacity to suffer harm and experience well-being. If it makes no sense to apply these concepts to nonhuman animals, then, it might seem, the ontological basis for moral concern is simply absent. The protesters and their supporters are, perhaps, well-meaning, but they are deluded by a mistakenly anthropomorphic view of animals.

Rights and Utilitarianism

So, there is no escaping the thorny question of the psychological status of nonhuman animals. As is well-known, Western philosophical traditions have tended to attribute a unique and elevated status to the human species, and, in general, the main means by which this has been accomplished has been some form of human/animal contrast: attributes supposedly peculiar to humans become definitive of our superior status within the order of nature, or of our elevation above it. The mark of distinction might be possession of an immortal soul, autonomous will, reason, language, or even sentience itself, as in Descartes' famous view of animals as automata.

Within the Western traditions, perhaps the most powerful challenge to this dualistic opposition between humans and animals came with Darwin's version of evolutionary thinking. In a striking passage of his 'Species' notebooks he writes:

> Animals – whom we have made our slaves we do not like to consider our equals. – Do not slave-holders wish to make the black man other kind? – Animals with affection, immitation, fear of death, pain, sorrow for the dead – respect ... The soul by consent of all is superadded, animals not got it, not look forward if we choose to let conjecture run wild, then animals our fellow brethren in pain, disease, death, & suffering & famine; our slaves in the most laborious work, our companions in our amusements; they may partake, from our origin in one common ancestor we may be all netted together (Barrett, 1987).

In this very dense passage, Darwin links together his conjecture that humans and other animals have a common ancestry with a series of observations of commonalities in the life-experience of human and nonhuman species, as well as noting forms of social relatedness across species-boundaries. We have in common a whole range of vulnerabilities to harms, in virtue of our organic constitutions and associated psychological capacities and dispositions. We establish social relations with animals through both enslavement of them and taking them as our 'companions' in our amusements. Finally, Darwin even postulates a parallel between the racist ideologies which legitimate slavery within the human species, and the human/animal dualism which legitimates the 'slavery' imposed by humans on other species. Whether or not Darwin was right to do so, he clearly thought that a deep revaluation of the moral character of our relations to other *animals* followed from his evolutionary thesis and related ethological observations.

Subsequent defenders of extension of moral concern beyond the species-boundary have commonly drawn on the authority of neo-Darwinian theory to establish the case for attributing to nonhuman animals whatever charac-teristics are required as a condition of application of their preferred moral theory. Peter Singer, for example, thinks that the similarities between vertebrate central nervous systems, together with the selective advantages conferred by sentience make it unlikely that vulnerability to pain is a uniquely human attribute. This, in addition to the common observation of cross-species similarities in behavioural expressions of pain, gives us strong theoretical and empirical grounds for thinking that the capacities to suffer pain and experience pleasure are widely shared across species-boundaries. Since, for utilitarian moral theorists, morality resolves itself into a matter of aggregate proportions of pleasure and pain in the world, animals clearly qualify to be included in the utilitarian calculus. Indeed, this was clearly acknowledged by Jeremy Bentham, in his much-quoted dictum to the effect that animal rationality was beside the point. For him, the question was 'Can they suffer?'. Of course, the utilitarian tradition has become both more diverse and more sophisticated since Bentham's day, so, for example, some latter-day utilitarians would speak of satisfaction or non-satisfaction of preferences in place of pleasure and pain. If this version of utilitarianism were to be accepted, then moral considerability could be carried across the species boundary only if nonhuman animals could properly be said to have preferences. Clearly the manufacturers of pet foods suppose this to be uncontroversial among their customers.

It is, therefore, not surprising that the utilitarian tradition has taken the lead in advocacy of a positive moral standing for nonhuman animals. Its moral theory is, so to speak, less metaphysically demanding than its main rivals. But the utilitarian tradition faces serious problems quite independently of its application to animals. Among the more commonly advanced criticisms, at least two might be thought actually less pressing when the theory is applied to nonhumans. The first of these arguments is that what is morally important in human life cannot be reduced to pleasure and pain. Some pleasures may be deemed good, others evil, while pain may be suffered for fine or noble purposes. Whilst there may be substantive moral disagreement about these judgements, it is clear that the relation between good and evil, on the one hand, and pleasure and pain, on the other is a contingent one. Similar considerations apply to 'preference utilitarianism': what is good is not *necessarily* what is preferred, neoclassical economics notwithstanding.

A second long-standing objection to utilitarianism is closely related to the first. It is that the quantitative focus of the doctrine limits its capacity to acknowledge qualitative differences among pleasures, or preferences. Different pleasures differ not just in amounts – intensities, durations, and so on, but also in kind, or quality. How many bars of a Mahler symphony are equivalent to a good meal? Since the possibility of subjecting pleasures, pains *and* preferences to moral evaluation, and to qualitative discriminations seems to be closely bound up with the culturally mediated, or formed character of human experience, it seems that these two objections are effective against utilitarianism solely in its application to the human case. So far as animals are concerned, perhaps the utilitarian identification of the good with an optimal ratio of pleasure to pain is more plausible than the same doctrine applied to humans. But to argue in this way would be to undermine the utilitarian case for animal liberation. For the doctrine to succeed in including nonhumans within the sphere of moral concern, it has to be supposed that human suffering and animal suffering are similar in kind, that each counts equally with the other in the utilitarian calculus.

There is another quite standard argument against utilitarian moral theory, one which has tended to be the most prominent in the debate about the moral standing of animals. This is the objection to the theory as a version of 'consequentialism'. Consequentialists deny that the moral character of an act, or a proposed rule of conduct is inherent in the act or rule itself. Rather, we can only decide on the rightness or wrongness of an act or rule by measuring or estimating its consequences. One uncomfortable implication of consequentialism is that it appears to allow that it would be right to mistreat an innocent individual if it could be shown that some aggregate benefit could be achieved by it. This cuts against very widespread moral intuitions that it is wrong to punish the innocent, no matter what the consequences, that some forms of treatment, such as torture and enslavement, are simply unacceptable, and cannot be justified in any circumstances.

These moral intuitions find justification in another tradition of moral theory which assigns a central place to the integrity of autonomous individuals, who are authors of their own ends, or purposes and should never be treated solely as means. One way of grounding this moral view is to say that individuals have basic, or 'natural' rights to respectful treatment in virtue of their 'inherent value'. Tom Regan is the leading advocate of this version of non-consequentialist, or 'deontological' moral theory in the 'animals' debate. At first sight, this seems to be a most unpromising approach. Unlike utilitarianism, the 'rights' tradition imposes quite stringent metaphysical conditions on the kinds of being that can be allowed into the moral universe. Kant's concept of autonomy, for example, presupposed a being rational enough to recognise its contemplated actions as falling under universal principles, and capable of acting in accordance with those principles, against the pull of contingent desires and preferences. To make such a concept stretch across the species-boundary would be a tall order!

Regan solves this problem by way of a crucial distinction between moral agents and moral patients. Something like Kant's account of autonomy would be needed to characterise full moral agency. Only moral agents in that sense are bearers of moral responsibility for their actions. Since there are close conceptual ties between the necessary rational capacities, language use, and full moral agency, it seems reasonable to accept that only individuals of the human species are moral agents. Of course, there may have been other hominids with such capacities, and, indeed, it may yet be discovered that other living species share them. Certainly research on other primates and some marine mammals has already produced results which have challenged the ingenuity of the stalwarts of human uniqueness. But for the immediate purpose of Regan's argument these questions are not central. Even if it could be shown that moral agency was possessed by one or two nonhuman species, to base the argument for animal rights on those grounds would be to abandon concern for the vast majority of individuals and species.

Regan's view is that there are no good reasons for limiting the class of beings entitled to moral consideration to those (that is, moral agents) who can bear moral responsibility. So, moral agents may have direct duties to other individuals who are not moral agents. Such beings are 'moral patients'. Moral agents have obligations to moral patients, to treat them with respect, to refrain from harming them, and so on, in virtue of their possession of inherent value. How far the status of moral patienthood can be stretched out beyond the human species will therefore depend on how individuals qualify as possessors of 'inherent value'. On Regan's view, a sufficient (but not necessary) condition for possession of inherent value is to be a 'subject of a life'. Though it includes sentience, this criterion is more demanding than the utilitarian doctrine. To count as a subject of a life, individuals must have preferences, purposes, some sense of self-identity through time, and enough capacity to be harmed or benefited by the actions of others to be said to have 'interests'.

Regan's claim is that mammals above the (seemingly rather arbitrary) age of one satisfy this criterion, and so must be held to possess 'inherent value' in the required sense. It follows that moral agents have moral obligations towards them to treat them with respect, refrain from harming them, and so on. Since animals which satisfy the subject-of-a-life criterion have a justified moral claim on moral agents, who are both responsible and able to meet it, they may be properly said to have rights. Regan's advocacy of rights is designed to give a more morally powerful and unconditional protection to animals than utilitarianism can offer. It does not make prohibition on maltreatment turn on calculations of aggregate benefit, and it rules out the use of animals as mere means to human ends.

However, the rights-view has one significant disadvantage, compared with the utilitarian view, and it also may even not have the main advantage it proclaims. Its disadvantage stems from its greater metaphysical stringency. The rights-view is faced with a harder job than is utilitarianism when it comes to showing that many nonhumans deserve moral consideration. That many other species are sentient is, these days, hardly controversial. Those who dispute that nonhumans have the various powers and capacities which go to make up 'subjecthood' have more of a case. R.G. Frey for example, has argued that to have preferences one must also have beliefs about the objects of those preferences. Beliefs, in turn, are always beliefs that something is the case – that is to say, they have a propositional content. Only a being with the capacity for language could be properly said to have beliefs, and so, also, preferences (see Frey, 1980 & 1983). M.P.T. Leahy (1991) also uses a version of the later philosophy of Wittgenstein as grounds for denying that psychological capacities can be coherently applied to non-participants in human 'language games'. More cautiously, Peter Carruthers (1992) introduces the idea of non-conscious mental states in questioning whether animal experience is sufficiently like human experience to ground the extension of moral concern to them.

Regan offers a 'cumulative' argument against such sceptics. This draws upon the authority of Darwinian evolutionary theory, as we have seen, but also takes common sense beliefs *and* language as a touchstone. This is not to claim that just because we ordinarily do refer to the cat as wanting to get closer to the fire, or the dog wanting to go for a walk, the metaphysical commitments carried by these forms of speech must be justified. Regan's claim is, rather, that the onus of justification is on those who would seek to replace these ways of thinking and speaking about animals with non-intentional descriptions of a behavioural or neurophysiological kind. So far such programmes have, he claims, been unsuccessful. On the contrary, it might be added that research on the lives of animals in their natural habitats, as well as much psychological research on captive animals has revealed complexities and flexibilities in their modes of life that render such reductive programmes ever more implausible.

Though, as Regan admits, the case for attributing 'subject-of-a-life' status to (some) nonhuman animals is not conclusive, it is certainly well-grounded. The reasonableness of this case will be assumed in the rest of this chapter. More difficult questions arise, however, when we turn to a consideration of the moral implications of what I have elsewhere called 'human/animal continuism'. Carruthers (1992, p. 21) recognises the possibility of alternative interpretations of Regan's position, but decisively rejects it if read as a form of moral intuitionism. Regan's talk of 'inherent value' does rather invite this interpretation, but it seems to me that a good deal of what Regan tries to establish with this concept can be convincingly argued without it. Both Regan and Singer make use of examples of human individuals who lack full moral agency, such as very young infants, and seriously mentally retarded or psychologically disabled adults. The challenge that such cases as these pose for someone committed to denying a positive moral status to animals, is to find good reasons for including these classes of human individuals which are not also good reasons for including nonhumans who are, similarly, 'subjects of a life'. To discriminate in this way without good reasons would be an injustice, comparable to racism or sexism.

To the extent that this argument works, it can offer a way to avoid the 'intuitionist' risks of the idea of inherent value. We can leave aside questions about the moral grounds for treating human 'subjects of a life' who are not moral agents as worthy of moral consideration, and simply rely on the premise that it is proper to do so. If this premise is accepted, then the onus is on those who would deny this status to nonhumans to demonstrate a morally significant difference, given the reasonableness of 'human/animal continuism'. If the premise is not accepted, then the argument has to be diverted into a consideration of the moral status of human moral patients. However, it seems unlikely that anyone initially not inclined to assign a positive moral status to human moral patients would be convinced by the simple device of attributing to them the somewhat mysterious property of inherent value. There are, of course, numerous attempts in the literature to identify differences between nonhuman animals and human infants, the deeply psychologically damaged, and so on, but few, if any, which rise to the challenge by denying moral status to human moral patients.

Though there is not space here to do the subject justice, it seems to me that there are, indeed, very significant differences between the different kinds of human moral patients, both among themselves, and between them and nonhuman animals. Some of these differences are clearly morally significant. However, it is quite another thing to show that these differences are of an order, and have a patterned distribution such that the boundary of appropriate moral concern coincides exactly with the species-boundary at every point. Once the distinction between moral patients and moral agents is accepted, so that we recogise that beings, of whatever species, which are incapable of *full* moral agency, may still be proper objects of moral concern, there is little to prevent the inclusion of animals within the scope of human morality. Attempts to persist in this increasingly take on the appearance of defensively motivated 'special pleading'.

So, whilst again, the case is far from conclusive, it is nevertheless reasonable, and well-grounded, both empirically and philosophically, to recognise the individuals of at least some nonhuman animal species as proper objects of moral concern. This far, it seems to me, the case on behalf of animals is well made. However, what remains to be considered, if we accept that animals do have positive moral status, is the question of just what that moral status is. Since, for both the utilitarian and the rights-view, the argument on behalf of animals works by extending an established moral theory across the species-boundary, a weakness in either theory in an application to the human case will, *a fortiori*, tell against it as as a theory of the moral status of animals. Since there are powerful arguments against the utilitarian position, in particular the familiar implications of its consequentialism, I will focus, in the rest of this chapter, on the case for rights.

Active and Passive Rights

So far most of the debate about animal rights has focused on the question: 'Are nonhuman animals the sort of being to which it makes sense to attribute rights?' This is, indeed, a relevant and important question. However, it is not the only relevant and important question to be asked in this area. There are, of course, philosophical sceptics for whom it makes no sense to attribute rights to humans, particularly the sort of 'basic' rights (a notion closely related to alleged 'natural' rights) upon which Regan's argument rests. My provisional assumption here is that these sceptics are mistaken, and that some notion of 'basic' human rights is defensible. But even on this assumption, we may still ask what is the point or purpose of assigning and respecting rights. Once we have an answer to this, the question then arises: 'What kinds of being stand in need of rights, and in virtue of what do they need them?' Finally, these questions take us on to a further set of considerations about rights which have typically been raised by radical critics from the left, from socialists, feminists and communitarians of various stripes. These considerations bring into the picture the social relations, especially power-relations which hold between the individuals who are assigned rights. Can the purposes for which rights are assigned be achieved in the case of those with insufficient social power to exercise them? More fundamentally, is it only because of the persistence of (alterable) social relations of mutual competitiveness, self-interest, and unequal power that individuals need rights in the first place? My central argument will be that since these are questions of importance for the discourse of human rights, the thesis of human/animal continuity suggests that they will also have an important bearing on the *animal* rights debate.

But let us deal, first, with the question whether nonhumans can qualify as (basic) rights-holders (assuming humans can). To the extent that at least some nonhuman animals have purposes and preferences of their own, are able to benefit, and are vulnerable to suffering at the hands of moral agents, they, like human moral patients, can be said to have an interest in respectful treatment. If the analogy with human moral patients holds, they have a justified moral claim to such treatment, and it is a moral obligation on the part of the relevant human moral agents to answer the claim. This is all that is required, on the concept of rights which Regan adopts.

Even accepting this rather 'thin' concept of rights, however, there are problems. The first problem concerns the symmetry between rights and obligations. I have already accepted the case for obligations on the part of moral agents towards moral patients of other species. But do obligations always confer correlative rights? One way of thinking about this is to ask whether, and when, attributing a right is doing anything over and above the attribution of the correlative obligation. When Regan and others appeal to their readers' acknowledgement of the rights of human moral patients, they do, indeed, tap into an established usage. However it is arguable that these rights-attributions amount to no more than could be said by way of a specification of the obligations which adults who do have full moral agency have towards their immature or unfortunate fellow beings: to care for them.

This contrasts markedly with the way the concept of rights has been used in the context of such movements as the American civil rights movement and the feminist movement. Above all these have been expressions of self-assertion, in which rights are, centrally, claims for self-definition and self-determination. These moral claims do, indeed, entail moral obligations on the part of others, but what those obligations might be could not be established independently of the claims made. Provisionally, I shall mark this distinction with the terms 'active' and 'passive'. Passive rights-holders are the subjects of moral obligations on the part of moral agents, while active rights-holders are also entitled to contribute to the processes of establishing what those obligations are and how they are to be implemented. Though suffering many kinds of material deprivation, social disadvantage, and lack of esteem has played its part in fuelling these social struggles, their aims go beyond the requirement for ameliorative reform. To be a mere recipient of the benevolence of others would not merely fall short of the rights which are claimed, but would itself be an instance of their denial.

This difference between active and passive rights does seem to mark out a significant moral boundary, more or less coextensive with the distinction between moral agents and moral patients. While passive rights may be attributed, as Regan argues, to all 'subjects of a life', active rights do seem to require a range of conceptual and other cultural capacities possessed only by moral agents. One way of making this clearer is to consider an intermediate case. In all human societies, children are assigned a status different from that of adults, usually with ritual marking the passage from one status to another. In modern Western societies, the law defines the ages at which the various rights and responsibilities of adult citizenship are acquired. So, for example, there is a legally defined age at which a young adult may be held capable of giving consent to sexual relations, another at which individuals acquire the right to vote, and so on. Recent attempts to bring down the age of consent for homosexuals in the UK to that already adopted for heterosexuals were widely presented as a matter of rights. For an individual sufficiently grown up to make autonomous choices, the choice of when and with whom to engage in consensual sexual activity is, indeed, a matter of rights, and, in the terms of my distinction, a matter of active rights. Though there may be controversy over the precise age at which the approriate capacity for autonomous choice is reached, and also about the injustice of setting it differently for people of different sexual orientations, there is general, and well-grounded agreement that there should be an age of consent set *somewhere*.

If we consider the situation of someone below an appropriately fixed age of consent, what does their lack of a right to give consent to sexual relations amount to? It is not, as it would be in the case of a fully autonomous individual, an unjust deprivation. Indeed, if a child does engage in even apparently 'consensual' sex, it is not the child who is held to be legally culpable, but her or his (presumably adult) partner. The rationale for this is that in the absence of fully developed agency, chidren need to be protected from self-seeking and exploitative behaviour on the part of adults, even when they (the children) may sometimes behave in ways which, in an adult, would be taken as consent. Set against this, there is a trend towards taking children's preferences as authoritative in, for example, custody cases. We may make sense of these sorts of considerations in terms of an obligation on the part of moral agents to protect the interests or seek the well-being of those who lack full moral agency, even if that involves a course of action contrary to the preferences of the subject of concern. For those who insist on assigning correlative rights wherever there are obligations, this may involve a (passive) right to be protected from one's own preferences. However, to the extent that a child matures towards full agency, its own preferences come to have more authority as defining the interests or well-being of that individual, to the point at which overriding that self-definition becomes an oppressive denial of its (active) rights.

The upshot of this is that there is a fairly minimal use of the term rights, as 'passive' rights, according to which rights are merely the formal correlates of obligations on the part of moral agents, in which animals may properly be said to possess rights. However (so we may reasonably suppose), animals generally lack the range of conceptual and cultural learning capacities to become bearers of the kinds of active rights for self-definition and self-determination which have been at the heart of the human struggles which advocates of animal rights are inclined to use as analogues. It may still be held that these struggles have a special and distinctive character, without conceding to a 'speciesist' denial of the positive moral standing of animals.

A second set of problems in the way of attributing rights to nonhuman animals has to do wth the absence of any relational element in Regan's 'subject of a life' qualifying condition. A thoroughgoing communitarian moral theorist would hold that animal rights are an absurdity, since to be a right-holder is necessarily to be a member of a human community whose normative order assigns both rights and responsibilities. But this communitarian view of rights faces the difficulty that it cannot readily make sense of the critical role of rights as moral claims on communities to revise their existing normative structure in favour of universalistic standards. This is precisely the aspect of the historical role of rights-claims that advocates of animal rights seek to draw on.

However, without going the whole distance with the communitarian position, it does seem that the rights-view's abstraction from any consideration of the social-relational conditions of rights presents some problems. So, whilst we may be convinced that any subject of a life, whether human or animal, may be worthy of moral consideration, we are left pretty much in the dark about just what this requires in the form of specific rules of action, and to whom which responsibilities are to be assigned. Do we have an obligation to come to the aid of a wild animal under attack from a predator? Should we take account of the interest of populations of wild animals in planning decisions which affect their habitats? Is pet-keeping an infringement of an animal's rights? Is there a moral difference between 'factory' farming and traditional methods of animal 'husbandry' for meat? Rights-theory is capable of devising secondary rules to answer such questions as these, but it does so in ways which smack of *ad hoc* reconciliation of the theory with (reflective) intuitions. But what is missing in these attempts is any recognition that the moral considerations at stake may vary depending on the kinds of social relations between humans and animals in which they arise. Reflective intuition (and legal codes) would, for example, acknowledge a moral responsibility on the part of a pet owner for the well-being of the pet, whilst denying any such responsibility on the part of a passer-by to rescue a wild animal from a predator. At least part of the justification for this difference would be grounded in the moral consequences of the very different human/animal relationships involved. This case could be made out quite independently of any difference in the status of the animals involved as 'subjects of a life'.

Do Rights Serve a Useful Purpose?

So, whilst animals may not be eligible as rights-holders in all of the respects in which (human) moral agents are, and there may be problems in connection with the social relational conditions of rights for them, there are still good reasons for holding that animals are not ruled out from the status of rights-holders by their substantive natures. It is at this point in the argument that the other questions I posed earlier become pertinent. What is the moral purpose of rights-attribution, and why do individuals stand in need of rights? If we agree with Regan and the tradition of rights-theory upon which he draws, then the answer to the first question is that rights afford protection of the basic interests, or welfare of the rights-holder. On this supposition, the answer to the second question *must* be that the bearers of rights require them because they are vulnerable. To say this much may be enough of an answer in the case of 'passive' rights. However, for moral agents, their capacity for self-definition and self-determination implies that what counts as their welfare cannot be fully known independently of their own active participation in defining it. Moreover, the social movements which the supporters of animal rights usually use as analogues provide evidence that recognition and preservation of the powers of self-definition and self-determination are likely to figure centrally as elements in the substantive views of their own welfare which they advance as rights-claims.

On this view of the purpose of rights-attributions, then, we can establish a connection between passive rights and vulnerability, on the one hand, and between active rights and the capacity for self-determination, on the other. Henceforth, I will speak of 'vulnerability-rights' and 'self-determination-rights', respectively. The moral force of attributing vulnerability rights to moral patients is now clear. Since, by definition, moral patients are incapable of making claims on their own behalf, they are likely to be particularly vulnerable, compared with individuals who do have this ability. They stand in need of a moral agent who will accept the obligation to speak and act on their behalf.

However, now we have briefly addressed the question of the moral purpose of rights-attributions, it is possible to go on to ask further questions about how far, under various actual or possible conditions, the attribution of rights succeeds in achieving that purpose; whether that purpose is itself made necessary only because of alterable social conditions; and whether some other set of moral concepts might not serve the subjects of rights-attributions better. The supporters of rights for animals have generally hoped that the moral authority of the idea of human rights could be drawn upon and extended for the benefit of nonhumans. Understandably, they have been less concerned with addressing the long tradition of radical criticism of the discourses and practices of rights in the human case. Understandable though this is, I shall argue that it is mistaken. More specifically, the liberal-individualist concept of rights which Regan adopts is open to a number of powerful objections, many of which apply equally or even more strongly when that concept is applied across the species-boundary.

The most widely shared criticism, levelled particularly by socialists, feminists and other tendencies on the left, is that there is a gap between being assigned rights and being able to exercise them. In societies marked by deep inequalities of economic wealth, social or political influence, and 'cultural capital', *formal* equality in access to education, health-care, legal representation and so on may coexist with *profound substantive inequalities* in these respects. What do legal rights amount to for someone unable to afford solicitors' fees? Short of wholesale social transformation, the left has attempted to address these problems piecemeal by such devices as legal aid, socialised health-care systems, and so on. The underlying point, here, is that rights as mere prohibitions on interference presuppose a view of individuals as capable of securing their own welfare so long as no one prevents them from doing so. In fact, various sorts of personal, socioeconomic, and cultural disadvantages, oppressions and exclusions may disempower individuals. When this is the case, mere non-interference amounts to neglect, so that for rights to *fulfil* their purpose of substantive protection requires a concept of rights whose correlative obligation is a duty of positive action to enable or empower the rights-holder.

This concept of positive rights already takes us some way beyond the concept of rights employed by Regan. In particular, there is an implicit commitment to the idea of pooled, or collective responsibility. Insofar as an individual's lack of power to secure her or his welfare, or basic interests is a result of pervasive features of an established social order, there will be no individual moral agent to whom the obligation of positive action can be assigned. On the concept of rights which Regan adopts, the rights-claim must fall in such circumstances. This might mean, for example, that pet animals could be assigned rights, because their welfare is the responsibility of an identifiable individual, whereas the harms done to many millions of animal victims of intensive rearing regimes would not count as rights-abuses. In this latter case, the practices are highly institutionalised ones in which causal and therefore moral responsibilities are diffuse and indeterminate. To whom do we attribute the responsibility for the harms suffered by the animals: wage-workers at the farm? The designers of the rearing-systems? The owners of the plant? The suppliers of feed and other materials? The consumers of the meat products? The retailers and distributors? The politicians who fail to enact protective legislation? Citizens who fail to protest?

The apparent limitations of liberal-individualist, negative concepts of rights in the face of harms to which beings are vulnerable because of their location in particular patterns of social relationships can be addressed in two possible ways. The first is the route already outlined: the attempt to construct a 'positive' concept of rights, sensitive to the social relational setting of the individual right-holder, and open to the idea of pooled or collective responsibilities not just to refrain from harming, but also to actively enable. The second possibility is the more radical one of abandoning the concept of rights as such, in favour of some alternative moral framework (I will ignore a possible third strategy of moral scepticism, or 'amoralism').

The strategy of abandoning rights in favour of an alternative, 'emancipatory' moral discourse is often (mistakenly, I think) attributed to Marx. Steven Lukes offers one of the most thorough critical investigations of this strategy (Lukes, 1985) and the argument I sketch here owes a lot to his work. The core of the emancipator critique of rights is that the prevailing pattern of social relations in liberal-capitalist societies has effects which run deeper than simply obstructing disadvantaged individuals in the exercise of the rights that are attributed to them. The very concept of rights, and the need to attribute them at all are products of this pattern of relationships. So, on this view, liberal-capitalist social relations are doubly at fault. They render individuals vulnerable to harms, from which protection is offered by the allocation of rights, which, in turn, cannot fulfil their promise in practice. The discourse of rights therefore adds to oppression by helping to legitimate in terms of formal entitlements a social and political regime which is *substantively* oppressive.

The source of the concept of rights in conditions of life specific to liberal-capitalist societies is already evidenced in the marked tendency of rights-theorists to take as their paradigms situations in which automomous individuals are at risk of harming one another in the course of pursuing their own interests. The allocation of rights is designed to set moral or legal restraint on the pursuit of self-interest in such contexts of interaction. We have already considered the limitations of the 'autonomy-assumption'. Autonomy is not something which can be taken to be unproblematically 'given', but has organic, psychological, developmental, cultural, socioeconomic and political conditions, and moreover, is not an 'all-or-nothing' possession. Second, what we might call the 'intentionality of harm' assumption makes this concept of rights relatively ineffectual in relation to risks which individuals run as a result of inadequate health and safety provisions at work, unsafe forms of transport, environmental pollution and so on, for which the allocation of individual responsibility may be impossible or just inappropriate.

However, these problems, as we have seen, might be addressed by developing a concept of rights which presses against the limits of this liberal-individualist moral ontology. This strategy starts to look less promising when we consider still further assumptions of the discourse of rights. There are two which are especially telling. The first is the concept of 'basic' interests, or welfare that rights are set in place to protect. The key assumption here is that such interests can be attributed to individuals in abstraction from their social context. This cuts against the commonplace experience of powerful social and emotional bonds both among individuals and between individuals and valued aspects of their social or cultural belonging. So, for example, it would be hard to make a concept of basic interests plausible if it did not include recognition of the importance of being able to maintain one's relationship with one's children or parents. More broadly, opportunities to participate in identity-affirming cultural practices, or in the normatively expected activities common to one's community are 'basic' in the sense that deprivation of them commonly deprives individuals of their sense of self-identity and meaning in life.

The second, related, assumption of the rights-discourse is the one which the radical critique finds the most objectionable. This is the assumption that individual action is always, or, at least, characteristically motivated by self-interest. The radical critique does not deny that there is an element of empirical truth in both assumptions, but to the extent that these assumptions are likely to be borne out by everyday experience, this is a consequence of the shaping of individual character, combined with the external constraints imposed by institutional structures. A society which rewards competitive performance, and punishes 'failure' is one in which we might expect individuals to adopt a narrowly-focused view of self-identity and interest, and devote most of their efforts to securing it. For the radical critics of rights there are important sources of evidence that competitive individualism is not a universal feature of human nature. Even in the context of a society in which all the pressures point in this direction, all individuals at least some of the time are motivated by love, compassion, and benevolence. Substantial minorities, even majorities, in these societies experience distress, often extreme distress, in the face of the dominant competitive ethos. There is, too, plenty of historical and anthropological evidence which bears out the enormous variability of patterns of human society and associated forms of individual character and motivation.

Finally, it might be argued that even if it were the case that individuals naturally tend to act self-interestedly, there is no necessity that they should threaten one another's interests in doing so. Only on the assumption that individuals pursue self-interest in a context which prevents simultaneous satisfaction of the interests of all does one individual's pursuit of satisfaction necessarily threaten the interests of others. The radical critic's claim is that liberal-capitalist social forms do produce precisely such conditions. There are two mechanisms at work. One is the tendency of markets to remove traditional normative restraints on desire, and render qualitatively different desires quantitatively equivalent through monetary exchange: desire loses its specificity, breaks its bounds and becomes insatiable. Secondly, individuals are set into mutual antagonism by socially induced relative scarcity. Against Malthus, Marx and other socialists have argued that material deprivation is not an unavoidable feature of the human predicament, but is rather a form of social discipline through which, in specifically capitalist societies, the competition between workers for jobs forces down wages, enhances the power of capital over labour, and obstructs the formation of collective power among the workers.

On this view, then, 'rights' are only required when individuals live in societies which induce limitless desires, create unnecessary scarcity, promote self-interest at the expense of mutual identification and benevolence, and reward only competitive success. The requirement for rights is, then, only a symptom of social pathology and moral disintegration. This leaves us with two tasks. One is to evaluate this set of arguments as they apply to human individuals. The second is to see how far what may be reasonable in it applies also to the situation of nonhuman animals. Obviously I have space for only a fraction of the exploration that these questions require.

Should Rights be Abandoned?

First, can and should humans do without rights? The answer to this turns in part on whether the set of conditions of life which necessitate rights can be thcroughly transcended by any emancipatory practice. If we consider, first, scarcity, it is clear that a vast proportion, if not all current material deprivation can be attributed to maldistribution, socially generated waste, and the effects of past ecological destruction. There is little doubt that radical social reorganisation could eliminate famine, poverty *and* mass disease, as well as bringing material aspirations within sustainable bounds. Nevertheless, the ecological insight that any form of human society must remain within the resource-constraints and waste-absorption limits of its environment implies that what Marx called the 'realm of necessity' is, after all, an unavoidable feature of the human condition. Parallel considerations apply to the possibility of mutual benevolence. Anyone who has lived through the privatisation or commercialisation of a public service will have first-hand experience of the destruction of wider identifications, of the withering of benevolence and solidarity which accompanies the imposition of performance indicators, performance-related pay, job-insecurity and enhanced differentials. Clearly, the balance of antagonism and mutual benevolence is deeply affected by institutional forms and can be altered very quickly. But can we be sure that mutual relations between humans could ultimately be wholly pacified? Psychoanalysis is one tradition of thought about human nature which offers some quite persuasive reasons for thinking that they could not.

Steven Lukes adds two further reasons for thinking that the need for rights could never be finally dispensed with. Even without scarcity and competitive antagonism, there might still be plural value-systems, so that one individual might harm another by benevolently imposing a view of the other's interests which the victim might reject. Further, since none of us has complete or infallible knowledge of the consequences of our actions, we may behave towards one another with the best of intentions, but still do one another harm.

The upshot of these considerations is that there are good grounds for thinking that a society in which humans were not vulnerable to harms to their basic interests deriving from the intended or unintended activity of other humans is in principle not achievable. It follows that moral or legal regulation by means of allocation of rights, or some functional equivalent would be a requirement for individual well-being in any foreseeable society.

However this does not mean that the radical critique of rights falls. The above discussion, so far as it goes, lends support to three important conclusions which are broadly favourable to the radical critique. The first is that the limitations of a specifically liberal-individualist conception of rights are confirmed. Any concept of rights adequate to the task of protecting the basic interests of individuals would have to take into account a number of features of human social being which tend to be obscured or marginalised in the liberal tradition. The second is that for even such an expanded, socialist view of rights to offer practical protection would require large-scale social transformation in the direction of conformity to socialist, feminist and ecological norms and insights. The third conclusion is that, in such a transformed society, the role for rights would be residual. Rights would, so to speak, plug the gaps left by an extended and pervasive network of solidarity and co-operatively established common purpose. With less work to do, the discourse of rights might be expected to do it more successfully.

To return to our earlier question of choice between a strategy of developing a richer, more socially sensitive and expansive concept of rights, and abandoning the discourse of rights as such in favour of an alternative moral framework, it is now possible to see a way of having our cake and eating at least part of it. Insofar as it can be shown that institutional and associated cultural changes would be likely to foster individual well-being as their spontaneous consequence, a morality of communal solidarity, benevolence, and mutual recognition could be expected to do much of the work of protecting 'basic' interests that in the present order of society is assigned (relatively unsuccessfully) to the discourse of rights. Much would depend, then, on developing strategies for social change which facilitated the re-emergence and strengthening of these alternative moral values and the sentiments which motivate them. As we have seen, this would be unlikely ever to wholly eradicate the various sources of human vulnerability which have been taken to necessitate rights. An enriched, socially and ecologically informed concept of rights would still be required, as a basis for authoritatively institutionalised protection of individual interests. In short, what is required is a *combination* of an expanded concept of rights alongside other, more solidaristic moral values and sentiments.

I fully acknowledge that I have done no more, here, than to indicate the desirability of a certain value-orientation and direction of social change. In view of the current pervasiveness of scepticism about emancipatory change, and widely shared feelings of helplessness in the face of global destruction, I am well aware that these arguments will seem far from convincing to many readers. Much more does, indeed, need to be done to consider how existing social movements might overcome divisions and broaden their appeal so as to breathe new life into the struggle for a better way of living together on our finite planet.

Nonhuman Animals and the Radical Critique of Rights

For now, however, my task is to try to draw some lessons from the foregoing discussion of the radical critique of rights as it bears on the question of the moral standing of nonhuman animals. To do this, I shall start with a provisional distinction between animals in the wild and those which are in some way or another bound up in human social life. I shall consider the latter first. Since it seems unlikely that any of these are capable of full moral agency, it makes no sense to attribute what I have called 'self-determination' rights to them. Since these animals, or, more generally, their ancestors, have been removed by human social practices from their 'natural' habitats, it is these same human social practices which shape their present conditions of life. Humans have, therefore, rendered the populations of these species in 'domestication' peculiarly dependent on human social practices and relations for their well-being. The presupposition of a 'negative' liberal concept of rights, that the right-holder can be assumed capable of autonomously securing its well-being so long as it is not interfered with, is simply absent in these cases. Where animal-involving practices by their nature harm the interests of animals in ways that cannot be morally justified, then there is a duty to transform or abolish those practices. Where the practice is one within which the animals can flourish, then the obligation on the relevant human agent is a positive duty to act for that end. In either type of case, it seems unlikely that a concept of 'basic' rights will be sufficient.

Though Regan seems to dismiss it, the notion that humans have 'acquired' quasi-contractual responsibilities towards 'domesticated' animals is not obviously absurd. Once it is accepted that animals are proper objects of moral concern 'in principle', then there is nothing to rule out the notion that, as in the relations among humans, *particular* individuals or groups might acquire *specific* obligations in virtue of past actions, or relationships entered into. Developing such a concept of 'acquired' responsibilities would go a long way towards rectifying the excessive abstraction of Regan's concept of rights, render more tractable the question of how to distribute responsibilities among human social agents and offer more conformity to widely shared moral 'intuitions'.

Another criticism of specifically liberal-individualist concepts of rights was, as we saw, their tendency not to recognise how far individual well-being is bound up with often life-long emotional investments in relationships with both other individuals and aspects of the wider community. Though other species are not social in the same way as are humans, many of them are, nonetheless, still social in ways which have comparable moral consequences. For fairly obvious reasons, most of the relatively small number of species that have been domesticated by humans are themselves highly social species, with relatively 'open' and malleable social modes of life.

In determining what might be meant by 'interests' or well-being for nonhuman species, it obviously will not do simply to extrapolate from the human case. If we accept, for the purpose of the present argument, that the point of moral regulation is to secure individual well-being, then the content of this notion must be specified differently to take into account the species-specific requirements for each mode of life. In the case of domestic social animals, most notably pets such as dogs, at least some of the social needs of the animal are met through learned adaptations to human social norms. This implies that, if humans have obligations to secure the well-being of such animals in their charge, that responsibility includes responsibility for emotional and social well-being, beyond ensuring that the animal is fed and watered.

For other species, such as sheep and cattle, which, under traditional forms of husbandry, retained much of their pre-domestication forms of social life, the responsibility is to provide the conditions for those patterns of social life among the herds themselves to be maintained. This moral requirement would rule out intensive rearing regimes, but would not, as in the case of Regan's rights theory, of itself rule out animal husbandry as such. However, the forms of animal husbandry which would be acceptable on this more socially-informed view of 'vulnerability' rights would be ones which also acknowledged the wider biophysical conditions of the mode of life of social species: that is their habitat requirements are to be understood as central to any full understanding of their well-being.

The remaining criticisms of the discouse of rights are aimed not just at the limitations of liberal versions, but at the idea of rights as such: first, the claim that rights are needed only because of the antagonisms set in motion by relative scarcity. If, as I suggested above, there are good reasons for thinking that any form of human social life would continue to be bounded by ecological constraints, with the consequent necessity for some rules governing allocation by rights and justice, these considerations must also cover nonhuman animal populations. In fact, since what humans treat as their own 'habitat requirements' have progressively transformed, and often completely destroyed the actual habitats of almost all other species on earth, these considerations are raised rather acutely. In the case of 'livestock' animals, fulfilling the responsibility to enable them to live according to their species-specific modes of life would entail much more extensive agricultural systems than those now established in most parts of the world. That would, in turn, entail much more restraint on the part of human populations in their land-use strategies.

But, at this point, moral consideration of 'wild' populations becomes relevant. Even someone convinced by the arguments of both utilitarians and rights-theorists that vegetarianism is morally required will surely accept that the growing of sufficient vegetable food will itself have ecological effects. Large areas of land will still be required for the growing of food for humans which might otherwise have sustained large populations of herbivorous animals, and their predators. It is also hard to imagine how such purely arable systems could operate without some method of *prima facie* rights-infringing pest control.

The philosophy of animal rights seems not well placed to deal with these issues. On the face of it, a 'non-interference' view of rights, with its liberal assumption of autonomy as 'given', might seem particularly appropriate in relation to animals in the wild. It would also be consistent with a widely shared ethic in favour of the preservation of 'wilderness'. But it is a measure of the overwhelming significance of the human impact on the contemporary world that the preservation of wilderness is now a moral and political issue. In a real sense, there are no 'wild' animal populations left. Such habitat as is not yet directly under human management is largely so because of socially agreed and enforced restraint. So, unqualified, the demand not to interfere is insufficient. How are the individual rights of wild animals not to be interfered with to be balanced against the rights of 'livestock' animals to sufficient grazing land, and the rights of human populations to grow and protect their crops, establish settlements, and so on? An undifferentiated concept of rights does seem inadequate to provide decision-procedures which would respect the complexity of these questions.

Perhaps more seriously for the rights view, moral issues arise in this context upon which the concept of rights seems to have little or no purchase at all. For example, widely shared moral intuitions, even enshrined in international conventions, place a high significance on preserving diversity of living species. On this view, protecting habitat from 'development' might be justified in terms of the vulnerability of a species from extinction, rather than in terms of the well-being of whatever individual animals happened to live there. More seriously still, most greens and other environmentalists would accept a responsibility towards an immense diversity of species, including plant species, the individuals of which do not even come close to satisfying Regan's 'subject-of-a-life' criterion. Of course, Regan offers this as a sufficient condition for moral considerability, not a necessary one. So, it remains open that we should develop a range of other moral concepts and rules to regulate our relations with the nonhuman world. This would not deny that there is important work for the concept of rights to do, but it would entail an acknowledgement that there is a great deal of morally necessary work that even a more socially and ecologically nuanced concept of rights cannot do.

Next, the question of benevolence: does the need to attribute rights to animals at all arise only because of socially removable sources of antagonism between the species? This question is closely related to another commonly held objection to the animal rights position. It is sometimes said that the doctrine is coldly rational, and fails to evoke the feelings of compassionate outrage that are required to motivate action in defence of animals. Of course, I reject the counterposing of reasons and emotions which this objection assumes. Having good reasons may strengthen or correct our feelings, and emotion in the absence of sound thinking can be a dangerous thing.

However, there is a sound point to be made here. It is that good moral reasoning cannot of itself produce right action: for this to happen, actors must be motivated to act in ways prescribed by moral reasoning. Actors may act morally because they want to do what is morally right, or they may act morally because that is what they would wish to do independently of moral considerations. Also, a variety of different moral considerations might each produce grounds for the same action. So, accepting that the purpose of the philosophy of *animal* rights is to protect the interests, or well-being of nonhuman animals, it may be that this purpose may be served by other means than action motivated by reasoned conviction that animals have rights. In particular, transformed social relations between humans and animals in the direction of eliminating the kinds of institutionalised 'reification' and 'commodification' I mentioned at the beginning of this chapter, might be expected to facilitate more benign and compassionate moral sentiments. In such a transformed context, the need for moral or legal regulation, whilst still present, would be far less pervasive.

However, as our earlier discussion revealed, the need for rights arises not just from scarcity and lack of benevolence, but also from value-diversity and lack of full knowledge of the consequences of our actions. Since nonhuman animals do not participate in culture as humans do, there is considerable doubt whether the argument from value-diversity can be made sense of at all across the species-boundary. However, that other species do have different modes of life from our own has been insisted upon in this chapter. So, there is a parallel to action in the human domain, which causes harm through failure to respect the self-defined good of the recipient of the act. Animals may be harmed by actions not properly grounded in an understanding of their species-specific mode of life and the needs which it carries with it. This consideration, in turn, leads to a deep problem affecting any attempt to develop a moral framework for human/animal relations. This is the problem of our limited understanding of the nature and conditions of the well-being of other species. In fact, we know more than some opponents of animal rights will admit. Ethology *is* a rich and scientifically well-grounded source of such knowledge. Equally, the kinds of sensitivity that are built up between particular human carers and pets or working animals are valuable sources of insights. However, and somewhat paradoxically for the rights-view, for the more psychologically complex animals our lack of access to the 'phenomenology' of their mode of being in the world is a permanent barrier to cross-species understanding just in that aspect of well-being which is most important for both the rights view and utilitarianism.

3   Animal Rights: An Incremental Approach

Gary L. Francione[1]

Those concerned about animal protection have for some time now debated the relative merits of animal rights and animal welfare as alternative approaches to ameliorating the plight of nonhumans. This debate has aspects of both philosophical theory and political strategy that are somewhat complicated, at least in part, because those involved in the debate often use the terms in confused and inconsistent ways. For the most part, however, the rights position maintains that at least some animals are rightholders and that treating animals solely as means to human ends violates those rights. Rights advocates argue that practices that violate animal rights should be abolished and not merely regulated. The welfare position maintains that animal interests may be ignored if the consequences for humans justify it. Although welfarists may disagree about what counts as a consequence that will override an animal interest, all welfarists accept that animals may be killed or subjected to suffering based on some consequential considerations.[2]

The rights/welfare issue has, however, gone in a most peculiar direction in recent years. On one hand, many in the animal protection community appear to regard the rights/welfare distinction as involving a tedious and irrelevant philosophical distraction in light of the perceived inevitability of animal welfare and the supposed utopian and unrealistic nature of animal rights. On the other hand, many who support animal exploitation seem not only to recognise the philosophical, political, and economic relevance of the distinction but also to understand that animal rights is a concept that poses practical and immediate threats to at least some forms of animal exploitation.

In this essay, I want to take issue with some of the notions that currently inform the rights/welfare controversy. Firstly, I will describe briefly the respective positions of animal exploiters and animal advocates on the welfare/rights debate. Secondly, I will argue that the reliance by animal advocates on animal welfare as a means of achieving animal rights is completely misplaced and that, in addition to moral and empirical problems, there are *structural* difficulties with animal welfare that make it highly unlikely (if not impossible) that animal welfare could ever lead in the direction of animal rights. Thirdly, I will argue that although the prevailing theory of animal rights, as articulated by Tom Regan (1983), advocates the immediate abolition of virtually all forms animal exploitation, Regan allows for a more piecemeal approach to animal rights, and that an incremental approach is not inconsistent with rights theory. Fourthly, I argue that there are important aspects of the rights approach that can quite realistically and practically be implemented even within the current legal system that characterises animals as property.

Prevailing wisdom is that animal welfare is the only realistic approach to achieve justice for animals. I will argue that animal welfare cannot serve this purpose and that, ironically, rights theory offers a realistic paradigm for the very incremental change sought by the welfarists.

Rights/Welfare: An Important Distinction or an Irrelevant Distraction?

There is absolutely no doubt that many of the most powerful opponents of the animal protection movement see a very important difference between animal welfare and animal rights. For example, Americans for Medical Progress (AMP), is a tax-exempt organization whose self-stated goal is to 'educate the public, the media and policy makers about the role of medical research in curing disease, easing pain and making quality medical care more affordable'. AMP lists as members of its board of directors theologians, educators, researchers, politicians, business people, and lawyers. In a recent mailing, AMP wrote to law school deans around the country in order to warn of a 'dangerous philosophy that is quickly emerging as a popular course of study in our law schools'.[3] This 'dangerous philosophy' is the philosophy of animal rights, which, according to AMP, 'goes beyond legitimate animal welfare issues'. We are told that although 'most Americans fully support animal welfare (the humane treatment of animals)', the 'misguided philosophy' of animal rights, which recognizes that animals, like humans, may be rightholders, 'is held only by a small minority in this country'.[4] The AMP warns that the popularity of animal rights courses in law schools is a 'foreboding sign for anyone concerned with health care. These lawyers will be asked to protect these extremists who destroy research facilities and cripple biomedical research with excessive regulation.' Such activities will 'cost researchers time and money, causing Americans to wait longer for cures and treatments and pay more for their health care'.[5]

The AMP position is far from unique. The Administrator of the Alcohol, Drug Abuse, and Mental Health Administration of the Department of Health and Human Services, Frederick K. Goodwin, claims that the animal welfare movement has had 'a distinguished history' and that 'our responsible stewardship of animals involves humane care'.[6] Animal rights advocates, on the other hand, subscribe to the view that 'humans and animals have equivalent rights' and that 'animals have intrinsic rights of their own, a notion that conflicts with the foundation of our entire legal system'. In a letter to Representative Dante B. Fascell, Goodwin distinguishes between animal welfarists and 'adherents of the animal rights movement'. The former are 'reasonable individuals [who] believe that we have a moral obligation to treat the animals in our charge humanely'. Goodwin characterizes scientists as adhering to the principle of animal welfare because they 'have a responsibility to make sure that they are properly fed, watered and housed in decent quarters'. The latter, he suggests, 'argue that animals are the moral equivalent of humans'. Like the AMP, Goodwin links the animal rights position as 'terrorist.'[7]

A recent book critical of the animal rights movement claims that 'according to the philosophy of the animal rights movement, humanity does not have the right to use any animal for any purpose' and that the animal welfare philosophy, on the other hand, is concerned to preserve people having 'control over animals' (Lutherer & Simon, 1992, p. 10; p. 13). Another academic defender of animal exploitation claims that 'the animal *rights* movement, in addition to holding the position that animals are entitled to the same moral rights as humans, has adopted terrorist tactics' (McLaughlin, 1990, pp. 12–13). Animal rights activists present an immediate threat to science through the 'demoralization of scientists, tremendous financial cost, and erosion of public opinion and political support for animal experimentation in biomedical research and education. The long-term threat is loss of the privilege to use animals and resultant retardation of progress.' The rights position is contrasted with the welfare position, which 'generally holds that animals may be used for human benefit, or for the benefit of other animals, provided the animals are treated humanely. Animal welfare is couched in terms of obligations of humans to provide humane care and treatment of animals rather than in terms of moral or legal rights of animals.' The author adds (p. 13) that despite any ambiguity concerning the concept of animal rights, one thing is clear: 'animal rights *is not* an extension of animal welfare'.[8]

On the other hand, many animal advocates, some of whom seem to show no reluctance in flying the banner of animal rights as a purely rhetorical matter in media and fundraising contexts, regard any substantive discussion of the rights/welfare issue as really nothing more than a philosophical distraction and as having absolutely no real-world application. For the most part, these advocates claim that animal rights is an all-or-nothing state of affairs and cannot realistically be achieved at present. As a result, any welfarist measure must be seen as a desirable step along the road to animal rights, and it is thought that animal rights will only be achieved as the result of incrementally improved animal welfare. For example, some animal advocates who claim to regard all uses of animals in experiments as impermissibly violative of animal rights in an ideal world nevertheless support amendments to the federal Animal Welfare Act on the ground that (supposedly) strengthening the welfarist norms contained in the Act will lead eventually to an abolition of vivisection. Animal welfare is regarded as part of a supposed 'evolution' toward animal rights that is necessitated by practical concerns and is regarded as necessary for the ultimate recognition of animal rights.[9]

Expressions of this view are articulated by many prominent animal advocates. For example, Ingrid E. Newkirk, director of People for the Ethical Treatment of Animals has stated that the position articulated by Regan and others is 'unrealistic' and although she endorses a rights position, she argues that 'total victory, like checkmate, cannot be achieved in one move' and that we must endorse welfarist measures as necessary 'steps in the direction' of animal rights (Newkirk, 1992). Newkirk regards animal welfare as the practical approach in contrast to the supposedly unrealistic and idealistic animal rights philosophy. Don Barnes of the National Anti-Vivisection Society has stated that he finds the philosophical distinction between rights and welfare to be 'artificial' and that philosophical positions simply do not matter as long as efforts are made to reduce animal suffering. Barnes states that in his view, most of those in the animal rights movement 'could not adequately differentiate between the theories' of rights and welfare (Barnes, 1994). Andrew Rowan endorses an 'evolutionist' position based on 'incremental proposals' of animal welfare. He rejects the distinction between animal rights and animal welfare as a 'false dichotomy' and concludes that 'drawing a hard and fast distinction between animal welfare and animal rights is neither accurate nor valid' (Rowan, undated). Animal welfare is seen as a means to the end of animal rights, and the only practical way in which to achieve that end.

In sum, then, we see that there are notions embedded in the current rights/welfare debate. The first is that animal welfare is a desirable or even necessary step in the struggle for justice for animals. Ironically, animal welfare is embraced by both the exploiters and many animal advocates; the primary general differences between the two camps concern what constitutes 'humane' treatment or 'unnecessary' suffering and whether animal rights is or is not regarded as a desirable end point. For example, Barnes argues that nothing more matters as long as 'one feels compassion toward other animals and seeks to aid their plight' (Barnes, 1994). The problem is that *everyone* – including vivisectors – claims to feel compassion for animals and to be working to improve animal treatment. Indeed, the comments of the animal exploiters discussed above are entirely consistent with Barnes's standard. And to the extent that the debate is shaped in these terms, it becomes centered on how generously welfarist notions are to be interpreted, rather than on more progressive measures that might be implemented to aid the plight of animals.

The second notion, adopted by many in the animal community, is that animal rights is not an alternative to animal welfare because, unlike the latter, the former does not offer a realistic alternative. I will now argue that these notions are mistaken.

Myth #1: Animal Welfare Works

There are a number of objections that may be lodged against the animal welfare position. For example, if animals really do have moral rights, then it is simply impermissible to sacrifice the rights of animals today in the hope that animals tomorrow will have rights. Moreover, there is little empirical evidence to suggest that animal welfare works. Although a recent study by Tufts University (Rowan & Loew, 1994) claims that the number of animals used in experiments has decreased by 50 per cent since 1967, that study is based on some data that the authors of the study acknowledge as 'unreliable' and a survey about which the authors state: 'it is not clear how much confidence can be placed in the survey's methodology or results'.[10] In any event, even if there were a decrease, and even if the reporting procedures, which are wholly inadequate, allowed us to measure this decrease with some remote degree of accuracy, there would be no reliable way in which that decrease could be linked causally to animal welfare measures, such as the federal Animal Welfare Act. Critics of the rights position often point to the decrease in the production and sales of fur as proof that animal welfare works. The success of the fur campaign (especially in the US) is, however, debatable and, in any event, the efforts against fur have all been articulated in the language of rights – that is, the abolition of the practices of producing or wearing fur – and not in the language of welfare – that is, that fur coats ought to be produced more 'humanely' and that 'unnecessary' suffering in fur production should be regulated. Moreover, despite the existence of literally hundreds of animal welfare laws that require the 'humane' treatment of animals, eight billion animals annually in the United States alone are raised in barbaric conditions of intensive agriculture and slaughtered on brutal assembly lines of death. Current standards of animal welfare also permit the use of animals for completely trivial purposes, such as circuses, zoos, rodeos, pigeon shoots, and the wearing of luxury items like fur. Indeed, in light of the development of intensive agricultural practices, the uses of animals in bioengineering, and the destruction of entire ecosystems to accommodate ostensibly limitless human expansion, it may be argued that the plight of animals in 1994 is much worse than it was in 1894. And throughout that entire period, there were animal welfare laws that protected animals from 'unnecessary' cruelty. In the United States, animal welfare laws go back to colonial times with the first anticruelty statute enacted in 1641 by the Massachusetts Bay Colony. If animal welfare works – if animal welfare is a step along the road to animal rights – then why has there been no really appreciable gain in any area of animal exploitation? How long do nonhumans have to wait until animal welfare delivers on the promise that it will 'evolve' into animal rights?

The answer to these questions may be found in a more rigorous analysis of what animal welfare really *is* and how it operates as a regulatory paradigm in a legal system that is based on a strong notion of private property, including that property ownership is a matter of the freedom of the individual property owner and that state regulation of private property ought to be scrutinized suspiciously and rejected unless justified, for the most part, by economic efficiency. Animal welfare provides that we ought to balance human and animal interests in situations of human/animal conflict, and that we ought to avoid imposing 'unnecessary' suffering on animals. The problem is that when we balance these interests in order to see whether the suffering or death of an animal is 'necessary', we actually balance two very different normative entities.[11] Human beings are regarded by the law as having interests that are protected by rights. To the extent that the law recognizes that nonhumans have interests, those interests are virtually never protected by right and can always be sacrificed if the benefits to humans (however measured) justify the sacrifice. This lopsided approach is exacerbated when the property rights of humans are involved because animals are a form of property. As such, humans are entitled under the law to convey or sell their animals, consume or kill them, use them as collateral, obtain the offspring and natural dividends from animals, and exclude others from interfering in the owner's dominion and control. Indeed, to characterize animals as property is precisely to regard them solely as means to human ends, and without any inherent value recognized under the law.

A property owner's treatment of an animal may ostensibly be limited by anticruelty laws, but property rights are paramount in determining the ambit of protection accorded to animals by law. Moreover, property rights have an explicit constitutional basis, and are considered 'natural rights' reflecting the moral ontology of John Locke whose views helped to shape both our views of the human right of property and the status of animals as property. Locke believed that the right of property was a natural right because its binding force existed even in the state of nature and in the absence of convention. The right does not depend on any sort of consent and cannot be abrogated as society deems appropriate. Locke believed that a person acquired property in something by mixing her labour with the thing, and that although animals were given by God to humans in common, humans had to 'appropriate' animals in order for animals to serve humans. Interestingly, Locke recognized that once animals were regarded as property, a primary concern of law and morals was to ensure only that people did not 'spoil or waste' animals for 'no purpose' (see Francione, 1995, ch. 2). In other words, animals could be exploited except when their exploitation would serve no socially useful benefit.

The property aspect of animals is almost always a major component in the resolution of human/animal conflicts, because even if the property aspect is not explicit, in almost all circumstances in which human and animal interests conflict, a human is seeking to act upon her property. As far as the law is concerned, it is as if we were resolving a conflict between a person and a lamp, or some other piece of personal property. The winner of the dispute is predetermined by the way in which the debate is conceptualized in the first place. The human interest in regarding animals as property is so strong that even when people do not want to consider animals as mere 'property', and instead, view animals, such as dogs and cats, as members of the family, the law generally refuses to recognize that relationship. For example, in most states, if a veterinarian negligently kills Joe's dog, and Joe sues the veterinarian, damages will be limited to the fair market value of the dog (which usually amounts to very little), and the court will not award damages for emotional distress.

To put the matter in another way, the current standards of animal welfare are determined not by reference to any moral ideal, but by the property status of the animal and by what conduct is perceived to maximize the value of animal property. Property rights in animals have historically been allocated to people and animals remain property because that allocation of rights is thought to maximize the value of animals to humans. Indeed our allocation to humans of rights in the bodies of animals reflects precisely the notion that it is more efficient to relegate animals to property status than it is to value animals for themselves or to accord them dignity and respect. We do not recognize that nonhumans have *any* type of inherent value, and we do not find animal protection measures to be desirable to the extent that these measures go beyond what is necessary to ensure the efficient exploitation of those animals. For example, as long as the laboratory animals are, in the opinion of those doing the experiment, providing reliable data, or as long as food animals are efficiently yielding products for the market, there is no incentive to regulate further; indeed, any further regulation would be considered as inefficient because it would represent an overall diminution of social wealth. In 1985, the Congress amended the Animal Welfare Act to provide for, among other things, psychological stimulation of primates and the exercise of dogs used in labs. The initial standards, which were promulgated by the United States Department of Agriculture (USDA), the federal agency to which Congress has delegated enforcement of the Act, established specific standards (that is each dog must be walked a certain number of minutes per day unless certain very limited conditions applied), and the biomedical community objected so vociferously that the government withdrew the standards. The objections reflected the concern of researchers that these specific standards would make research much more expensive and there was no need for such expense in light of the prevailing view (among researchers) that current standards already exceed what is necessary to obtain reliable research data. In place of the specific standards, and in clear deference to the research community, the government promulgated standards that left primate psychological well-being and canine exercise in the discretion of the individual research facility, which is not likely to improve standards as long as its researchers believe that the current level of 'care' is sufficient to ensure reliable research data. The Animal Welfare Act is there to ensure that we do not, in Locke's words, 'waste' or 'spoil' animal resources 'for no purpose'. The Act simply does not go beyond that standard and it never has done so. If my thesis is correct, it never will do so.

For the most part, the suffering of animals represents what economists call an 'external' cost of animal use because there is no easy way to quantify that cost and internalize it for the purpose of determining what course best serves the goal of economic efficiency. Indeed, to the extent that animal welfare measures may be said to produce a social benefit (some people will attach an economic value to that value animal protection), we do not measure that benefit from the point of view of the animal because the animal is only property that has no interests protected by right. *Any* animal interest that is recognized under animal welfare laws is subject to being traded away for human benefit, and, under welfare laws, we allow the property owner to decide whether the benefit is sufficient. So, for example, the federal Animal Welfare Act prohibits the infliction of 'unnecessary' pain on animals used in experiments, but allows the experimenter virtually unfettered discretion to determine what constitutes 'necessity'. To the extent that animal welfare regulation produces any identifiable social benefit, such benefit must be measured in terms of benefits that are perceived by the public and the measurement of such benefit is extremely difficult. The USDA, has put the matter this way: 'animal welfare is an anthropomorphic attribute' that requires measurement of the 'increase in the level of public perception in animal welfare as the level of stringency of the regulations also increases'. Such measurements involve a 'lengthy and cost prohibitive study of the marginal increases in social welfare or utility'.[12]

The tension that arises from the perceived need to maximize the value of the property – in this case, animal property – and the costs of regulation of property use means, in effect, that 'unnecessary' suffering or 'cruel' treatment will come to be understood in terms of that suffering that does not serve some *legitimate* (that is, socially accepted) purpose. And without any notion of absolute prohibitions on animal use (in light of the property status of animals and our deference to property owners to determine the value of their animal property), virtually all uses of animals will be permitted, and, in fact, most uses of animals, however barbaric, *are* permitted. If animal use results in the infliction of pain and suffering, but the suffering facilitates the activity and generates social wealth, then, however 'inhumane' the activity may be in terms of the ordinary language use of 'humane' behavior, any pain and suffering are regarded as 'necessary' and beyond the ambit of animal welfare laws. If there is no social benefit generated by the conduct, or the conduct involves activity to which is attached some social approbation (such as gambling at cockfights), then the activity may be prohibited by animal welfare laws. For example, if a farmer for absolutely no reason allows farm animals to die, the action may be punished under anticruelty laws as a 'waste' of animal property; if, however, the farmer brands, dehorns, castrates, force-feeds, or mutilates an animal incidental to preparing the animal for a socially accepted use – meat eating – then the action will generally be permitted as long as it is accepted husbandry practice.

A defender of animal welfare may agree that the current standards of animal welfare are inadequate, but may argue that the solution is to *improve* animal welfare and not reject it in favour of animal rights. The problem with this approach, however, is that all forms of animal welfare, including the theory articulated by Peter Singer in *Animal Liberation* (1990) are linked by the notion that it is morally justifiable to support the institutionalized exploitation of animals under some circumstances. All versions of animal welfare necessarily involve the use of a balancing construct; because animals are regarded as property, it is difficult to understand how this balancing construct *could* be adjusted to ensure greater animal protection.

It is, of course, possible to conceive of a situation in which animals were not regarded as property but were also not regarded as rightholders. Presumably, animal interests would be taken more seriously were animals not regarded, as a matter of law, as solely means to human ends. The problem is that if humans are still rightholders and animals are not (although they would no longer be regarded as property), then any welfarist balancing of human and animal interests would still weigh interests protected by right against interests unprotected by right.

Alternatively, we might eliminate the notion of rights entirely and rely solely on interest balancing in the absence of any rights considerations related to humans or animals. This is the sort of position advocated by Peter Singer. This is, however, an unrealistic option; it is highly unlikely that we would agree to forgo our rights precisely because most of us do not want our most important and fundamental interests to hinge on purely consequential considerations. Singer, who is at least consistent in his utilitarian views, accepts that there may be circumstances in which animal *and human* exploitation (including the use of nonconsenting human subjects in medical experiments) could be morally justified in light of consequences. Even those people who are more communally minded would, I think, reject this position precisely because we cling to a notion that at least some of our interests ought not to be subject to abrogation simply because of some aggregation of consequences.

Finally, any balancing of human and animal interests, whether or not animals are regarded as property, is likely to be problematic as long as no rights considerations serve to limit the balancing process. The utilitarian notion of 'consequences' simply cannot be interpreted in a way that does not prejudice the issue of animal protection. Even if we do accept that animals have interests, it is very difficult to make determinations about those interests from our humanocentric and patriarchal perspective; it is precisely because we systematically devalue and underestimate the interests of disempowered populations that rights concepts are necessary in the first place. Perhaps the most compelling evidence of the structural defects of animal welfare can be found in the present-day reality of pervasive and barbaric animal abuse despite myriad animal welfare laws stretching back to the earliest days of the Anglo-American legal systems. These laws have failed miserably in providing protection to nonhumans.

Myth #2: Animal Rights is not a Realistic Alternative to Animal Welfare

The flip side of the myth that animal welfare works is the myth that rights for animals is an unrealistic and unachievable alternative. Just as the efficacy of animal welfare has been challenged, so too will the supposed inefficacy of animal rights.

The notion that animal rights represents an unworkable or unrealistic approach is based on the supposed status of the philosophy of animal rights as an all-or-nothing philosophy that demands an immediate and complete cessation of all types of animal exploitation and can tolerate nothing less. In certain respects, this is a correct characterization of the rights position as articulated by Regan, and in certain respects, it is not.

Regan argues that it is morally wrong to regard animals as nothing more than receptacles for intrinsic value that lack any value of their own. Animals have inherent value apart and it is inappropriate to treat them solely as the means to the end of value maximization. Regan claims that evolutionary theory, common sense, and ordinary language all point to the possession of consciousness – indeed, of a complex mental life – by nonhuman animals. Normal mammals aged one year or more (human and nonhuman) share mind states such as perception, memory, desire, belief, self-consciousness, intention, a sense of the future, emotion, sentience. Human and nonhuman animals possess equal inherent value precisely because they share a crucial similarity; almost every mammal – human or nonhuman – is the subject of a life that is meaningful to that being, irrespective of the value of that being to anyone else. The basic moral right possessed by all moral agents and patients is the right to respectful treatment. This right is based on the respect principle, which precludes treating the rightholder merely as a means to an end. Rather, the rightholder must be treated in a manner consistent with the recognition that she possesses an inherent value that is the same as any other holder of such right. Inherent value and respect support the harm principle, which holds that we have a *prima facie* duty not to harm individuals and we owe this duty directly to the beneficiaries of the duty. Although the harm principle imposes a *prima facie* and not absolute obligation, we need valid moral reasons to override the obligation and cannot do so simply by appeal to consequences, as is the case with animal welfare.

After presenting his basic argument, Regan argues what implications arise from accepting that nonhumans share with humans this right to respectful treatment. He concludes that virtually all forms of animal exploitation are morally indefensible and that animal exploitation should be *abolished* and not merely regulated. For the most part, he advocates the total and immediate cessation of the use of animals for science, food, clothing, and entertainment, and other practices condoned by a Cartesian dualism that sees animals as fundamentally different from humans. Regan considers the major forms of animal exploitation as resulting from a general failure to regard animals as subjects-of-a-life. This failure is the direct result of the status of animals as property – a status that Regan argues should be abolished.

There are two ways (at least) of looking at all of this. First, Regan's theory may, indeed, be viewed as entailing an all-or-nothing proposition in that it requires that we relinquish completely all property rights in animals, and that we cease immediately all forms of exploitation that are based on the instrumental status of animals as property. Regan unequivocally endorses this 'abolitionist' position, which, of course, makes perfect sense in light of his view that our treatment of animals and our treatment, say, of slaves, are based on the same underlying notion that it is morally permissible to treat certain sentient beings in a completely instrumental manner that regards any interest of the being as subject to sacrifice upon a finding that the aggregation of consequences favors that sacrifice. If this is the *only* possible interpretation of the rights view, then, although it may present a sound moral theory that ought to be adopted immediately, the realistic possibilities for such a situation occurring, especially in light of the increasingly reactionary political and legal systems, are slight to none. But that does not mean that there is no alternative other than animal welfare, which does not work anyway and is no real alternative. The concept of animal rights, I will argue, allows for a third choice: the incremental achievement of animal rights through the use of deontological norms that prohibit rather than regulate certain conduct, that recognize that animals have certain interests that are not subject to being sacrificed, and that do not prescribe alternative, supposedly more 'humane' forms of exploitation as substitutes for the original conduct.

In the remainder of this section, I want to offer an explanation of why there are some very good reasons why the rights approach does, in a very important sense, entail an all-or-nothing approach in that acceptance of the rights position means that virtually all animal exploitation, including our use of animals as sources of food and clothing, is immoral and should cease immediately. I will then discuss what I regard as a practical incremental approach to animal rights that is theoretically consistent with the general theory of animal rights.

Basic Rights

In order to understand the complexity surrounding the concept of animal rights, it is necessary first to explore a very central – and peculiar – feature of rights discourse when applied to nonhumans. This exploration requires that we first examine the notion of a 'basic' right. Although the notions of 'basic' and 'absolute' rights are discussed in much philosophical literature, its most lucid presentation for present purposes may be found in the illuminating analysis presented by Professor Henry Shue in his book, *Basic Rights* (1980).

According to Shue, a basic right is not a right that is 'more valuable or intrinsically more satisfying to enjoy than some other rights'. Rather, a right is a basic right when 'any attempt to enjoy any other right by sacrificing the basic right would be quite literally self-defeating, cutting the ground from beneath itself'. Although 'non-basic rights may be sacrificed, if necessary, in order to secure the basic right ... the protection of a basic right may not be sacrificed in order to secure the enjoyment of a non-basic right'. The reason for this is that a basic right 'cannot be sacrificed successfully. If the right sacrificed is indeed basic, then no right for which it might be sacrificed can actually be enjoyed in the absence of the basic right. The sacrifice would prove self-defeating.' Shue emphasizes that basic rights are a prerequisite to the enjoyment and exercise of non-basic rights, and that the possession of non-basic rights in the absence of basic rights is nothing more than the possession of rights 'in some merely legalistic or otherwise abstract sense compatible with being unable to make any use of the substance of the right'.

Although Shue identifies several basic rights, the most important of these is the 'basic right to physical security – a negative right not to be subjected to murder, torture, mayhem, rape, or assault'. Shue acknowledges that it is not unusual in a given society that some members of at least one ethnic group receive less physical protection, 'few, if any, people would be prepared to defend in principle the contention that anyone lacks a basic right to physical security'. If a person does not enjoy the basic right to security, and may be murdered at will by any other person, then it is difficult to understand what *other* rights that person might enjoy (Shue, 1980, pp. 19–21).

Shue is most certainly correct to note that we always assume that humans have basic rights to physical security, whether or not there are social differences in terms of the actual distribution of the right. In order words, recognition of the basic right of physical security is a right *as a matter of law* irrespective of whether the state enforces this right in an even-handed manner. In the case of animals, however, the situation is precisely the opposite. Although we talk about the rights of animals, animals do not have the basic right of physical security and they do not possess it *as a matter of law*. Because animals are regarded as the property of their human owners, animals can be killed for food, used in experiments, and exploited in numerous other ways. Moreover, because animals do not have the basic right of physical security (or any other basic rights), it is senseless to talk about animals having rights at all.

If animals are property, and property status is inconsistent with the existence of basic rights, such as the right of physical security, then the achievement of animal rights may well be impossible as long as animals are regarded as property. That is, if animals are to have any rights at all (other than merely legalistic or abstract ones), they must have certain basic rights that would then necessarily protect them from being used as food or clothing sources, or as experimental animals. If animal rights requires at a minimum the recognition of basic rights as Shue understands them, then animal rights may very well entail an all-or-nothing state of affairs.[13]

It is not clear, however, that the rights theorist is compelled to settle for nothing less than a basic right that would, by eviscerating property rights in animals, abolish virtually all animal exploitation. Shue's basic right of physical security is, even when applied to human beings, a rather fuzzy concept. That is, even where the right exists both as a matter of law and as applied (however unfairly), the content of the right may be unclear. For example, if a country has military conscription during time of active conflict, does that type of coercion vitiate the right to physical security? Do patriarchal laws about rape and spousal abuse vitiate the basic right of security for women? It would seem that the right of physical security is something that doesn't just exist or not; it may exist by degrees. What is essential to any such right of physical security, however, is that there be at least *some* interests concerning physical security that are not subject to violation in the absence of valid and compelling moral reasons. To the extent that there is this protection that is not determined by aggregation of consequences, the beneficiary of the protection does, indeed, have a meaningful claim against others that is central to the notion of rights. Beyond that, the precise content of any such basic right is vague. So, although the notion of animal rights may be understood to require a radical and immediate social transformation, it may also be amenable to incremental measures that erode the property status of animals over time without requiring that property status to be eliminated immediately. It is to this question that I will now turn.

Animal Rights: A Piecemeal Approach?

According to political theorist Robert Garner, Regan's philosophy is an 'absolutist approach' in that he recognizes that rights theory requires the immediate and total abolition of all animal exploitation. Garner recognizes, however, that the rights theorist is not necessarily committed to this state of affairs. He states that Regan acknowledges that rightists 'can support a gradual programme but each step must, in itself, be abolitionist' (Garner, 1993a, p. 248). Garner doubts that this approach is workable. For example, he argues that 'surely there is much that can be done to improve the lot of animals short of abolition of a particular practice' (p. 248). More to the point, however, Garner argues that the incremental rights approach, which requires abolitionist steps, might work in the context of particular practices involved in vivisection (for example, an abolitionist step would be the elimination of certain toxicity tests altogether), but 'this position does not regard reforms to animal agriculture as acceptable because, whatever the methods used, killing animals for food continues' (Garner, 1993b, p. 7).

Although Garner's concerns about the implementation of animal rights are legitimate, I do think that he is incorrect to regard the incremental approach as being more problematic in the case of farm animals than in the case of animals used in vivisection. Assume that a law is passed that absolutely prohibits using animals in toxicity tests. The same animals that are banned from use for these experiments will most certainly be used for some other type of experiment. That is, even an absolute prohibition does not guarantee that animals will not be exploited. Indeed, that is the problem with 'gradual abolition' as opposed to abolition; as long as legally-sanctioned exploitation exists, then prohibitions of activities that are constitutive of the institutionalized exploitation will not serve to eradicate that exploitation.

The same is true of animals used in agriculture. It is a routine practice to castrate bulls without anesthesia. Even if that practice were abolished entirely, the steer will still be consumed. This is, however, no different from the laboratory rat. Some law may prohibit the use of the rat for toxicity tests, but the rat will be used for some other type of experiment. Contrary to what appears to be Garner's view, the rat and the steer are very similarly situated with respect to the notion of incremental abolition of animal exploitation. The reason why vivisection is supposedly amenable to this 'gradual reduction' is because Garner assumes that vivisection is a practice that can be divided somehow so that we can 'abolish' its constituent parts. To the extent that this is true for vivisection, it is also true in the case of farm animals.

The question remains, then, whether a rights approach can accommodate this notion of incremental change that still leaves animals as the property of human owners. Although I think that the issue is quite complicated, I will as a preliminary matter present an argument that an incremental approach is logically and practically feasible. The cornerstone of this approach is the rejection of the foundational principle of animal welfare – that all animal interests (to the extent that any are even recognized) are subject to being balanced against human interests that are protected by deontological rather than consequential norms. In order for an incremental step to count as a 'rights' rather than 'welfare' measure, the norm must satisfy three conditions:

Firstly, the norm must recognize a non-tradable interest. As we saw above in the discussion of animal welfare, the primary defect of that theory is that all animal interests are regarded as tradable as long as there is some benefit for humans that will result. In light of the property status of animals, and the status of humans as rightholders with considerable discretion in their use of their property, this sacrifice is largely inevitable.

Secondly, the norm must prohibit, rather than regulate, the conduct that constitutes a violation of the non-tradable interest. Under the current legal systems of most western countries, there is very little conduct toward animals that is prohibited outright. Indeed, the primary form of legal control consists in laws that require that animals be treated 'humanely'. This means that virtually any action toward animals will be permitted as long as the requisite human benefit is identified. To the extent that specific acts are prohibited, such as cockfighting or dog fighting, those prohibitions are often more related to class issues than to animal protection, and are not, in any event, enforced for the most part.

Thirdly, the norm must not prescribe an alternative form of exploitation although animals that will be beneficiaries of such prohibitions may still be subject to other exploitation because, by definition, incremental abolition leaves the underlying institutionalized exploitation intact. For example, a prohibition on the dehorning of steers based on respect for the animals' interests in not being subjected to the procedures, and that did not require some other, supposedly more 'humane' procedure, would satisfy this requirement. This third requirement is needed both to identify true prohibitions and to avoid incorporating welfarist balancing through the back door of rights. That is, a rule that prohibits four hens from being placed in a 12 inch square battery cage, and requires instead that the hens be confined in a cage that is 16 inches square may in one sense be said to constitute a prohibition in that confinement of the hens in the smaller cage is prohibited. But this rule cannot really be said to be a prohibition in the sense that we talk about when we speak of incremental abolition of animal exploitation or incremental achievement of animal rights. Indeed, such a prohibition would be completely indistinguishable from a welfarist regulation. Moreover, if the rule substitutes another, supposedly more 'humane' form of exploitation, or substitutes a standard that prohibits 'unnecessary' suffering, we are right back where we started from with animal welfare: what constitutes the 'necessity' of suffering or the 'humane' treatment of animals will be determined by a balancing process in which animal interests will be at risk.

These three conditions satisfy key elements of the rights approach. To the extent that the law recognizes that at least some animal interests are not tradable, animals stop being treated solely as means to human ends although they will still be treated as means to human ends. Incremental abolition recognizes the status of the nonhuman as a sentient being with inherent value. Each incremental measure erodes the status of animals as property. That is, the property status of animals means that animals are *only* means to ends and that their interests are protected only insofar as that protection is consistent with norms of property ownership and the efficient use of property. To the extent that the law recognizes that animals have non-tradable interests, it undermines, albeit gradually, that property status. Finally, each incremental recognition is consistent with the precise type of protection that constitutes Shue's basic right of physical security. Although no particular incremental change will result in Shue's basic right, each step represents a rejection of

the institutionalized structure of exploitation that presently precludes
attributing any content to that basic right as far as animals are concerned.

An incremental approach to animal rights is also politically acceptable
because it does not threaten the complete and immediate elimination of the
property status of animals. This is, of course, not to say that incremental
abolition will be welcomed. It will certainly be resisted by animal exploiters,
who, by the way, just as vehemently fight the most moderate of animal
welfare measures. One need only read the legislative history of the federal
Animal Welfare Act and its various amendments to see how the biomedical
establishment fought that law at every stage despite the generally accepted
view that the Act has done little, if anything, to benefit animals. Nevertheless,
the level of social concern about animals has not been higher in recent years,
and this concern can be harnessed effectively to support such measures as
prohibitions on particular experiments or procedures, prohibitions on certain
practices used in animal agriculture, and prohibitions on the use of animals
for entertainment.

This incremental use of deontological norms, is, of course, woefully short
of the state of affairs envisioned by animal rights advocates. Most troubling
is that problem identified by Garner with respect to farm animals but, as
argued above, applied to all instances of incremental abolition. Until the
property status of animals is abolished, there will never be true abolition and
even abolitionist measures will result in animals being exploited. Of course,
the rights advocate can rely on the principle of moral agency, and make clear
that it is not her moral responsibility if someone chooses to exploit animals
in some way other than the one that has been banned on moral grounds as
the result of her efforts. Perhaps the best that the rights advocate can do is
to say that 'I have succeeded in abolishing this particular practice; its abolition
does not, in and of itself, prescribe or require the substitution of another form
of exploitation'. The very same animals may be used in other experiments,
or other animals of a different species may be used in other experiments
simply as the result of banning certain animal uses. Nothing in a rights-
oriented prohibition, however, would require or prescribe this result. In
addition, all of these deontological protections must be accompanied by a
continuing and unrelenting political demand for the end of the property
status of nonhumans and all the animal exploitation that is made possible
by that status.

Conclusion

The debate about animal rights and animal welfare has foundered on two
notions – that animal welfare works and that animal rights cannot. I have

argued that there are serious structural problems with animal welfare in that it requires that we balance normatively dissimilar entities: the interests of animals who cannot under the law have rights and are characterized as the property of humans and the interests of humans who have rights and, in particular, the right of private property. When these interests are balanced, the animal virtually always loses. That animal welfare simply does not work is indicated by the fact that although there is a high level of social concern about animals, animals are still routinely used for what the overwhelming majority would say are frivolous purposes.

I have also argued that the theory of animal rights does, indeed, provide a viable theoretical and political alternative to animal welfare. Although the complete abolition of all animal exploitation is – at least in my view – morally required, that state of affairs is not realistic at the present time. Incremental abolition is realistic and achievable through prohibitions that recognize that animals have non-tradable interests and where those prohibitions do not substitute alternative forms of exploitation.

NOTES

1. This essay is adapted from Francione (1995). I acknowledge the marvellous assistance provided by Anna Charlton, the co-founder and co-director of the Rutgers Animal Rights Law Center. I have benefitted greatly from discussions with Tom Regan, Nancy Regan, Priscilla Cohn, Patty Shenker, Doug Stoll, and Shelton Walden. This essay is dedicated to The Bandit, one of my nonhuman companions who most generously supplies ideas and inspiration in the most unexpected ways, and who has very much informed my notion of what personhood really means.
2. Although animal welfare comes in different shapes and sizes, the underlying theory of animal welfare is obviously closely related to utilitarian thought. Animal rights describes generally those positions that regard some animal interests as not being able to be sacrificed, or at least not based on the aggregation of consequences. The theory of animal rights is a manifestation of deontological or nonconsequentialist moral theory.
3. Letter from Susan Paris to Dean Lewis Kerman, dated 7 April 1994. This letter was contained as part of a national mailing from Americans for Medical Progress Educational Fund.
4. There are indications, however, that the animal rights position is more popular than the defenders of animal use would have us believe. Although the AMP claims that the acceptance of the 'dangerous philosophy' of animal rights is restricted to 'a small minority', other materials in the same AMP mailing explicitly contradict the AMP description of the support for animal rights. For

example, the AMP reports that in a poll conducted by the *Los Angeles Times*, 61 per cent of those aged 18–29 years agreed with the assertion that 'animals are just like humans in all important respects'. These observations by AMP about the popularity of animal rights are consistent with other polls which indicate that an increasing number of people accept the rights perspective. The AMP observations are, however, inconsistent with AMP's proclamation that animal rights is a view held only by a small number of 'extremists'.

5.   The AMP approach is problematic not only for reasons concerning justice for nonhumans, but also for reasons concerned with justice for humans. The AMP position is a complete repudiation of freedom of speech and of the presumption of innocence in criminal trials. Indeed, the AMP position advocates standards that would be illegal under current interpretations of constitutional law.

6.   F. Goodwin, 'Animal Rights vs Animal Welfare', a manuscript to accompany a slide show, 1989.

7.   Letter of Frederick K. Goodwin to Dante B. Fascell, 10 February 1992 (copy on file with the author).

8.   It should also be noted that the rights position is often mischaracterized in the quoted materials. For example, no animal advocate argues that animals have the same rights as humans. And the overwhelming majority of the animal rights community has condemned violence.

9.   The precise relationship between animal welfare and animal rights is not clear. That is, those who argue that animal welfare is a step in the evolution toward animal rights may have different views about the precise relationship between welfare and rights. For example, animal welfare measures may be thought to educate the public about animal exploitation so as ultimately to facilitate the achievement of animal rights. Similarly, welfare measures may be regarded as making the political system more amenable to rights-oriented changes. The relationship between welfare and rights, however, need not be seen as causal in any sense.

10. Despite the defects that the authors acknowledge, they conclude that the 50 per cent decline indicated by the suspicious study are confirmed by other data that the authors also find problematic, as well as studies by pharmaceutical companies and a PhD thesis that reports a reduction in animal use by the United States Department of Defense.

11. For a more detailed discussion of the structural problems of animal welfare see Francione (1994 & 1995).

12. 56 Fed. Reg. 6486 (1991) (preamble to rules promulgated by the United States Department of Agriculture).

13. I do not wish to give the impression that Shue argues that animals ought to have basic rights as his book does not even address the question of animal rights.

Part II: Medical Science, Agriculture and Animal Welfare

Having considered some of the moral issues relating to our relationship with nonhuman animals and the way in which they inform the strategy of the animal rights movement, this section moves on to examine some of the substantive contexts in which animals are exploited. Animals are exploited in a wide variety of ways and for a wide variety of human purposes – food, health, clothes, companionship and entertainment to name the main categories. It is appropriate, however, as this section does, to focus on the use of animals in agriculture and the laboratory. The importance of these two categories derives not only from the fact that billions of animals worldwide are utilised for food and research and that they involve some of the severest examples of animal suffering, but also because they represent the kind of systematic, institutionalised exploitation which the animal rights movement was born to challenge (see Mason & Singer, 1990; Johnson, 1991; Ryder, 1975).

Animal Welfare Law

The section begins with Mike Radford's detailed account of the British law relating to the treatment of farm and laboratory animals. Such an account is crucial since it emphasises that rigorous legislation is a necessary, if not sufficient, prerequisite for the protection of animals. In addition, pinpointing the weaknesses of existing legislation allows the animal protection movement to prioritise its campaigning focus, thereby maximising its chances of success before moving on to more ambitious objectives.

What Radford's analysis does reveal is that, whilst British animal welfare law is fairly comprehensive in comparison to other countries – including the United States and many other European states – there are a number of serious flaws which ought to exercise the concern of reformers. It is a salutary fact, for instance, that the fairly moderate recommendations of the Brambell Committee (set up in the 1960s to examine the welfare of farm animals) have been only partly accepted by successive British governments and that some of the reforms – such as the prohibition of sow tethers and stalls – have only come about as a result of considerable pressure through the mobilisation of public opinion and the use of the Private Member's Bill procedure. Likewise, although in theory the 1986 Animals (Scientific Procedures) Act provides fairly stringent controls on researchers wishing to use animals, the legislation prohibits no particular procedures – such as the use of animals for testing household products and cosmetics – and decisions on what is to be permitted is left in the hands of ministers and officials in the Home Office who are likely to be strongly influenced by the research community. At the very least, the secrecy surrounding the working of the legislation leads to suspicions that it is not operated in the best interests of animals.

Radford also identifies some general weaknesses of animal welfare law. There are co-ordination problems because a variety of government departments are responsible for different aspects of animal welfare (a point also made by Ryder in chapter 9), there are doubts about the effectiveness of enforcement and there is the ever-present danger of standards in Britain being undermined by the international contexts in which policy relevant to animal welfare is increasingly made (see Rosemary Goddard Svendsen's article in chapter 8). Crucially, too, much animal welfare legislation seeks, negatively, to prohibit certain practices rather than positively promoting the welfare of animals. This situation, Radford suggests, derives from the fact that animals are regarded in law as property and a positive version of animal welfare – involving the imposition of 'a general duty to ensure their physiological and psychological needs *except* in such situations as the law defined' – necessitates a legal status which recognises animals as sentient beings. Whether this can be achieved without rejecting the whole notion of animal welfare in favour of a rights-based theory and practice, as Gary Francione implores us to do, is a moot point.

A legal account, of course, only takes us so far. A political analysis would seek to explain the existence and character of animal welfare law by considering the motivations and influence of the actors involved in the formulation and implementation of legislation. We will return to the political context in the third section of this book but here it should be noted that it is extremely significant that in Britain the law relating to farm and laboratory animals has been the responsibility of government departments who have traditionally been dominated, respectively, by agricultural interests and the research community.

Benefits, Harms and Human Interests

Following on from Radford's account of animal welfare law, the contributions by Andrew Rowan and Michael Fox focus specifically on the issues of animal experimentation and agriculture. Significantly, whilst both eschew the language of rights, they make constructive contributions to the debate about our treatment of animals and the future direction of the animal protection movement. Indeed, it might be argued that they are able to achieve this precisely because the avoidance of rights-based arguments allows them to be more flexible.

From an animal rights perspective, animal experimentation is illegitimate irrespective of the human and/or animal benefits deriving from it. As Regan points out, such benefits may be considerable but they are still ill-gotten gains (Regan, 1983, p. 393). In reality, the animal rights movement has in recent years spent a great deal of time seeking to challenge the utility of using animal models in research designed to apply to humans (see, for instance, Sharpe, 1988). This 'practical anti-vivisection' approach can be distinguished from Regan's 'ethical anti-vivisection' and a genuine welfarist position, the latter differing from the other two by accepting both the empirical claim – that animal research has benefited humans – and the moral claim – that it must therefore continue until valid alternatives can be found. In the light of this, Rowan's concern is to assess the technical case against animal experimentation. This case is based on two propositions: that animal experimentation is unnecessary and that animal research causes too much suffering for too little or no benefit. In terms of its necessity, Rowan questions the contribution of preventive medicine, the role of public health and clinical measures. The development and use of alternatives, on the other hand, has played – and will continue to play – Rowan suggests, a major role in the reduction of animal usage. Here, he makes the controversial claim (challenged by many in the animal rights movement – see Stephens, 1994) that the number of animals used worldwide has fallen by between 30–50 per cent in the last two decades or so. Whether or not this is true (and there are enormous methodological difficulties involved in confirming or refuting the assertion) Rowan does admit that it is not clear how far this has come about as a direct result of the search for alternatives as opposed to the unintended by-product of more efficient research techniques.

On the second proposition, Rowan shows how difficult it is to weigh the benefits of animal research against the suffering inflicted. There is relatively little data on the suffering part of the equation and evaluating harm is to a large degree dependent upon prior moral assumptions, particularly in relation to the rightness and wrongness of killing. Indeed, a characteristic of the practical anti-vivisectionist campaign is the extent to which the moral objection impinges on the interpretation of the empirical evidence relating to the necessity of animal research, the extent of animal suffering in the laboratory, and the benefits accruing from it. Thus, for example, whether or not one thinks that cosmetics should be tested on animals will depend upon weighing up the suffering inflicted on animals against the benefits to humans. Increasing numbers of people now think that the suffering outweighs the benefit in this case, but they only do so because they think the moral status of animals is such that they should not be used to satisfy the relatively trivial interests of humans.

It is obviously more difficult to justify the claim, often made by practical anti-vivisectionists, that animal research provides no beneficial outcomes in medical research. It is possible to point to some cases where animal research has not only failed to lead to advances but has also led researchers up the wrong path, thereby holding back progress. As Rowan demonstrates in his case studies of the discovery of insulin and the development of the polio vaccine, however, it is extremely difficult to pinpoint the contributions made by animal research. If animal research sometimes led researchers up blind alleys then so, on occasions, did clinical observations. In the end, it is difficult to dispute his conclusion that a 'mixture of chance, technique availability, clinical observation and animal experimentation' led to advances in knowledge. Prohibiting animal experimentation, then, would not, as some scientists insist, lead to the total collapse of medical research but it would remove one possible avenue which, at times, has made a difference.

The practical anti-vivisection case has been a useful strategy, putting advocates of animal research on the defensive and enabling campaigners to focus on challenging the utility of animal research without needing to get involved, overtly at least, in a philosophical debate about animal rights which, presently at least, is unlikely – particularly where medical research is concerned – to convince the mass of the public. The success of Singer's *Animal Liberation* was at least partly to do with the cases of animal exploitation he documents, a tactic he also used in the article reproduced in chapter 1 of this volume. Such an approach is justified on the grounds that his intention was to demonstrate the levels of pain inflicted on animals. His philosophical position, however, stands alone without the need for such extensive empirical information demonstrating the futility of much animal research. The fact that the practical anti-vivisection strategy has worried the research community is indicative of its utility.

One practical success has been the growing recognition – amounting now to something approaching a consensus amongst the general public at least – that using animals for cosmetic testing is illegitimate, because trivial. Governments have not so far prohibited such testing, although intelligence reveals that the Animal Procedures Committee in Britain has rejected project applications for such a purpose. However, consumers, as Radford points out, have been keen to buy products not tested on animals and, particularly in the United States, enormous pressure has been applied on cosmetic manufacturers, most notably by the campaigns run by Henry Spira, to find alternatives to the infamous LD50 and Draize tests. In Britain, Home Office figures reveal that the number of procedures used to safety-test cosmetics and toiletries declined from some 15000 at the beginning of the 1980s to little more than 4000 by the end of the decade (Garner, 1993a, p. 121). One can assume that at least part of this decline has come about as a result of the growing public demand for an end to animal testing.

An agricultural equivalent of the practical anti-vivisection strategy is provided in the chapter by Michael Fox. Fox explicitly seeks to expand the notion of the harm caused by factory farming to encompass not just the suffering inflicted on animals (which actually receives very little attention in his article) but also the harm done to the environment, human health, the poor in the developing world and the small-scale family farms which have suffered at the hands of giant agribusiness concerns. Fox is not, of course, the first to draw attention to this interdependence (see, for instance, Johnson, 1991; Mason & Singer, 1990; Wynne-Tyson, 1975; Robbins, 1987). He is, however, more concerned than most – and unlike the practical anti-vivisectionists – to deny that his major concern is with the consequences for animals of factory farming in particular and meat eating in general.

Fox makes it clear that he has no objection to ecologically sound animal agriculture. Indeed, farm animals, he writes, 'play a vital economic role in sustainable crop production and range management'. Likewise, the animal rights rejection of meat eating is cast aside. 'The question of the rightness or wrongness of meat eating and of killing animals', Fox continues, 'is not the central issue or primary bioethical concern of the humane movement'. As a result of this he is able to offer a pragmatic programme for reform involving a reduction in the production and consumption of meat, a refinement of the ways in which animals are reared, transported and slaughtered and the gradual replacement of animal protein and fat with healthier and more environmentally benign alternatives.

The kind of analysis which Fox engages in and the claims of the practical anti-vivisectionists which Rowan seeks to examine are open to similar objections. Fox, as indicated above, eschews an animal rights position but his arguments can be adopted from within an animal rights perspective. The problem with so doing is that those who oppose animal experimentation and the killing of animals for food on moral grounds, but who seek to challenge it on empirical grounds by pointing out that it does not serve human interests (henceforth the 'human interest strategy'), can be accused of intellectual dishonesty (Finsen & Finsen, 1994, p. 279). In the hard world of practical politics, however, such a criticism can be overstated. Clearly, there is little objection to pointing out that the benefits of intensive agriculture and animal experimentation can be exaggerated and that, particularly in the case of the former, the costs to humans and animals can be great. Another response might be to say that the dishonesty objection is, as Fox seems to suggest, reason enough to abandon a rights position so as to avoid such charges. It should also, finally, be pointed out that to some extent the emprical and moral claims are not mutually exclusive. Most notably, the human problems caused by intensive agriculture are a product of an ethical disregard for nature. As Mary Midgley (*Guardian*, 21 March 1996) pointed out in the context of the British BSE crisis: 'How can we expect to be safe and prosperous ourselves if we show no respect for the life around us?'

A more telling objection is that the human interest strategy involves shifting the debate from a preoccupation with ethics to areas (relating to scientific procedures, the welfare of animals on farms, the health and environmental implications of intensive agriculture and so on) about which the movement's opponents can claim to have expertise. This is potentially hugely problematic for the animal protection movement. Even if, as is often the case, animal protection groups provide a rigorous and scientifically informed case, they are open to the patronising retort often made by opponents that whilst the hearts of animal protection advocates are in the right place, they are misguided because their rational judgement is clouded by their compassion. At the very least, the animal protection movement needs to attract the backing of experts in a wide variety of academic disciplines in order to provide as much respectability as possible for its claims. Rowan's work is itself, of course, indicative that such a development has already begun to occur.

A related objection is that the logic of the human interest strategy requires its proponents to accept that when human benefits can be discerned from the exploitation of animals they are morally justified. In effect, this is to deny, as Fox does, the possibility of achieving the ultimate abolitionist objectives animal rightists want. This is an important consideration and is particularly relevant to the medical benefits which it is difficult to deny sometimes derive from animal experimentation. We should weigh this objection, however, against the opportunities for coalition-building offered by the human interest strategy which may be hindered by an isolationist rights-based strategy. Further, the objection is to assume that the abolition of animal agriculture and experimentation is a possibility in the medium term. However much animal rightists might wish it were so, this assumption is unrealistic and is likely to remain so for the foreseeable future.

4 Partial Protection: Animal Welfare and the Law

Mike Radford

> My message is that animal welfare, in the general and in the particular, is largely a matter for the law ... There is no complete substitute for the law. Public opinion, though invaluable and indeed essential, is not the law. Public opinion is what makes laws possible and observance widely acceptable.
>
> Rt Hon. Lord Houghton of Sowerby CH
> (in Patterson & Ryder, 1979)

The purpose of this chapter is to consider the law of Great Britain in relation to two specific areas: the treatment of animals in agricultural production, and the use of animals for scientific procedures. The intention is not only to explain the relevant legal provisions, but also to identify some of the important shortcomings which are associated with the legal process.

It is not suggested that those who wish to see an improvement in the treatment of animals are wrong to look to the law for achieving reform. Clearly, such a focus is essential, not only because of the authority and status which is inherent in the law, but also because there is no alternative: if one wishes to change the rules which determine how animals are to be treated, then it must be through the law.

Moreover, not only are weaknesses in the present law detrimental to the welfare of individual animals, they also provide legitimacy for that treatment. It is a common defence to criticism to assert that 'I'm doing nothing wrong; I'm acting within the law', or 'I'm merely doing what I have a legal right to do'. The significance of such arguments is that they provide apparent justification for what is being done, and place an onus on the state, on the basis of notions of the rule of law, to ensure that those concerned can continue to go about their lawful business, regardless of the strength of opposition it might engender. Thus, while hunting with hounds remains a lawful activity, the police will see it as their duty to protect those who wish to participate. Similarly, protesters against the trade in live animals have found themselves confronted at ports and airports by hundreds of police, many fully-equipped with riot equipment, who had been drafted in to ensure that trade which was lawful could continue.

So, those who wish to see change must look to the law to achieve their ends. In so doing, they are continuing a proud tradition of campaigning which dates back to the early years of the nineteenth century. Indeed, it was inevitable that the early reformers should have made the law the focus of their attention: at common law – that is, the law handed down over time by the judges – domestic animals are regarded merely as private property. As such, the owner was free to treat them however he pleased. It was only through statute that this situation could be rectified, hence the need to persuade Parliament to intervene.

It is right, therefore, to say that 'There is no complete substitute for the law'. Equally, however, it must be appreciated that the law is not the panacea which some would like to think: changing the law does not of itself provide all the answers or solve all the problems. In seeking to rely on the law, it is important also to appreciate the weaknesses of the legal process: to have due regard to the pressures which are brought to bear in determining the content of the law itself, and the context in which it is – or is not, as the case may be – enforced.

Background

The legislative regimes relating to both agricultural animals and those used in scientific procedures operate against the backdrop of the Protection of Animals Acts, particularly that of 1911 – in Scotland, the Protection of Animals (Scotland) Act 1912. Notwithstanding that the Act is more than 80 years old, and both its wording and underlying concepts owe much to its nineteenth-century predecessors, it remains the statute which defines the general offence of cruelty. As such, it is the foundation on which the law relating to the treatment of domestic and captive animals is built.[1] Under the Act, an offence of cruelty can be committed in a number of specific ways, such as to cruelly beat, kick, ill-treat, over-ride, over-drive, over-load, torture, infuriate or terrify an animal. The central test of cruelty, however, rests on the notion of causing an animal unnecessary suffering.

Thus, the Act provides that it is an offence to convey or carry an animal in such a manner or position as to result in unnecessary suffering; to tether any horse, ass, or mule under such conditions or in such a manner as to cause unnecessary suffering; or without reasonable cause or excuse to abandon an animal in circumstances likely to cause unnecessary suffering. Most importantly in practical terms, it is an offence wantonly or unreasonably to do or to omit to do any act which causes unnecessary suffering.

The advantage of a broad, general test such as this is that it can be applied in a wide range of situations. The problem, and it is a significant problem, is its subjective nature. In short, it is ultimately up to the courts to determine, on the basis of the particular circumstances of each individual case, what constitutes unnecessary suffering. This produces uncertainty: only in the most extreme situations is it possible to predict with any degree of confidence that an offence has been committed. Moreover, the notion of unnecessary suffering means not only that the law contemplates there to be situations in which suffering can be regarded as necessary, and therefore lawful, but also treatment that might be regarded as unlawful in one context – on the basis that is causes unnecessary suffering – can be considered lawful in another because the court takes the view that the suffering is necessary.

It will be appreciated from the foregoing that the Protection of Animals Act 1911 is not all that its name implies. In practice, the Act affords animals partial protection. Only those animals for which man is directly responsible through domestication or captivity receive any protection under it – although under the Wild Mammals (Protection) Act 1996 it is now an offence to subject a wild mammal to certain specific acts of cruelty – but even this is sporadic. The combined effect of the 'unnecessary suffering' test and the provisions of other legislation relating to the treatment of animals in specific circumstances is that the degree of protection varies according to the circumstances in which man has placed it. A rabbit, for example, is subject to different degrees of protection depending on whether it finds itself in a person's home, a pet shop, a zoo, on a farm, or in a laboratory. Determining what is lawful, then, is not so much by reference to the physical and psychological needs of the individual animal, but rather by its relationship with man and the purpose for which it is being used. This is the triumph of pragmatism over principle.

Agricultural Animals

The first animal protection legislation in Great Britain was introduced with the specific intention of improving the way in which agricultural animals were treated. In 1822 Parliament enacted 'An Act to Prevent the Cruel and Improper Treatment of Cattle', although subsequently it became better known as 'Martin's Act' after Richard Martin MP who, with Lord Erskine, had been the driving force in getting it onto the statute book. The Act broke new ground in making cruelty to animals a criminal offence. The owner's unfettered property right was qualified in that it became unlawful to 'wantonly beat, abuse, or ill-treat any horse, mare, gelding, mule, ass, ox, cow, heifer, steer, sheep, or other cattle'. The principle that, regardless of an agricultural animal's eventual fate at the hands of the slaughterman, it is entitled to a

basic standard of humane treatment during its life is therefore well established
in English law.

Animal Husbandry

Until the end of the 1960s control over the way in which farm animals were
treated relied essentially on the Protection of Animals Act 1911. However,
as the nature of farming and animal husbandry changed, becoming more
intensive, less personal, and undertaken on a much larger scale, public
unease began to grow, and it became apparent that to rely merely on the
general provisions of the 1911 Act to regulate these new practices was no
longer appropriate. Such concerns were both represented and increased by
the publication in 1964 of Ruth Harrison's important book, *Animal Machines*
(1964) the first informed critique against the growing practice of 'factory
farming'. In response, the government appointed a technical committee of
inquiry to 'examine the conditions in which livestock are kept under systems
of intensive husbandry and to advise whether standards ought to be set in
the interest of their welfare and if so what they should be' – the Brambell
Committee (HMSO, 1965a).

The Committee failed to condemn outright the use of intensive forms of
husbandry. It observed that an animal kept under such conditions was 'no
more, and is probably less liable than any other' to suffer wanton cruelty as
a result of either intent or neglect (paragraph 35). More controversially, it
concluded that the use of intensive husbandry methods 'should not in itself
be regarded as objectionable and may often benefit the animals'. The
Committee did accept, however, that 'certain practices are contrary to animal
welfare and need to be controlled' (p. 63, paragraph 1), and agreed that the
existing legislation failed adequately to safeguard the welfare of farm animals.

Notwithstanding that the Committee accepted the principle of intensive
farming methods, and its recommendations failed to lead to radical change,
the significance of its work should not be overlooked. Thirty years on, the
tenor of its report comes across as both informed and enlightened. Indeed,
the approach of the Brambell Committee represents something of a landmark,
for it was the first official body to put the interests of the individual farm
animal firmly at the heart of its deliberations, and to assess the welfare of
livestock on the basis of the physiological and psychological needs of a
sentient being, rather than as merely an instrument of agricultural production:
'We consider that it is morally incumbent upon us to give the animal the
benefit of the doubt and to protect it so far as is possible from conditions
that may be reasonably supposed to cause it suffering, though this cannot
be proved' (paragraph 30).

For example, the Committee categorically rejected the argument, which is still regularly advanced by the proponents of intensive methods, that the rate of growth of an animal, or the level of egg production in the case of laying hens, provides an objective measure of welfare, describing such a proposition as 'an over-simplified and incomplete view' (paragraph 30). In contrast, the Committee emphasised that there were many factors to be taken into account, and only by giving attention to all of them could an animal's welfare be measured and, ultimately, improved. Thus, it attached importance to animal health (paragraph 31); to threats posed by hazards such as fire risks, failure of environmental control and automatic feeding systems, slippery floors, the risk of entanglement or strangulation in caged or tethered animals; and the need for adequate ventilation and lighting, and appropriate temperature controls (paragraphs 33, 40, 41, 42 & 43). On the basis that farm animals belong to species which have an organised social life, it was said that they needed companionship, and should not be kept in solitary confinement (paragraph 38); the practice of providing a diet that is deficient in some essential component was condemned, regardless of whether it led to an overt pathological condition (paragraph 39); floors should be constructed in such a way that made an animal feel secure on its feet, and not so as to produce undue strain on the legs or feet or to result in malformation of them (paragraph 40); there should be an appropriate balance between periods of illumination and darkness (paragraph 44); and appropriate measures taken to prevent or minimise undesirable habits which can arise because of confinement, such as fighting, feather-picking, tail and ear biting (paragraph 45).

What makes the Committee's approach particularly significant, however, is the importance it attached to ensuring that animals could indulge in their natural behaviour. All mutilation of animals was condemned 'in principle', but mutilation which affected their normal behaviour and was carried out to counter a defect in the system of husbandry was singled out for particular criticism. According to the Committee, mutilation of an animal is only acceptable in circumstances 'where the overall advantage to the animal, its fellows, or the safety of man, is unmistakeable' (paragraph 34).

Turning to the central question of confinement, it was recognised that this could be advantageous to an animal, in providing shelter and protection. However, the Committee cautioned that the advantages must be weighed against the inherent disadvantages, and in determining whether particular situations were acceptable, it suggested that two factors should be taken into account. Firstly, the degree to which the animal's behavioural urges were affected; and, secondly, the duration of the confinement: 'In principle we disapprove of a degree of confinement of an animal which necessarily frustrates most of the major activities which make up its natural behaviour and we do not consider such confinement or restraint permissible over a long period unless the other advantages thereby conferred upon the animal are likely to be very substantial.' At the very minimum, the Committee considered that an animal should have 'sufficient freedom of movement to be able without difficulty, to turn round, groom itself, get up, lie down, and stretch its limbs' (paragraphs 36 & 37).

Although the Committee made a large number of specific recommendations, it appreciated that the nature of an animal's welfare was more than the sum of these individual requirements, and expressed concern that, even if they were all fulfilled, animals could still suffer pain or cruelty. The Committee therefore considered it necessary to establish a clearer definition of 'suffering' over and above that contained in the Protection of Animals Act 1911. To this end, it adopted the relatively sophisticated concept which had been included in the report of an earlier inquiry looking at animal experiments (HMSO, 1965b) which suggested that suffering existed where there was:

(a)   discomfort (such as may be characterised by such negative signs as poor condition, torpor, diminished appetite);
(b)   stress (that is a condition of tension or anxiety predictable or readily explicable from environmental causes whether distinct from or including physical causes);
(c)   pain (recognisable by more positive signs such as struggling, screaming or squealing, convulsions, severe palpitation).

The Committee recommended that any legislation resulting from its Report should make it an offence 'to cause, or permit to continue, avoidable suffering so defined' (HMSO, 1965b, paragraphs 223 & 224). Note that not only is the meaning of suffering widely drawn, but the offence would turn on avoidable suffering – an objective test – rather than the subjective test of unnecessary suffering.

The Brambell Committee's Report merits rereading. Indeed, one could do worse than use it as a benchmark against which to compare current practice and legal protection. Whatever its shortcomings, the Committee was ahead of its time in its approach and its recommendations; it did, after all, consider that the debeaking of hens, the docking of pigs' tails, and the close tethering of sows and veal calves should all be prohibited forthwith. The latter practices have, eventually, been banned, but it took more than 20 years. Debeaking hens and docking pigs' tails both remain lawful and widespread practices.

The fact that Brambell did not lead to radical legislative reform was not the fault of the Committee; responsibility lies with the politicians of the day. If its recommendations had been implemented in full they would have represented a major advance in farm animal welfare. As it was, Parliament's response was to enact the Agriculture (Miscellaneous Provisions) Act 1968, which adopted a much more gradualist approach than Brambell had urged.

The 1968 Act, together with the relevant provisions of the Protection of Animals Act 1911, form the basis of the current law relating to the treatment of farm animals. It makes it an offence to cause, or knowingly allow, livestock to suffer unnecessary pain or unnecessary distress whilst they are on agricultural land. The nature of the offence is not so vague as that of unnecessary suffering under the 1911 Act, as ministers are empowered to make regulations and issue codes of practice which together provide further detail about how livestock should be treated. However, the concepts of unnecessary pain and unnecessary distress are much weaker than the definition of suffering recommended by the Brambell Committee. Most significantly, the 'unnecessary' qualification continues to rely on a subjective test.

Regulations made under the authority of the 1968 Act are legally binding. They have been used to advance the welfare of animals, by, on the one hand, laying down requirements which must be complied with and, on the other, prohibiting practices and procedures which have come to be regarded as unacceptable. Thus a number of practices such as hot branding cattle and devoicing cockerels are prohibited, and detailed requirements are proscribed regarding the conditions under which livestock must be kept.[2] The codes of practice issued under the Act are advisory rather than mandatory, but failure to observe them can be used in evidence by the prosecution in criminal proceedings brought under the Act. To date, codes have been issued in respect of cattle, pigs, domestic fowls, turkeys, sheep, ducks, rabbits, farmed deer and goats.

Ministers may authorise individuals to enter premises to ensure that the legal requirements concerning the treatment of livestock are being complied with. In practice, enforcement of the Act's provisions is the responsibility of the State Veterinary Service, which operates under the auspices of the Ministry of Agriculture, Fisheries and Food in England, and the Scottish Office and Welsh Office respectively. However, there is nothing in the legislation to preclude an individual taking a prosecution, and the Royal Society for the Prevention of Cruelty to Animals, for example, brings a number of prosecutions under the Act each year, either on its own initiative or in co-operation with the State Veterinary Service.

One recommendation of the Brambell Committee which was implemented at an early stage was the establishment of a Farm Animal Welfare Advisory Committee, to advise ministers on welfare issues. It was replaced in 1979 by the Farm Animal Welfare Council (FAWC).

Transport and trade

The Agriculture (Miscellaneous Provisions) Act only applies to livestock while they are on agricultural land; the law relating to their treatment once they are moved away is governed by the Animal Health Act 1981, under which ministers may make Orders for the purpose of protecting animals from unnecessary suffering (again!) during transit, in markets, or while being exported.[3] The most important single measure regulating animal transport, and the most controversial, is relatively recent. Under the Welfare of Animals during Transport Order 1992 (SI 1992/3304), which was introduced to bring British law into line with the terms of the European Community's Directive on the Protection of Animals During Transport (91/628/EEC 19 November 1991), it was prohibited to transport an animal in a way which causes or is likely to cause it injury or unnecessary suffering; or to transport an animal which is unfit for the journey. Those in charge of animals being transported were made responsible for ensuring that they had been appropriately fed and watered both before the journey began and at suitable intervals thereafter. In respect of cattle, sheep, goats, pigs and equine animals, it was specified that the interval between the provision of rest, food and water should not exceed 15 hours.

The issue of transport has been the subject of considerable controversy, particularly in the United Kingdom and especially in relation to animals sent for export to the European mainland. The debate has centred on two separate but connected issues: the conditions attached to the journey itself, and the treatment inflicted on the animals at their final destination, in particular where the standards of animal welfare are not so high as in the United Kingdom – the practice of keeping veal calves in crates and the methods used for slaughtering livestock are matters which have generated particular concern.

Animal welfare organisations such as the RSPCA and Compassion in World Farming would like to see an end to the routine export of live animals for slaughter, arguing that meat should be exported 'on the hook' as carcasses. While the live trade continues, however, both organisations have mounted a vigorous campaign to introduce a maximum journey time of eight hours, and succeeded in attracting considerable public support which culminated in widespread protests at docks and airports during 1994 and 1995. As a result, the government was placed under considerable pressure to act. In response, it revoked and re-enacted the 1992 Regulations, introducing further requirements in relation to the loading and unloading of animals, and the information which was required to be included on journey plans.[4] However, the government has consistently refused to interfere with the trade itself, claiming that to act unilaterally would be an infringement of European Community law. This position is currently under challenge by the RSPCA and Compassion in World Farming; having been granted the leave for judicial review by the High Court, the question has now been referred to the European Court of Justice.

After long and tortuous negotiations in the Council of Ministers, agreement was finally reached in June 1995 which has now been enshrined in Directive 95/29/EC. This provides that from the beginning of 1997, all animals must be fed, watered and rested for at least 24 hours after eight hours on the road, *except* when they are being transported in lorries which meet additional specific requirements. These include having aboard the vehicle adequate bedding straw and appropriate feed; allow direct access to the animals through a side-door; and be equipped with adjustable ventilation, compartments for different animals, and facilities for connection to a water supply during stops. Where such a lorry is used, the eight hour journey time will not apply. Instead, young animals may be subjected to a journey of 18 hours travelling time, provided there is a rest period of at least an hour after nine hours on the road; in the case of adult cattle and sheep, the limit is extended to 28 hours travelling, on condition that there is an hour's rest after 14 hours travelling; in recognition of the greater degree of stress suffered by pigs, their journey time will be limited to 24 hours, provided they have continuous access to water en route.

In practice, the requirements imposed on hauliers are not stringent and they will have little difficulty in complying with them. It is not immediately obvious how an arrangement which replaces a 15 hour journey limit, with a journey of 28 hours, albeit with the requirement of an hour's rest in the middle, advances the interests of animal welfare, despite the protestations of the Minister of Agriculture that the agreement represented the 'historic beginning of proper legislation to improve the treatment of animals in transport'.

Moreover, the issue of whether governments are empowered under the Treaty of Rome to interfere with trade in live animals on the basis of the way in which they may be treated at their journey's end remains unresolved for the present.

Slaughter

The manner in which animals are slaughtered and their treatment prior to being killed is regulated by the Welfare of Animals (Slaughter or Killing) Regulations 1995 (SI 1995/731), which were introduced to give effect to European Community provisions on the protection of animals at the time of slaughter or killing (Directive 93/119/EC). These place a general duty on those involved with slaughter to ensure that animals are not subjected to any avoidable excitement, pain or suffering. Not only does this wording represent a welcome move away from the 'unnecessary suffering' test, but the inclusion of the word 'any' would suggest that the smallest degree of avoidable suffering would amount to an offence. At all times when there are live animals on the premises, there must be available a person who is both competent and has the authority to take whatever action is necessary to safeguard the welfare of the animals. In addition, those whose duties include handling the animals are required to have the necessary knowledge and skill to perform the task humanely and efficiently.

The Regulations specify provisions in respect of the construction, equipment and maintenance of slaughterhouses and knackers' yards;[5] the treatment of animals awaiting slaughter; and requirements as to their restraint prior to being killed. Only those licensed as being competent may undertake the restraint, stunning, slaughter or killing of an animal.[6] Where appropriate, stunning must be by means of captive bolt, concussion, or electronarcosis (the latter referring to causing insensibility by the application of an electric shock); where an animal has not been stunned, the method of killing is by free bullet or electrocution, except in the case of pigs, which may be gassed, or birds, which may be gassed, decapitated, or have their necks dislocated. In respect of all these procedures, the Regulations specify in detail how they are to be carried out. Additionally, the Minister has the power to issue codes of practice for the purpose of providing further guidance. Slaughterhouses and knackers' yards are subject to inspection by persons authorised by the Minister. This provides a right of entry and the power to carry out such checks and examinations as are necessary. Controversially, slaughter by the Jewish or Muslim methods is still permitted. This entails cutting the animal's throat without pre-stunning.

Scientific Procedures

There is no realistic prospect in the foreseeable future of an end to the use of animals for either basic research or product testing; a combination of academic, commercial, economic, medical, and scientific interests, together with a significant proportion of public opinion and a variety of legal constraints will see to that. Whatever one's view about the necessity of such activities, it is surely desirable that, while they continue, they should be regulated. In the United Kingdom this is the function of the Animals (Scientific Procedures) Act 1986, which replaced the Cruelty to Animals Act 1876.

The regulatory system is administered by the Home Secretary, assisted by a team of inspectors and an advisory body, the Animal Procedures Committee. In general terms, the legislation requires that where an experiment or other scientific procedure which may cause pain, suffering, distress or lasting harm (a 'regulated procedure') is carried out on a vertebrate (other than man) or the common octopus ('protected animals'), those undertaking the work, the relevant research programme, and the premises at which it is carried out, each have to be individually approved by the Home Secretary.

The legal effect of the scheme is significantly different from that of other legislation concerned with the treatment of animals. Such measures prohibit specified practices and lay down basic standards of care, contravention of which may lead to prosecution. In contrast, the Animals (Scientific Procedures) Act makes those who comply with its terms exempt from these provisions. In other words, the Act only affords animals indirect protection; it is the scientists who enjoy direct protection because practices which might otherwise amount to a criminal offence are deemed lawful. So, for example, activities which would constitute cruelty under the Protection of Animals Act 1911 are not illegal if carried out in accordance with the terms of the 1986 Act; similarly, the duty to prevent unnecessary pain and distress under the Agriculture (Miscellaneous Provisions) Act does not apply in such circumstances. Such suffering, pain and distress which is caused is, by implication, regarded as necessary.

Everyone who carries out a regulated procedure must hold a personal licence, which is subject to review at least every five years. It specifies the nature of the procedures the holder is authorised to undertake, the type of animal involved, and the place at which they are to be carried out. The Home Secretary may include such conditions as he thinks fit, but it is mandatory for there to be a requirement that precautions are taken to prevent or reduce to the minimum consistent with the purposes of the work any pain, distress or discomfort to the animals used.

In addition, a project licence must be issued by the Home Secretary authorising the application of designated regulated procedures as part of a specified programme of work. It states the types of animals to be used, and the place where the work is to be carried out. The maximum duration for a licence is five years, thereafter it is necessary to apply for a renewal.

Under guidance issued by the Home Office, applicants for a project licence are required to provide details of:

(a) the purpose and scientific justification for the work;
(b) a full description of the procedures which would be involved;
(c) an estimate of the number of animals of each species which may be required;
(d) the status, qualifications and experience of the project licence holder;
(e) an assessment of the anticipated level of suffering – mild, moderate or substantial. (HMSO, 1990, paragraph 4.1)

The Act imposes a number of significant constraints on the Home Secretary in deciding whether to grant a project licence. Firstly, he may only grant such a licence if he is satisfied that it will further one of the following objectives:

(a) the prevention, diagnosis or treatment of disease, ill-health or abnormality, or their effects, in man, animals or plants (including the testing of appropriate products);
(b) the assessment, detection, regulation or modification of physiological conditions in man, animals or plants;
(c) the protection of the natural environment in the interests of the health or welfare of man or animals;
(d) the advancement of knowledge in biological or behavioural sciences;
(e) education or training otherwise than in primary or secondary schools;
(f) forensic enquiries;
(g) the breeding of animals for experimental or other scientific use. (Animals (Scientific Procedures) Act, (1986) s. 5(3))

Secondly, in determining whether and on what terms to grant a project licence the Home Secretary is required to weigh the likely adverse effects on the animals concerned against the benefit likely to accrue as a result of the intended programme of work. Thirdly, he may only grant a project licence if he is satisfied that the applicant has given adequate consideration to the feasibility of achieving the purpose of the programme by means not involving the use of protected animals.

A project licence authorising the use of cats, dogs, primates or equidae may only be granted if the Home Secretary is satisfied that animals of no other species are suitable for the purposes of the programme or that it is not practicable to obtain animals of any other species that are suitable for those purposes. With effect from 1 October 1993 project licences can authorise the use of endangered species only if the research is aimed at the preservation of the particular species, or for essential biomedical purposes, but only if the species in question is exceptionally the only one suitable.

In addition to the above statutory requirements, the Home Secretary has advised applicants that in determining whether to grant a project licence, he will take a number of other factors into account, including:

(a) the suitability of the design of the project in relation to its stated objectives;
(b) the consideration which has been given by the applicants to reducing the number of animals used, refining the procedures to minimise suffering and replacing animals with alternatives; and
(c) the justification for using the animals which are proposed.
    (HMSO, 1990, paragraph 4.32)

No place may be specified in a project licence unless the Home Secretary has issued a certificate designating it as a scientific procedure establishment. Such a certificate must specify a person responsible for the day-to-day care of the protected animals kept there and a veterinary surgeon or other suitably qualified person to provide advice on the animals' health and welfare. All premises used to breed mice, rats, guinea-pigs, hamsters, rabbits, dogs, cats or primates for use in regulated procedures require a similar certificate, as do establishments which supply protected animals, regardless of species. All these certificates remain in force indefinitely, although they are subject to revocation.

In deciding whether to grant a personal licence, project licence, or designation certificate, the Home Secretary is required to consult an inspector appointed under the Act. In addition, he may consult an independent assessor or the Animal Procedures Committee. Should he decide to refuse, vary or revoke a licence or certificate the applicant or holder must be informed of the decision and the reasons for it. Anyone affected in this way, or who is dissatisfied with the conditions attached to a licence or certificate, is entitled to make representations to a person appointed by the Secretary of State, and the matter is then reviewed. However, anyone who may wish to object to the granting of a licence or certificate has no formal access to the procedure. In a case of urgency, the Home Secretary may suspend a licence or certificate forthwith for a period of up to three months if he considers it necessary for the welfare of protected animals.

Inspectors are appointed on the basis of their medical or veterinary qualifications. While this may be advantageous in having an inspectorate which is familiar with the use of animals in scientific procedures, it does mean that they are drawn from a relatively narrow base and there is always the suspicion – which may or may not be justified – that they are inherently sympathetic to the use of animals. The number of inspectors appointed is by agreement between the Home Office and the Treasury; it seems to have settled down at around 20.

The inspectorate's function is two-fold; it acts as expert adviser to the Home Secretary in carrying out his duties under the Act, and polices its provisions by visiting designated establishments to ensure that regulated procedures are being undertaken in compliance with statutory requirements and the conditions attached to the relevant licences and certificates.

In addition to the inspectorate, the Act provides for the appointment of an Animal Procedures Committee (APC) to advise the Home Secretary on matters of policy and practice associated with the use of animals in scientific procedures. In performing its functions, the APC is required to have regard both to the legitimate requirements of science and industry and to the protection of animals against avoidable suffering and unnecessary use in scientific procedures.

The APC consists of a chairman and at least 12 other members, of whom at least two-thirds must be doctors, vets, or those who have qualifications or experience in a relevant biological discipline; at least half of the membership must be persons who do not hold any licence under the Act, or have not done so within the previous six years. In making appointments to the Committee, the Home Secretary is required to have regard to the desirability of ensuring that the interests of animal welfare are adequately represented.

Any person who carries out a regulated procedure on an animal without holding a personal licence, or without a project licence, or at premises other than specified in the personal or project licence, is guilty of an offence. So too is a project licence holder who allows a person under his control to carry out a regulated procedure otherwise than as part of the programme specified in the licence or otherwise than in accordance with that person's personal licence. The consent of the Director of Public Prosecutions is required to bring proceedings for an offence under the Act.

Although the 1986 Act has been criticised for failing to prohibit any specific scientific procedure, it does represent a major strengthening of the controls which were formerly available, and since its introduction there has been a small, but steady decline in the number of experiments. However, that still represents around 3 million procedures a year (see the Home Office, *Statistics of Scientific Procedures in Great Britain* which is published annually).

The Cruelty to Animals Act 1876 was restricted to 'experiments calculated to cause pain'. In licensing individuals to perform specific techniques, it exerted minimal control over the way in which such techniques were used.

The current statutory framework is wider in its ambit and much more thorough in the detail and extent of its regulation. Most significantly, every individual programme of work is required to obtain specific authorisation, as part of which the use of animals has to be justified and the likely benefits of the proposed work are weighed against the severity of the procedures involved. In theory, then, these arrangements allow for rigorous scrutiny of licence applications, enable inspectors to make a fully informed evaluation of proposals, and provide a detailed basis on which to determine whether the terms of a licence have been complied with.

Issues

The United Kingdom has developed a sophisticated and detailed legislative framework in an attempt to protect animals from the worst excesses of abuse by humans. It is surely incontrovertible that without it, animals would be in a much more vulnerable position, and have to endure far greater suffering. Moreover, the degree of regulation is significantly more extensive and effective than that in many other comparable countries. These are all benefits which should not be overlooked. It is, however, the case that there are significant weaknesses in the legislation relating to animals and the way in which it operates. Furthermore, notwithstanding the effects of legislative intervention, it must be appreciated that the law alone cannot solve all the problems.

The Nature of the Law

The nature of much animal welfare law is negative in character – it states what must not be done, rather than attempting to impose positive duties. It is submitted that rather than merely seeking the prevention of cruelty, the law should engage in the positive promotion of welfare (see Everton, 1989).

But it is arguable that the law should go even further. It was explained above that the first anti-cruelty legislation sought to qualify the absolute right of owners under common law to do with their property, including animals, what they like. Contemporary animal welfare legislation has the same effect. The legal status of a captive or domestic animal remains one of property, indistinguishable from that of any inanimate possession; the law simply places restrictions on the way in which it may be treated, the nature of those restrictions being entirely dependent on the circumstances in which the animal finds itself. They are not determined by the needs of the animal, but rather by the demands of man. A more principled approach, it is submitted, would be for animals – at least vertebrates – to be given a legal status which recognises them as sentient beings, and as such, imposes a general duty to ensure their physiological and psychological needs, except in such situations as the law defined. This would turn the present position on its head: at the moment one may treat an animal as one sees fit provided it is within the generally vague and pragmatic limits specified by statute. This question of the appropriate legal status of animals is often discussed in relation to European Union law, but it is surely equally relevant to the law of individual states, including the United Kingdom.

Of course, the degree to which the same species may be treated differently, depending on the circumstances of the individual animal, is in part due to the way in which the legislative process works. Threats of increased regulation can arouse opposition from interest groups which have considerable economic and political influence, especially in respect of both agriculture and scientific procedures. Too often, legislation is a compromise reflecting the lowest common denominator. Indeed, United Kingdom governments are well aware of the dangers inherent in legislating on animal matters; it can easily be the case that no one ends up satisfied – animal welfarists want more, economic interests consider things to have gone too far. In such a situation, the government can decide that it is best advised to do nothing.

Such comparative inaction has been compounded by the degree to which oversight of animal welfare is spread across government departments: the Ministry of Agriculture, Fisheries and Food; the Home Office; the Departments of the Environment, Education, Trade and Industry; in addition to the Scottish Office, the Welsh Office, and the Northern Ireland Office. This diffusion of responsibility has two consequences: firstly, it creates problems in achieving co-ordination throughout government; and, secondly, given that – under the British system – the initiative for measures to be included in the government's legislative programme tends to come from within individual departments, animal welfare has to compete for scarce parliamentary time with the great variety of other matters which are overseen by them (see Ryder, this volume, for a similar view).

The result is that measures such as the Animal (Scientific Procedures) Act, which attempt a complete overhaul of a particular area are the exception rather than the rule. Legislation relating to animal welfare is characterised by *ad hoc* measures intended to deal with a particular problem which happens to be exciting public attention at the time, rather than introducing wide-ranging reforms. On occasions a campaign can attract the support of an individual Member of Parliament who is able to steer his or her own bill onto the statute book by means of the Private Member's Bill procedure (although, to be successful, such a measure requires the open or tacit support of the government). Alternatively, an issue may force itself onto the political agenda with such an impact that the government itself sponsors change. While these individual advances are to welcomed, they do result in a somewhat patchy legislative framework, with legal reform due more to successful campaigning for a particular cause than to rational changes based on objective need or principle.

The final problem with the nature of the law has already been touched upon, namely the subjective nature of tests such as unnecessary suffering, distress and pain. Consequently, it is up to the individual court to decide, on the basis of the circumstances of the case, whether in its opinion an offence has been committed. The result is that, on identical facts, different courts can come to different conclusions.

Moreover, as such decisions are regarded as questions of fact, rather than questions of law, the grounds of appeal are extremely limited. In general terms, to succeed on appeal one has to show that the court which heard the case has either misinterpreted or misapplied the law, or has reached a perverse verdict (that is, a decision which is at odds with all the evidence). Consequently, very few cases involving animal welfare reach the appeal courts, denying them the opportunity to consider and develop the concepts of unnecessary suffering, distress and pain. It is significant that most of the established precedents date back to the last century or the early years of this, and reflect a much less enlightened attitude to animals than we like to think now exists.

Enforcement

The second area of concern centres on the question of enforcement. It is self-evident that success in changing the law is only part of the story; to be effective, law must be enforced. It is not suggested that the impact of legislation is to be judged by the number of cases which are brought before the courts. After all, the most successful legislation would be that with which everyone voluntarily complies, and no one is prosecuted. Similarly, the number of prosecutions is not necessarily an accurate reflection of the rigour with which legislation is being enforced. Enforcement means ensuring that the law's provisions are complied with, and this can generally be much more effectively achieved through education, publicity, guidance and advice, than by hauling people before the courts.

However, if legal provisions are to be taken seriously it is essential that they are seen to be enforced; that is, it is apparent to the objective observer that those charged with implementing and policing the law are carrying out their duties conscientiously, and the appropriate sanctions are being used effectively against those who choose to disregard their legal obligations.

So far as agricultural animals are concerned, formal responsibility is divided between the State Veterinary Service (SVS), which has a duty to inspect farms, and local authorities, who are responsible for enforcing the law relating to transport. Both agencies are underpinned by the activities of animal welfare organisations, particularly the RSPCA (or the SSPCA in Scotland). Crucially, however, RSPCA inspectors do not have a right of access onto private land, which makes it difficult to ascertain whether offences are being committed on farms. Reservations about the SVS centre on whether they have the number of personnel required adequately to oversee all of the agricultural land where livestock is kept, together with their perceived closeness to the farming industry.

In 1993, the SVS carried out 4090 inspections of farms specifically to assess welfare standards, in addition to monitoring animal welfare on routine visits. In most cases where welfare problems were identified they could be resolved by advice coupled with follow up visits to ensure that appropriate action had been taken. However, during the year, the SVS initiated nine successful prosecutions. A further 111 successful prosecutions were brought to court through co-operation with the SVS and other agencies, such as the police, the RSPCA and the SSPCA (HMSO, 1994). These statistics suggest a reasonable level of activity to enforce animal welfare provisions, although, in the absence of any other explanation, it would appear that the animal welfare organisations are more vigorous in formally pursuing infringements than the SVS.

With regard to the role of local authorities in enforcing provisions relating to transport, the major problem arises from the number of authorities involved, the extent and variety of their other responsibilities, and the competition within authorities for available resources. This leads to a lack of uniformity in the level of enforcement. In some areas, and it is usually due to the initiative of one or two individual officers, there is strict enforcement; in others, it is at a very rudimentary level. This is unacceptable; it cannot be right that there is so great a variation in the level of enforcement to the extent that, in some authorities, the legislation is barely acknowledged.

The difficulties are even greater in the context of international road transport, where animals may be travelling through a number of different jurisdictions, the officials of which may have very different attitudes to the question of animal welfare. The best legal provisions can be rendered impotent by inadequate enforcement. In the 1995 agreement on animal transport, the Council of Ministers attached great importance to the introduction of compulsory training for drivers of livestock vehicles, a system of licensing (with the threat that licences could be revoked in cases of non-compliance), and requirements for detailed journey plans. However welcome these measures may be in principle, they will only be effective if they are rigorously and uniformly applied across the European Union. The issue of enforcement has certainly concerned the Farm Animal Welfare Council, which has expressed reservations about its effectiveness in a number of reports, and has devoted one report specifically to this subject (Farm Animal Welfare Council, 1990).

But a further problem arises from an apparent reluctance to apply the legislation and associated guidance for the full benefit of the livestock which it is intended to protect. Indeed, the whole question of the status of the codes of practice in particular has given rise to controversy. It will be recalled that they are not legally binding, but contravention of them can be used as evidence in proceedings brought under the Agriculture (Miscellaneous Provisions) Act 1968. There must be a question-mark, however, over how seriously they are taken by the Ministry when it can produce a leaflet, aimed specifically at farmers, which in referring to the codes states, 'The requirements are not onerous but they do require careful consideration!' (MAFF, 1991). This does not seem an accurate description of their provisions, if they were to be interpreted literally and applied in full. But they are not; neither are the requirements which are legally binding.

For example, it is a legal requirement that when laying hens do not appear to be in good health or show behavioural changes, steps are taken to establish the cause and appropriate remedial action is put in hand.[7] Further guidance is contained in the relevant code which states, 'All stockmen should know the normal behaviour of domestic fowls and watch closely for signs of distress or disease and, where necessary, take prompt remedial action' (MAFF, 1987). It is not obvious that these requirements are being complied with in many intensive units, given the conditions in which the birds live, and their resultant behaviour and physical condition. Yet, the practice of battery egg production is allowed to persist.

The preface to the codes, including that relating to poultry, is not formally part of the code but is, in its own words, 'intended to explain [the code's] purpose and to indicate the broad considerations upon which it is based'. The preface states:

> The basic requirements for the welfare of livestock are a husbandry system appropriate to the health and, so far as practicable, the behavioural needs of the animals and a high standard of stockmanship ... .

> Nearly all livestock husbandry systems impose restrictions on the stock and some of these can cause an unacceptable degree of discomfort or distress by preventing the animals from fulfilling their basic needs.

Provisions meeting these needs, and others which must be considered, include:

- freedom of movement;
- the opportunity to exercise most normal patterns of behaviour;
- flooring which neither harms the animals, nor causes undue strain;
- the prevention, or rapid diagnosis and treatment, of vice, injury, parasitic infestation and disease;
- the avoidance of unnecessary mutilation.

It is not immediately apparent how this agenda can be equated with keeping hens under battery conditions (or, indeed, the conditions under which many broiler chickens are reared). Perhaps those charged with enforcement are too ready to regard compliance with accepted practices within the industry as being sufficient to meet farmers' obligations towards their livestock. Alternatively, it may be that they are reluctant to challenge battery conditions when neither Parliament nor the government has seen fit to intervene.[8] Whatever the reason, it is arguable that treatment of animals which apparently falls below the standard required by law is currently being condoned by those responsible for its enforcement. As the Agriculture Select Committee observed in 1981:

> The authorities should therefore be ready to prosecute not only cases of wilful or persistent disregard of the law but also cases of neglect or carelessness in which exemplary consequences would have a useful deterrent effect. They should also seek occasion to bring some carefully chosen test cases under the 1968 Act ... to determine the adequacy of the terms used, to show that the legislation actually means something (Agriculture Select Committee, 1980–1, vol. 1 paragraph 38).

Turning to the enforcement of the Animals (Scientific Procedures) Act, much of the criticism stems from the secretive nature of the process. The lack of information about what goes on in designated establishments is perhaps unsurprising in view of the commercially sensitive nature of much of it, coupled with the potential threat to life and property from extremists opposed to such activities. Nevertheless, a significant proportion of the work is funded with public money, and it is submitted that the public are entitled to have some information about what is being done in their name. Moreover, the degree of secrecy together with the lack of prosecutions breeds suspicion that the legislation is not being effectively enforced.

In 1992 there were just 11 infringements resolved, the following year there were 12; of these, both the project and personal licence were revoked in one case, while only the personal licence was revoked in another. That is the extent of the disciplinary action taken under the Act during the course of two years.[9] Either it is working extremely well, or there are underlying weaknesses in the manner of its enforcement.

However well intentioned the inspectorate, there must be questions over its ability to perform its functions under the Act. As at 31 December there were, in Great Britain, 334 certificates of designation for scientific procedure establishments, 4083 project licences, and 16 823 personal licences. During 1993, eight certificates of designation, 1444 project licences, and 2779 personal licences were approved by the Home Secretary, each application having been assessed by the inspectorate.[10] As the Parliamentary Office of Science and Technology pointed out, in 1990, each inspector covered on average, 20 designated premises, 200 project licences and 800 personal licences under which 160 000 animal procedures were carried out (Parliamentary Office of Science and Technology, 1992, p. 75). This seems an impossible task. However, it is perhaps not so demanding as it at first appears because in the view of the Home Office 'the Inspectorate is not a police force; rather its role is seen as one of monitoring a system that is essentially self-regulatory' (p. 75). Whether those with an interest in the use of animals for scientific procedures are the most appropriate people to oversee such activities is open to question.

It may be misleading to judge the entire regulatory system on the basis of one case, but it is nevertheless instructive. Following the exposé of the work of Professor Wilhelm Feldberg at the National Institute for Medical Research which revealed many fundamental infringements and shortcomings of the statutory regime (MacDonald, 1994) – at all levels – no one was reprimanded, no one was prosecuted, only the 89-year-old Feldberg had his personal licence revoked. Such a response does not inspire confidence in the legislation. Was it just an isolated incident, as the scientific establishment claimed? Is it credible that the investigators just happened to alight on the one example in the whole system which undermines it? Why did all the regulatory requirements fail so spectacularly?

International Considerations

In the modern world, it is not enough simply to focus on domestic legislation. International influence, policies, treaties, law and economics all have a direct bearing on the national law of any individual country. In the case of states which are members of the European Union this is particularly significant, for the Union is unique in being a transnational organisation with its own legislative institutions and courts, and in enacting law which binds member states to the extent that it supersedes their own legislation. The original objective of the European Community (as was), and still its driving force, is the establishment of a free trade area. Animals are not given any special legal status; they are regarded essentially as commodities, and the Union's interest in animal welfare is largely derived from its concern that varying welfare standards between countries might lead to distortion of competition (see chapter 8 this volume).

The impact of the European Union on the treatment of animals has been mixed. Where considered appropriate,[11] European law sets basic standards which must be reflected in the law of individual member states. Where these European standards are higher than those formerly in operation, then clearly animals within that country stand to benefit (assuming the improved standards are actually implemented and enforced). Thus the Animal (Scientific Procedures) Act was drawn up with the intention of complying with the relevant European directive; similarly, the restrictions on the use of endangered species in experiments mentioned above were dictated by European law.

However, if the existing standards were better than those imposed by European law, then the effect can be detrimental. So, for example, prior to the implementation of the Directive on the Protection of Animals During Transport, United Kingdom law stipulated that food and water had to be provided at intervals not exceeding 12 hours, the only exception being if the entire journey could be completed within 15 hours. Similarly, it was a requirement that animals for export by sea were rested for at least 10 hours before embarkation at an approved lairage, where they were fed, watered and inspected by a vet. This arrangement has now been abolished.

In some situations national legislatures may improve on European standards, provided it does not interfere with free trade between states. Thus, the United Kingdom has prohibited rearing veal calves in crates, notwith-standing that such a practice is permitted under European law. But, as we have seen, the British government has taken the view that it is unable either to prevent calves being exported from the United Kingdom to be kept in such conditions, or to stop the meat produced from being imported for sale in British shops.[12] It is clearly undesirable that national law enacted to prohibit a practice which is considered unacceptable can be circumvented in this way.

The Union's equivocation about the treatment of animals stems largely from the different attitudes with which the various member states regard the topic. The issue is at least gaining attention, even if the eventual decisions of Union institutions leave much to be desired. A Protocol appended to the Treaty on European Union, agreed at Maastricht in December 1991, calls upon 'the European Parliament, the Council and the Commission, as well as Member States, when drafting and implementing Community legislation on the common agriculture policy, transport, the internal market and research, to pay full regard to the welfare requirements of animals'. While the sentiment of the statement is to be applauded, its impact is limited; unfortunately, its status is declaratory rather than legally binding.

However, the activities of the Eurogroup for Animal Welfare have been beneficial in raising consciousness about animal welfare and pursuing areas of concern within European Union institutions. Made up of representatives of animal welfare organisations operating within the Union, it can co-ordinate their activities and present a unified voice in campaigning and lobbying. Its influence and status is further enhanced by the fact that it acts as the secretariat for the European Parliament's all-party Intergroup on Animal Welfare.

In addition to the impact of the European Union, there are other factors of international significance which have a bearing on the protection of animals. At the present time much emphasis is being placed on deregulation and abolishing barriers to free trade. Such moves pose a significant threat to the ability of individual countries to prevent imports because of their origins. For example, the agreement which concluded the 'Uruguay Round' of the General Agreement on Tariffs and Trade (GATT) does not allow nations to discriminate between two like products because of the way they are produced. Such legislation is considered to be 'an unnecessary barrier to trade'.

However, the international threat to animal welfare comes not just from formal international agreements. Increasingly, markets are dominated by multinational companies who trade internationally and have the ability to move their activities around the globe. In such a situation, animal products can be brought into the home market from anywhere in the world. Furthermore, manufacturers in launching a product have to be aware of their legal obligations in different markets. Cheap food is always going to be attractive to retailers, and manufacturers are acutely aware of their legal duty to ensure that their products are safe and suitable for the purpose for which they are intended. These forces can too easily undermine laws intended to protect farm animals and those used in scientific procedures. And herein lies a very real dilemma: do proponents of improved animal welfare seek the highest possible standards of protection in the home market, and thereby encourage manufacturers and producers to move their activities to countries where animals benefit from minimal levels of protection? Or do they compromise so far as domestic regulation is concerned on the basis that it is better that animals are used under some, albeit inadequate, protection than that the activities are still undertaken, but in jurisdictions where the animals are protected significantly less well? This is an extremely difficult conundrum. In the long term the objective must be to raise international standards, but at the moment the trend is in the opposite direction: free trade and protective regulation do not sit well together. Perhaps the most immediate pressure that can be brought to bear is through the power of the consumer.

The Power of the Consumer

Consumer choice can have an impact where legislators are loathe to intervene or in situations where effective legislation is difficult to draw up and implement. For example, in the United Kingdom the crisis over animal transport came to a head during 1994 as a result of the major British ferry operators introducing a voluntary ban on exporting livestock to the European mainland because, one assumes, on balance they considered the opposition to such trade from passengers outweighed the income which it generated. Similarly, the consequences of modern farming methods, such as calcium deficiency in laying hens and the physical pressure under which dairy cows are kept, is very difficult to deal with by regulation, but consumers can bring pressure to bear through what they buy. The drastic effect on beef sales as a result of revelations about BSE in March 1996 is a pertinent reminder of this.

To be effective, however, this strategy relies on consumers being able to make a conscious, informed choice. It is essential, therefore, that the animal welfare organisations continue to give maximum publicity to the suffering inflicted on animals so that consumers can use their own judgement. Conversely, it is in the interests of the farming industry and those involved in scientific procedures using animals to be open about what they are doing and to demonstrate to the public that the highest standards of animal welfare are being maintained. In tandem with this, there is a need for more detailed product labelling, in order that potential purchasers know what they are buying, where it has come from, and how it has been produced. Where consumers lead, legislators follow.

Conclusion

This chapter has focused on the law of the United Kingdom, but the issues which it raises have a wider significance. Britain has a developed framework of legislation aimed at protecting animals from abuse; it serves animals well, but not well enough. In evaluating the effectiveness of the law it is necessary to have regard not simply to its substance, but also to the nature of the legal process, the levels of enforcement, and the national and international context in which it operates. Through its law, the United Kingdom has done much to promote animal welfare, but there is still much to be done.

NOTES

1. The ambit of the Protection of Animals Act 1911 is restricted to domestic and captive animals; its provisions do not apply to animals living in the wild.
2. The Welfare of Livestock (Prohibited Operations) Regulations 1982 (SI 1982/1884) as amended (SI 1987/114) and the Welfare of Livestock Regulations 1994 (SI 1994/2126).
3. The 1981 Act was a consolidation of previous legislation, and much of the delegated legislation relating to animal transport and trade which is in force in fact predates it.
4. The Welfare of Animals during Transport Order 1994 (SI 1994/3249).
5. The distinction between a slaughterhouse and a knacker's yard is that at the former the animals are killed for human consumption; at the latter they are not intended for human consumption.
6. Slaughter means causing the death of an animal by bleeding; killing refers to causing death by any means other than slaughter.
7. The Welfare of Livestock Regulations 1994 (SI 1994/2126), Sch.1 para. 11.
8. In 1981 the Agriculture Select Committee recommended an end to keeping hens under battery conditions, but this was rejected by the government.
9. Report of the Animal Procedures Committee for 1992, para 5.2; Report of the Animal Procedures Committee for 1993, para. 7.3.
10. Report of the Animal Procedures Committee for 1993, paras 2.1 & 2.3.
11. See, for example: Council Directive 86/609/EEC on the approximation of laws, regulations and administrative provisions of the Member States regarding the protection of animals used for experimental and other scientific purposes; Council Directive 91/629/EEC laying down minimum standards for the protection of calves; Council Directive 91/630/EEC laying down minimum standards for the protection of pigs; Council Directive 74/577/EEC on stunning of animals before slaughter; Council Directive 91/628/EEC on the protection of animals during transport.
12. Article 36 of the Treaty of Rome allows restrictions on imports, exports or goods in transit that would otherwise be in contravention of European law to be imposed on grounds of public morality, public policy, or the protection of the health and life of humans, animals or plants. Whether it could be relied on in this situation is currently unclear.

5 To Farm Without Harm and Choosing a Humane Diet: The Bioethics of Humane Sustainable Agriculture

Michael W. Fox

No other society past or present raises and kills so many animals just for their meat. No other society past or present has adopted such intensive systems of animal production and nonrenewable resource-dependent farming practices. These have evolved to make meat a dietary staple, and to meet the public expectation and demand for a 'cheap' and plentiful supply of meat. An agriculture that raises and slaughters billions of animals every year primarily for meat, depends on costly nonrenewable natural resources and precious farmland to raise the feed[1] for these animals to convert into flesh; land that critics now believe should instead be used more economically to feed people directly. To a hungry world, such conspicuous consumption is a poor model to emulate.

Supporters of intensive animal factory farming claim that America has the cheapest and most productive agriculture in the world and that humane reforms would increase costs and put an unfair burden on the poor. Critics of factory farming are judged as being more concerned about animals than people and against progress. Both these erroneous beliefs and conclusions need to be dispelled.

The real costs of factory farming have been well documented, ranging from price supports and subsidies at taxpayers' expense, to the demise of family farms, rural communities, waste of natural resources and animal stress, disease[2] and suffering. Coupled with corporate monopoly, these hidden costs have aggravated rather than alleviated poverty and malnutrition nationally and internationally. The fact is the real costs of factory farming are not accounted for by agribusiness, and its high productivity is neither efficient nor socially or ethically acceptable. Some of the reasons for reaching this regrettable conclusion will now be detailed.

The Harms of Overproduction

In some countries, like Brazil, raising livestock has become a major hedge against inflation, but overproduction cycles depress world market prices, fuel deforestation and other forms of environmental degradation. Price supports and subsidies to producers, especially in the developed world, encourage overproduction and cause further distortions and inequities in world market prices. One serious consequence is the 'dumping' of meat, dairy and other agricultural products in other countries that are sold to processors and wholesalers at prices much lower than local farmers can get for their own similar produce. Import tariffs to help protect local farmers from 'dumping' and from being forced out of business further compound the problems of agricultural surpluses and subsidized export commodities coming from more industrialized nations.

While raising tariffs and other forms of 'protectionism' by any country to protect its own farmers is an illegal 'technical barrier', under the GATT convention, local farmers raising food and feed for domestic consumption should have their market protected and fair market prices guaranteed, provided their farming methods are humane, socioeconomically just and ecologically sound and sustainable. And they should not be encouraged to adopt the capital intensive, high-input methods of animal agriculture that have become the bane of the industrial world.

The high-volume productivity of industrial-scale, intensive systems of livestock and poultry production is often touted as being the hallmark and miracle of progress and success. Poorer 'developing' countries are encouraged to adopt these methods in order to increase agricultural production and 'efficiency'. Yet ironically, the global industrialization of animal agriculture is now counterproductive in part because it is too successful. Industrialized countries are now passing on the burden of overproduction and commodity surpluses to the Third World while at the same time their industrial agricultural experts, agribusiness agents and development banks are trying to sell intensive livestock and poultry production systems to these countries.

The legal definition of 'dumping' is to put products on the market for sale at a price below the actual costs of production. This definition of such unfair and illegal trade needs to be broadened to include all marketing activities that undermine regional self-sufficiency, national sovereignty and local sustainable productivity of the same or similar commodities and services. The fair market price of commodities and services should be reflective of all costs, including social and environmental. On the basis of *full cost* accountability, more equitable trade policies could then be established, and markets encouraged or protected as the case may be. With a firm bioethical basis that considers social and environmental as well as economic factors, there will be incentives to promote the most ecologically appropriate farming methods and choice of crops for domestic use and for export. The scenario of one country or region harming its constituents or its ecology and natural resources by investing in large-scale production of grain, livestock, cotton or some other commodity, and then compounding this harm by 'dumping' such produce on the world market and lowering the fair market price would then be averted.

The final irony and tragedy of developing countries becoming dependent on imported food commodities and losing their own agricultural self-reliance is the spectre of malnutrition and hunger when there is rapid inflation, and when the world market demand and prices for food commodities like chicken and powdered milk suddenly increase. When a country's agriculture collapses, social strife is inevitable, and with political and economic instability, crime and violence and even civil war are likely. The possibility of a recovery of agriculture will become ever more remote as the poor and hungry try to raise their own food. Lacking the right inputs and resources, if not also knowledge, especially in sustainable and conservation agriculture, irreparable ecological damage to the land and loss of biodiversity are likely consequences.

These socioeconomic, environmental and ethical concerns cannot be ignored by GATT or by the World Trade Organization (WTO). To farm without harm clearly has international ramifications related to equity and world trade. The adoption and multiplication of non-sustainable, intensive livestock and poultry systems by industrialized countries directed toward high-volume production for export, needs to be looked at from an ethical as well as an economic perspective, and constraints applied for the good of all. The same can be said for new genetically-engineered products of agri-biotechnology, like analog cocoa, vanilla and nut oils, the production of which will harm those countries dependent on raising these products naturally for export revenues, needed in part to pay off the interest accrued by too often misguided development loans.

Ethical and moral imperatives notwithstanding, it would be enlightened self-interest for GATT and the WTO to protect and encourage local agricultural self-sufficiency in poorer countries, since the world market will become increasingly dysfunctional and may well collapse if poverty and socioeconomic inequities and strife continue to spread under the compounding pressures of population increase and environmental degradation. The application of bioethics to world trade, especially in the agricultural sector, will do much to help every nation and region maximize productivity and minimize adverse environmental and socioeconomic consequences primarily by encouraging mixed farming systems (including agroforestry and aquaculture) that are most appropriate ecologically and culturally for each biogeographic region.

Harm of Farm Animal Feeds and Wastes

Meat industry defenders counter the argument that importing food for livestock and poultry from the Third World contributes to hunger and poverty by insisting that much of this food comes from crop by-products[3] of cash crops grown for export, such as sugar cane, molasses, palm kernal cake, cotton oil seed cake, soya bean cake, rice, wheat bran, and rice polishings. In actuality, this market for by-products simply perpetuates unsound agricultural practices in poorer countries, undermines traditional sustainable farming systems and uses up good land that should be used to feed people first.

This aspect of animal agriculture, in enabling farmers to feed far more animals than the land can sustain from local resources alone, is a major support-structure of intensive livestock and poultry production. But it is ethically, economically and ecologically unacceptable, in part because of the by-product of animal waste that should, but is not and cannot be returned to enrich the land in other regions and countries from which the animal feed originated. Such animal waste has become a costly environmental management hazard and is a cardinal indicator of bad farming practices and agricultural policy. Nitrates, phosphates, bacteria, antibiotic and other drug and feed additive residues – such as copper, arsenic and selenium in farm animal excrement – overload and pollute the environment and food chain.

A related problem is dealing with the enormous volume of another form of animal waste that the meat industry refers to as *animal tankage*. The dried and processed residue of animal tankage from rendering plants contains the remains of dead, diseased and debilitated livestock and poultry, condemned and unusable body parts and even the remains of road-kills and cats and dogs from animal shelters. Slow, low-heat rendering neither sanitizes nor rids animal tankage of potentially harmful organisms, heavy metals and other hazardous residues. Farm animals, companion animals and consumers are all put at risk since this by-product of animal agriculture is added to pet foods, livestock and poultry feeds, and is even sold as fertilizer for farm, home and kitchen gardens. Studies have linked bacterial food poisoning in humans and bovine spongiform encephalopathy in cattle and other animals (that may also be transmissible to humans) with this industry practice of including animal tankage by-products in farm animals' food. Obviously if consumers responded wisely by reducing their consumption of meat and other animal produce, the magnitude of these problems would be significantly reduced with great economic savings.

Finding Solutions

Those who believe that farm animals do not play a vital ecological and economic role in sustainable crop production and range management are as wrong as those who claim that intensive livestock and poultry production are bioethically acceptable because they cause no harm. Now is the time for openness and objectivity and a coming together of all parties and sectors of society involved in the production, marketing and consumption of food to support the development, adoption and market viability of humane and ecological farming practices that enable farmers to farm with less harm.

The industrial factory-scale system that the animal component of modern agriculture has evolved is bioethically unacceptable. Making the retail price of meat 'cheaper' through tax subsidies and price supports, through better vaccines and biotechnology, through irrigation projects and further deforestation and draining of wetlands, makes it even less bioethically acceptable. So will innovations in meat safety inspection, handling and processing, including food irradiation, since a full and fair cost accounting will still show that producing meat as a dietary staple causes far too much harm.

The question of the rightness or wrongness of meat eating and of killing animals is not the central issue or primary bioethical concern of the humane movement. Our primary concern is the need to implement less harmful alternatives to contemporary animal agriculture, with its factory farms and feedlots. In the process of producing affordably-priced meat as a dietary staple, these intensive livestock and poultry production systems cause harm to farm animals in terms of environmental and production – or husbandry-related – stress and disease; harm to the agro-ecology, to wildlife, biodiversity, and natural ecosystems; harm to family farms and rural communities; harm to consumers and also to the indigenous peoples of the Third World. The antidote is in the adoption and public support of less harmful organic and other alternative, sustainable crop and livestock production practices that are humane and ecologically sound.

The ethic of reverential respect for life and for the land is the guiding bioethical principle of a humane, socially just and sustainable agriculture and society. To question agricultural practices, including new developments in genetic engineering biotechnology that may cause harm, be it to the environment, to sectors of society or to domesticated animals and wildlife, should not be judged as unscientific or as erecting hurdles to obstruct progress. Surely the essence of progress is to apply science and ethics in the development and adoption of agricultural and other practices and industries that cause the least harm and the greatest good to the entire life community of Earth. We cannot sacrifice the good of the environment or of rural communities for the short-term good of the economy, for society will suffer, if not this generation, then the next. Likewise we cannot sacrifice the good of farm animals or of the soil in the name of productivity and labour-substituting technological innovation and marketing, without ultimately harming the economy and the health of the populace (see Fig. 5.1).

Health and Sustainable Economy Triad

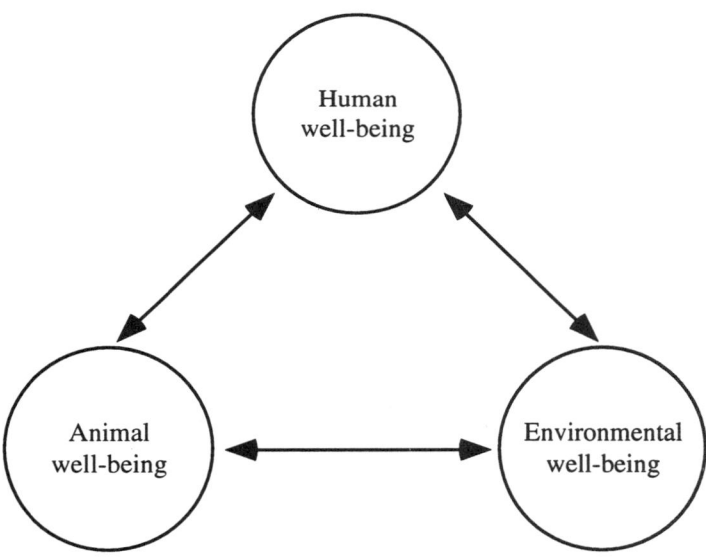

Figure 5.1

The rights, interest and well-being of humans, animals and the environment are inter-dependent and not mutually exclusive.

A Humane Diet

We humans are a highly adaptable primate species, one feature of our adaptive success being our physiological capacity to be omnivores. This flexibility in our capacity to utilize a wide range of food sources, from fruits to nuts and meats to maize, is universal. With rare exception, most peoples can eat and digest almost anything that other mammalian species can assimilate (with the notable exception of cellulose); and have developed remarkable ways to preserve and enhance the nutritive value and palatability of a diversity of natural foods. Cultural/ethnic differences in cuisine reflect biogeographic and seasonal variations in food types and availability. This ethnic diversity provides a rich cornucopia of culinary delights and is a source of new crops and food products for an increasingly cosmopolitan marketplace. From this cornucopia, we can select some of the most tried and true diets that have been 'human tested' for countless generations, and that are ecologically sound and sustainable. One classic example is what is generically termed 'Mediterranean cuisine' that integrates various ethnic foods from this biogeographic region to provide an extremely healthful, relatively low-cost and ecologically sustainable diet (see Fig. 5.2).

The Traditional Healthy
Mediterranean Diet Pyramid

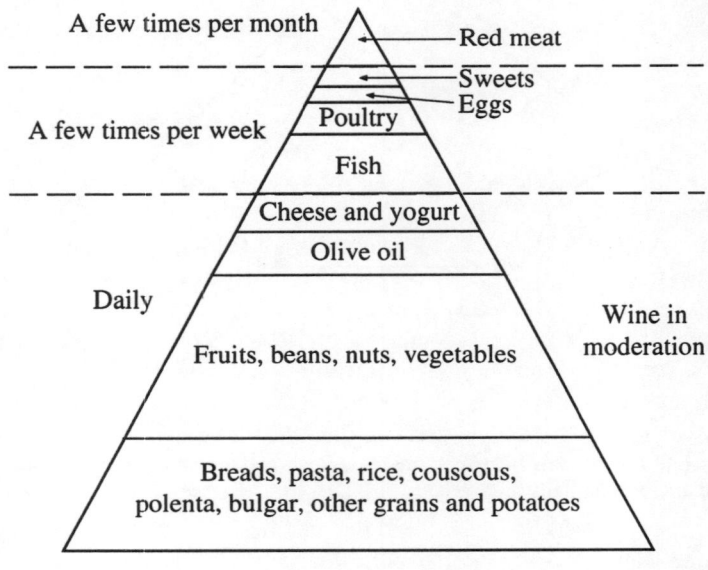

Figure 5.2

These diet guidelines are based on study of the traditional diet of Crete, much of the rest of Greece and southern Italy circa 1960.

This revisionist view of the USDA's Eat Right Food Pyramid accords with the aims of ethical vegetarians and 'conscientious omnivores' to reduce the amounts of animal protein and fat in their diets. These views, now being more widely accepted and promoted by health experts and authorities, like the

World Health Organization, confirm the connections between a healthful diet and humane and sustainable agriculture. The many benefits of farming without harm and eating with conscience are therefore gaining greater recognition. Such recognition will do much to encourage traditional farming practices and ethnic foods, and help prevent the loss of biocultural diversity in world agriculture as well as in the kitchen, which is under siege by the promoters of meat and other animal produce as dietary staples. The consumer trends in industrial society toward nutritional illiteracy, agricultural amnesia, and culinary catatonia, fostered by the microwaveable frozen meal industry with its prepared and processed convenience foods and relatively meaningless ingredient and daily recommended allowances labelling, are symptomatic of the disintegration of agriculture and culture. So are the diseases of an over-consumptive and malconsumptive (and malcontent) society that justifies health spas, costly coronary bypasses, and liposuction to remove excess calories, while the rest of the human population that might well aspire to live this way suffers from malnutrition and even starvation due in part to the insatiable appetites of the industrial world.

Farm With Less Harm

In order to farm with less harm, we must all consume and generally live so as to cause less harm to ourselves and the rest of Earth's creation. It means a *reduction* in the production and consumption of meat in those countries where meat is a dietary staple. It also means *refinement* in terms of how animals are raised, transported and slaughtered, and *replacement* of animal protein and fat with cheaper vegetable fats, oils and proteins. Our human population of a soon-to-double 5.4 billion (of which 1.6 billion are malnourished today) can only increase the current livestock population of some 4.5 billion to maintain the status quo and public demand for meat if it is prepared to accept the loss of biodiversity and nonrenewable resources, and cope with the attendant environmental and economic risks and costs. We have a better chance to predict and prevent these, if we begin to apply bioethics in the public and corporate policy decision-making process and in our collective vision of what kind of future world we are creating this and every day. And the first principle of bioethics in agriculture is like the good doctor's Hippocratic aphorism: do no harm.

Protecting Nature and Wildlife

The fact that an agriculture that is based primarily on using good land to raise feed for livestock is non-sustainable is at last being recognized by conventional agriculturalists. The conservative Council for Agricultural Science and Technology published a landmark report in 1994 by agronomist Paul E. Waggoner entitled *How Much Land Can Ten Billion People Spare for Nature?* In his introduction, Waggoner writes:

> Today farmers feed five to six billion people by cultivating about a tenth of the planet's land. The seemingly irresistible doubling of population and the imperative of producing food will take another tenth of the land, much from Nature, if people keep on eating and farmers keep on farming as they do now. So farmers work at the junction where population, the human condition, and sparing land for Nature meet.

With this premise, and using the latest data from around the world, Waggoner proceeds to show how 'smart farmers' can harvest more per-plot and thus spare some of today's cropland for Nature – if we help them with changed diets, never-ending research, and encouraging incentives. Among the points the report makes are:

- Calories and protein equally distributed from present cropland could give a vegetarian diet to ten billion people;
- The global totals of sun on land, CO_2 in the air, fertilizer, and even water could produce far more food than ten billion people need;
- By eating different species of crop and more or less vegetarian diets, we can change the number who can be fed from a plot;
- Recent data shows that millions of people do change their diets in response to health, price, and other pressures, and that they are capable of changing their diet even further;
- Given adequate incentives, farmers can use new technologies to increase food productivity and thus keep prices level despite a rising population. Even better use of existing technology can raise current yields;
- Despite recurring problems with water supply and distribution, there are opportunities to raise more crop with the same volume of water;
- In Europe and the United States, rising income, improving technology, and leveling populations forecast diminishing use of cropland.

The first most important step for every caring person to take is to choose a humane diet. This bioethical imperative should be on top of every nation's agenda, since choosing a humane diet is a vital component in the prevention of animal suffering; inhumane health-maintenance; and in biodiversity and natural resource preservation. But encouraging people to make this caring and enlightened choice is politically controversial and is still seen as an economic threat by those who have a vested interest in stopping real progress in agriculture.

Eighteen national agribusiness groups[4] purportedly representing the best interests of farmers, ranchers and farm animals, have publicly attacked The Humane Society of the United States' 'Choosing A Humane Diet' project. They claim that, 'This campaign for the first time really places The HSUS squarely in the lead of animal rights groups seeking a vegetarian society by using emotionalism to induce the public to both reduce and replace animal products with other foods.' By so doing, these groups seek to discredit the legitimacy of our concerns and to protect their vested interests in maintaining the status quo of factory farms and feedlots. We are also cast as the enemy of farmers and ranchers. Yet the real enemy is agribusiness, which has contributed to the loss of over 425 000 family farms over the past decade as animal factories and feedlots have proliferated and put smaller producers out of business.

But there are farmers and ranchers who care and support The HSUS. A revolution in agriculture is gaining momentum nationally and internationally to make it more ecologically sound and environmentally and consumer friendly. The buzzword is *sustainable* agriculture and our task is to make it humane. With the support of caring consumers, this revolution will succeed, but only if it is made humane. The ultimate goal *to farm without harm* is attainable provided those farmers and ranchers, and food wholesalers and distributors who care, are supported by all of us choosing a humane diet.

Bioethical Principles and Criteria

Many of the national agribusiness groups who oppose the humane sustainable agriculture movement today will support it tomorrow when there is a clearer understanding of our motives and of the bioethics and profitability of farming nonviolently. Such understanding will lead to a shared vision of a brighter future for all, beyond the short-term goals and imperatives of the world marketplace.

There are many academicians, politicians and others who still believe that factory farms and feedlots help America lead the world in producing meat at the lowest cost, and that to abolish them would hurt the poor who could not afford more humanely, and ecologically-raised, organically-certified meat and poultry. A broader bioethical perspective would enable them to see that factory farms and feedlots are neither efficient nor sustainable ways of producing food for human consumption.

The application of bioethics to evaluate developments and current practices in agriculture will facilitate the adoption of humane practices. All new agricultural products, processes and policies should be subject to rigorous bioethical evaluation prior to approval and adoption in order to promote the 'farm-without-harm' ideal, and the goal of sustainability.

The core principle of bioethics is *ahimsa*, meaning nonharmful, non-injurious and non-violent action. The future of agriculture, therefore, if it is to be sustainable, must be guided not simply by the imperatives of human need and greed, but by this compassionate ethic of *ahimsa*: of avoiding harm to other living beings, human and nonhuman, plant and animal, wild and domesticated, either directly, or indirectly as by damaging their environment.

The major criteria for bioethical evaluation demonstrates the interconnectedness of these interdependent criteria, that all converge on economics or full cost accounting. These bioethical criteria include safety and effectiveness; social justice, equity and farm animal well-being; environmental impact, including harm to wildlife, loss of ecosystems and biodiversity; socioeconomic and cultural impact, especially harm to established sustainable practices and communities; and accord with established organic and other humane sustainable agriculture practices, standards and production claims. To farm without harm and choosing a humane diet are coins of the same currency that will forge a strong alliance between urban consumers who care, and rural producers who share the vision of a humane and socially just agriculture and society.

Postscript – Change Agriculture, Change Consciousness

The challenge to farm with less harm entails more than a change in agricultural systems, technologies and policies. A fundamental change in attitude or consciousness is needed. We should reflect on the wisdom of Albert Einstein who surmised that: 'The significant problems of the world cannot be solved at the same level of consciousness at which they were created.'

The ethical and spiritual components of agriculture, like most other organized human activities, have become marginalized and superseded by the mechanistic and materialistic values of scientism, industrialism and consumerism. The process whereby nature, plants, animals and even humans come to be regarded as commodities and resources, as means rather than ends in themselves, is mental or conceptual. Their re-sacralization therefore entails a mental or conceptual change, a *metanoia* that incorporates ethical and spiritual principles and values. This more holistic or ecological and bioethical worldview does not negate such narrow, linear ideals and values of efficiency, control, productivity and profitability, but rather casts these mechanistic and materialistic goals in a more realistic, sustainable, humane and equitable framework. In order for this change in consciousness to occur, there must be such openness, honesty and humility that the rationalizations and denials that maintain the worldview that narrowly objectifies and commodifies life are transcended. Without such transcendence, the evolution of human consciousness will be arrested. The biological, socioecological and economic imperatives of a spiritual rebirth and ethical renaissance are now converging on the collective human psyche demanding an end to all forms of violence and injustice against all beings and nature. This demand is a call to conscience and the awakening of a reverential respect for the intrinsic value and sacred dimension of all life, expressed empathetically and rationally as humane, responsible planetary stewardship; in frugality (the essence of conservativism), in respect for biocultural diversity, and for eco-justice.

NOTES

1. According to the UN Food and Agriculture Organization, *FAO Production Yearbook 1990* (Rome 1991), some 800 kg of grain is used to feed livestock in the US to meet the annual per capita average consumption of 42 kg beef, 20 kg pork, 44 kg poultry, 283 kg dairy products and 16 kg of eggs.
2. According to a 1986 report by the Office of Technology Assessment, animal diseases cost US agriculture $17 billion annually (*Feedstuffs*, 14 March 1994).
3. Various domestic crop, food and beverage industry by-products (like citrus pulp and brewers' grains) do play an important role in providing feed for integrated livestock and poultry production.
4. These groups are as follows: American Farm Bureau Federation, American Feed Industry Association, American Meat Institute, American Sheep Industry, American Veal Association, Animal Health Institute, Animal Industry Foundation, Egg Association of America, Holstein Association of America, Livestock Marketing Association, National Broiler Council, National Cattlemen's Association, National Livestock Producers Association, National Milk Producers Federation, National Pork Producers Council, National Turkey Federation, United Egg Association, and United Egg Producers.

6 The Use of Animals in Experimentation: An Examination of the 'Technical' Arguments Used to Criticize the Practice

Andrew N. Rowan[1]

The use of animals in experimentation has a long history which, for the past few hundred years, has included a passionate debate over whether or not animal experimentation is moral. Despite the claimed productivity of animal research and our modern ability to take more or less effective steps to cure or ameliorate many diseases, the debate about the use of laboratory animals is today more heated than ever (Phillips and Sechzer, 1989). Opponents still challenge the morality and practice of animal research through the usual mechanisms of civic protest. A small group of activists are even prepared to risk arrest and imprisonment by engaging in acts of theft and vandalism to publicize their beliefs and arguments.

Why has society been unable to develop appropriate mechanisms to defuse the passion and the polarization of this debate? Part of the problem has always been the emotive loading given to particular terms. Thus, opponents will talk of torturing animals in laboratories (implying some level of sadistic motivation among scientists) and scientists will refer to animal activists in similarly unflattering terms. Both sides also tend to take refuge in relatively absolute positions when they are confronted by the media, or under threat, or seeking public support. It is not easy to develop a reasonable dialogue that leads to practical policy solutions under such circumstances. In addition to the unflattering attitude of each side for the other, there is no shortage of people on both sides who hold strong ethical positions and such views are also more likely to be publicized by the media because stark opposition is perceived to make for a better story in the age of the ten-second sound bite than subtle arguments and nuanced differences.

The current unproductive rhetoric over animal research comes at a time when it should be easier than ever to construct a reasoned dialogue around which to build a public policy consensus. According to most accounts, biomedical research (including research on animals) has produced tremendous advances in knowledge, life expectancy and health care (but see McKeown, 1979). At the same time, the biological sciences have made remarkable technological advances that have led to a relatively dramatic drop in laboratory animal use (30–50 per cent over the past ten to twenty years) and a greater ability to promote laboratory animal well-being and alleviate animal distress than ever before (Rowan and Loew 1994). By contrast, at

104

the end of the nineteenth century, when the animal research debate was almost as impassioned as it is today, very few therapeutic advances could be *demonstrated* to have emerged *solely and specifically* from animal research and animal care in the laboratory was very crude by today's standards.

One problem in trying to address the policy issues is the lack of detailed examinations of some of the arguments against the use of research animals. The moral arguments against animal research (for example Regan, 1983 and Singer, 1990) have received some attention although most of the papers in the philosophical literature appear to favor greater restrictions on animal use in the laboratory. Even two middle-of-the-road reports from America (Donnelly and Nolan, 1990) and the UK (Smith and Boyd, 1991) conclude that more attention should be given to the moral issues raised by animal research.

While the ethics debate is somewhat one-sided, there has been virtually no serious discussion of the technical criticisms that have been advanced to challenge the utility and propriety of animal research until very recently. The technical arguments have tended to be ignored because the research establishment either does not wish to 'give credibility' to the opposition or because the arguments are perceived to be so ill-founded as to be not worth a response. Nevertheless, these new technical arguments have garnered considerable respect from both movement members and the public and it seems inappropriate that a community of scholars (biological and medical researchers) should deal with contrary or disagreeable arguments with either nothing but silence or *ad hominem* attacks. Recently, a few scientists in the UK (Paton, 1993 and Botting, 1991a and b, and 1993a and b) and in the USA (for example Verhetsel, 1986) have mounted challenges to some of the arguments employed by opponents of animal research.

This paper represents an attempt to characterize and analyze such technical criticisms (most of which contain moral underpinnings or assumptions but the attacks on animal research are mainly framed in technical and scientific terms). This paper starts by categorizing and analyzing the validity of the various criticisms and then describes two specific cases, the discovery of insulin and the development of the polio vaccine. Both of these have long been regarded as triumphs of animal research but such views have recently been strongly challenged by critics of animal research (for example Reines, undated; Sharpe, 1993).

CRITICISMS OF ANIMAL RESEARCH: AN OVERVIEW

The various technical criticisms of animal research may be classified into the following two broad themes: first, the practice is unnecessary and, second, the practice produces too little benefit to balance the harm done to the animals.

Animal Research is Unnecessary

Some critics of animal research argue that animal research is not necessary because:

(i) better use of preventive medicine will eliminate the need for animal research;
(ii) greater use of and reliance on public health measures will eliminate the need for animal research;
(iii) clinical approaches provide all the clues we need while animal research merely dramatizes clinical discoveries; and
(iv) the development of alternatives eliminates the need to use animals.

(i) and (ii): Prevention and Public Health

Opponents of animal experimentation propose that the prevention of disease is the only truly effective way to insure universally good health. Sharpe (1988, p. 49) states that since 'treatment has little impact and often comes too late, real improvements can only come by preventing the disease in the first place'. But a healthful diet, regular exercise, and avoidance of harmful substances is not always sufficient to keep people free of disease nor even alive in the modern world. Risk of injury and disease cannot be eliminated and life involves making constant compromises between conflicting risks.

The first two arguments tend to overlap and are vulnerable to the same general rebuttal – namely, that both preventive medicine and public health initiatives are heavily influenced by the development of new biological and medical knowledge, a considerable amount of which is generated via the use of animals. Thus, it is certainly true that the incidence of many of the major diseases was declining steadily long before the advent of modern medicine (McKeown, 1979) and that nearly all the decline occurred before the discovery and application of antibiotics, vaccines and other drugs. However, the development of clean water supplies, better hygiene, improved food supply and nutrition, and other measures that have been identified as contributing to the decline in infectious disease mortality did not take place in a vacuum. They occurred as the germ theory was being confirmed, as our knowledge of pathogenic organisms exploded and as other advances in biomedical knowledge were being made. It would be very surprising if such research advances, which relied to at least some degree on animal studies, did not have a substantial impact on changing societal attitudes about hygiene and disease.

The historical context of new research discoveries must also be included in any analysis of the real world relevance (or lack of relevance) of earlier animal studies and clinical investigations. There are many historical examples of how prevailing dogma and knowledge were able to resist new insights and clever clinical detective work until the mechanism of the disease was more thoroughly understood. The connection between lung cancer and cigarettes is a more recent story of the linked role of epidemiology, pathology and laboratory research in supporting (all too little and too late) moves to introduce appropriate public health measures. One can, with the benefit of hindsight, legitimately argue that some animal and other laboratory research should not have been necessary to stimulate the public health authorities to act in these cases but not if we view these narratives in their historical context.

Furthermore, even though diseases such as tuberculosis were in steady decline through the nineteenth and first half of the twentieth century, there were still individuals who contracted tuberculosis and who were then helped by the new therapies. When isoniazid and streptomyocin became available to treat tuberculosis 40 to 50 years ago, there were still 50000 people in the United Kingdom with the disease. As Paton (1993) shows, these two drugs produced a marked improvement in the clinical outcomes of tuberculosis sufferers.

A potentially more serious problem for the claim that animal research was (and is) unnecessary derives from the fact that the charts and statistics usually cited to support the idea that public health measures could have replaced much animal research are based on *mortality* figures rather than measures of *morbidity and suffering* (although McKeown, 1979, does begin to address this issue). Relief of sickness and suffering has arguably been a more significant trend in improving health care but such improvements are almost completely ignored when one relies only on mortality statistics.

If a family member came down with pneumonia prior to 1935, symptomatic treatment was all that was available. Many individuals survived their bout with pneumonia but they, and their loved ones suffered through one to two weeks of uncertainty, high fever and considerable distress. The survivors then had lengthy weeks or months of recuperation ahead. After the sulphonamides and other antibiotics were discovered (involving a number of key studies on animals), pneumonia became a relatively minor inconvenience for most people. The sense of control over pneumonia and other diseases that modern advances in health care have provided may be much more important in improving our quality of life measures than we suspect (for example Sagan, 1987).

Thus, one can make some important arguments about the importance of prevention and public health initiatives in human health and even grant the argument that modern medical research has contributed only a small part directly to the increase in life expectancy. But one cannot imply either that these measures were not influenced by knowledge derived from animal research nor that prevention and public health by themselves are responsible for the considerable ability we now have to control *morbidity and suffering*. Modern dentistry is not generally viewed as extending life expectancy but it has had an enormous impact on the alleviation of human suffering.

(iii) Clinical Studies

The third claim in this category implies that animal research is unnecessary because we can achieve the same or better results by relying on clinical research. In the United States, a considerable proportion of Federal biomedical research funding (around 40 per cent) does support research on human subjects or human material (although the actual proportion of funding devoted to research in the clinic and at the bedside is much lower) while approximately one-third supports animal research. Thus, the call to support clinical studies is already being met to some extent. The question is whether the clinic can completely supplant all animal studies. Reines, a veterinarian with an avocation as a medical historian, has argued this issue most forcefully, drawing on a variety of case studies, including the discovery of some psychoactive drugs via clinical observation (Reines, 1990) and other case studies. In addition, Kaufman et al. (1989) have produced a critique of animal models which argues that animal models are rarely cited in the clinical literature and are, therefore, not useful in terms of actual clinical medicine.

The case studies cited by Reines draw on instances where astute clinicians (following William Osler's advice) use interesting cases and clues from the clinic to make conceptual or therapeutic leaps into new areas. For example, important psychoactive drugs (for example chlorpromazine) were discovered in this way (Reines, 1990). However, this naturally led to a whole range of additional research questions about the mode of action of such drugs and the possibility of developing other drugs with different (improved?) properties. Thus, the initial observation or intriguing clue, whether clinical or experimental, is only part of the process of developing new knowledge and new therapies.

A critical issue in the claims that clinical discovery is the key to medical advance is the way in which the term 'discovery' is used. For example, Reines appears to use the term very narrowly to refer to the moment of insight that unlocks a flurry of further investigation. Experimentation that confirms and expands the insight is consigned to a process referred to in part as 'dramatization'. This tends to elevate the importance of the moment of insight and downplay the further investigations that confirm and extend the insight. In addition, Reines' use of 'discovery' does not conform to its colloquial meaning which usually refers to a process rather than a moment of insight.

In the critique of animal models, Kaufman et al. (1989) analyze citations to ten randomly chosen animal models from the files at the Armed Forces Institute of Pathology. Of 693 citations to the 21 core papers describing the animal models, 78 (11.3 per cent) were clinical with most of these citations (61) referring to only three of the models. The authors note that many of these citations appeared to be clinically unimportant and they conclude their analysis by questioning the usefulness of these models in understanding and treating human disease.

This study represented an interesting (and to this date the most sophisticated) attempt to undertake an objective analysis of the utility of animal models. However, it is not without problems. Citation analysis has developed into a complex science with many potential pitfalls. For example, it is well known that older papers rapidly disappear from the literature and become subsumed by more recent reviews. Thus, their simple citation analysis tracked the influence of the primordial papers that first described the animal model but not the influence of the model itself. In addition, errors in citation are fairly frequent and one has to be careful to examine potential variants. Such variants can account for a significant proportion of the total citation record.

There are other problems aside from the technical difficulties of citation analysis. It is not clear how clinical 'value' was judged nor how the citing literature was divided into clinical papers and other types of research. The scientific literature is also notoriously neutral in assigning value to prior literature and it is likely to be very difficult to determine how much impact an earlier paper has had on an investigator merely by reading the journal report. The study also does not provide any control comparison, such as a citation analysis of the clinical studies of the same human diseases which the animals were supposed to be modeling. It may be that the clinical studies were similarly unimpressive in influencing the later literature. Finally, this analysis sets out to assess the idea of the usefulness of animal models. However, much animal research only uses the animal as a model in the sense that the research animal is a mammal, as are humans. For example, in toxicity studies, mice and rats are used because they are small, relatively prolific mammals for which a great deal of background information is available. It is well recognized by scientists that the animal models are not perfect models of a human disease process (in some cases they are far from perfect) and that care must be exercised in extrapolating from animals to humans (for example Norrby et al., 1993). In one recent book review of animal models in psychiatry, the word 'model' is criticized as being one of the most over-worked terms in animal research. 'In addition to denigrating the word, overzealous usage of the word *model* in animal research denigrates the science, suggesting that the phenomena studied are somehow not real, but merely representations of reality' (Silverman, 1994; emphasis in the original).

LaFollette and Shanks (1994) produced an interesting critique of animal models which is strongest when mounting an epistemological challenge to the idea of animals models. They criticize the assumption that we can generalize from animal experiments to humans and the lack of examination of this assumption in most scientific papers. Two responses to LaFollette and Shanks take issue with their paper but do not deal with their basic epistemological challenge (Willis and Hulsey, 1994; Steinmetz and Tillery, 1994). In fact, it is impossible to refute their criticism that animal models are always inexact representations of what would occur in humans and that, since we do not know to what extent the animal's system differs from the average human system (individual humans differ considerably too), we can never predict precisely how useful an animal model might be. One has to agree that animal models are not perfect (and frequently far from perfect) but then fall back on the claim that animal studies have produced knowledge that can be generalized to humans and therefore the use of animals in research does have utility. What we are then left with is arguing over how much utility animal models have.

In addition, it should also be noted that studies of phenomena in animals produce knowledge in their own right that could be argued to have value independently of any potential application to human health or well-being. However, it is very rare to find any research scientist or research institution defending animal research on this basis. In nearly every case, reference is made to the benefits that humans and other animals have reaped from laboratory research.

(iv) Alternatives

The best available statistics indicate that the use of laboratory animals worldwide has fallen by 30–50 per cent after peaking between 1975 and 1980. Several reasons have been put forward to explain this decline. Firstly, it is argued that laboratory animals and their care have become increasingly expensive leading to an economic disincentive to use research animals. This is true but there is no data showing that animal research costs have risen any faster than general research costs. Secondly, it has been suggested that animal use has fallen because of economic uncertainty and recessions. During the last 15 years there have been two recessions and one boom period but animal use fell steadily throughout. In addition, Hoffman-La Roche reported that it cut its animal use from 1 million to around 300000 per annum over ten years while maintaining the same number of Investigational New Drugs under study.

Third, it is argued that alternatives have played a major role. This is most likely true but it is not clear how much of the fall has been due to the *specific search for and use of alternatives* and how much has been due to the development of more efficient and powerful research techniques that also happen to reduce animal use. Thus, cell culture technology has improved considerably in the last 15 years as has our knowledge of basic biological mechanisms. Partly as a result, the National Cancer Institute has replaced its use of the mouse cancer model for screening for new chemotherapeutic agents with cultures of human cancer cells at a saving of around 3–4 million mice per annum (Rowan, 1989) but the switch was made for scientific rather than animal welfare reasons. The pharmaceutical industry has also made very good use of new techniques to reduce animal use in screening for potential new drugs.

Even given the progress made in reducing animal use (and in reducing animal distress in research) over the past 15 years, it is difficult to see how animals could be eliminated now or in the foreseeable future from many research areas. By combining clinical, public health, cell culture and other approaches to research, it may well be possible to reduce animal use still further (perhaps substantially), but it is not realistic to expect to eliminate all animal use in the laboratories of the OECD countries *and* also argue that biological and medical research would be unaffected.

Animal Research Causes Too Much Suffering For Little/No Benefit

Another approach used in criticisms of animal research addresses the cost–benefit balance. Some suggest that animal research produces a tremendous amount of suffering and little human benefit. For example, Singer (1990) states that he thinks that much animal research 'is of minimal or zero value' while it causes considerable suffering. Others suggest that no animal research is useful while it causes considerable harm to animals. For example, the Australian Association for Humane Research (1988, p. 1) states: 'We know of no animal experiments, as such, which ever led to a cure of a human disease.'

Finally, others argue that animal experiments are not only useless, but are actually misleading. Sharpe (1988, p. 200) states that: 'the real choice is not between dogs and children, it is between good science and bad science; between methods that directly relate to humans and those that do not. By its very nature vivisection is bad science: it tells us about animals, usually under artificial conditions, and not about people.' All three approaches are found, sometimes together and sometimes not, but all aim to refute the research argument that animal studies have proved to be very useful at a relatively small cost in animal suffering.

How Much Suffering is Caused by Animal Research?

We have relatively little data on animal suffering in research and testing and what we do have depends heavily on what is perceived to constitute suffering. There are two issues. How much suffering and distress is caused by standard laboratory animal housing and husbandry and how much by the actual research. While there has been considerable concern in recent years about the housing and care standards for the larger laboratory species (for example primates and dogs), there has been much less worry about laboratory rodent facilities. Generally, it appears to be assumed in scentific circles that the standard shoebox cage with bedding provides a more than adequate home for rats and mice, especially when compared to rodent life in nature. For the most part, the available assessments of animal pain and distress in research do not currently consider the effect of animal care and housing practices on the animals. Nearly all the attention is concentrated on what happens during the experimental process itself.

The authorities in The Netherlands have collected data on the potential pain and suffering experienced by laboratory animals under study. The 1990 Annual Report on animal experimentation notes that 53 per cent of the animals experience minor discomfort, 23 per cent were likely to experience moderate discomfort and 24 per cent were likely to experience severe discomfort. About one-fifth of the animals in this last category were given medication to alleviate pain. Examples of procedures that would place animals in the 'severe' category are prolonged deprivation, some experimental infections, tumor induction, LD50 testing, and immunization in the foot pad or with complete Freund's adjuvant (The Alternatives Report, 1992). Nearly all of the research animals will be euthanized so they will also experience the harm of death.

In Great Britain, the only indication of pain control that is available is the recording of anesthesia use. In 1978, 3 per cent of the 5.2 million procedures involved anesthesia for the whole procedure (they were terminal) and 14 per cent involved anesthesia for only part of the procedure. In 1988, 19 per cent of the 3.5 million procedures involved anesthesia for the whole procedure and 17 per cent involved anesthesia for only part of the procedure. It is not clear why anesthesia use doubled from 1978 to 1988 although the 1986 Act that revised British controls over animal experimentation placed greater emphasis on the control of pain and distress (The Alternatives Report, 1990).

According to 1992 US Department of Agriculture (USDA) statistics (which do not include rats, mice and birds or 90 per cent of all laboratory animals), 5.63 per cent of the animals used in research in the USA experience pain or distress that is not alleviated by pain medication. However, USDA statistics on pain and distress are regarded with justifiable suspicion by critics of animal research, especially in light of the tremendous variation in the way different institutions report their use of animals by pain category. States vary dramatically in the proportion of research that is reported to be painful and for which pain relief is not provided. Kansas (45.5 per cent), Washington (30.4 per cent) and Colorado (26.0 per cent) all reported that more than a quarter of their animal research involved unrelieved pain while some relatively big research animal users like Arkansas (0.03 per cent), Delaware (0.65 per cent), Florida (0.70 per cent), Maryland (0.82 per cent), Massachusetts (0.98 per cent), Nebraska (0.13 per cent) and Texas(0.70 per cent) reported less than 1 per cent of animal research in the unrelieved pain category. It can be concluded that the USDA statistics cannot be used as a reliable assessment of research animal pain and distress. There is also some direct evidence that actual use of post-operative pain relief is lower than stated by scientists (Phillips, 1993).

Despite the problems of assessing animal pain and distress and the questionable reliability of some of the numbers, the available evidence does not indicate that all, or even a majority of research animals experience severe and unrelieved suffering. Of course, how one judges the total extent of animal suffering (and whether it is excessive) will be heavily influenced by one's personal values and interpretation of the data, and by one's assessment of the level of harm caused by the killing of animals.

What are the Benefits of Animal Research?

Having attempted to address the cost side of the equation, what of the benefits? These are no easier to judge. Nonetheless, our knowledge of the natural world and human biology has expanded enormously in this century (although one may question whether human wisdom has increased by a commensurate amount over the same period). Our ability to develop vaccines, antibiotics, public health initiatives and reasonably good nutritional advice is much greater than it was even 40 years ago. While about 40 per cent of the research that has produced this knowledge used animals (at least according to NIH analyses of its funding allocations), it is, in practice, not really possible to separate different research approaches to apportion credit. Research tends to be an endless circle with insights flowing from the clinic to the laboratory to the theoreticians and back again. If the flow is disrupted, then one will lose much more than the portion removed.

There is also some question about what should be valued in research. Is the simple increase in knowledge that is produced by a well-designed study sufficient to justify the death and possible suffering of some animals? Or should one insist that the research produces knowledge that has some applicable benefit to human or environmental health? In attempting to develop a cost–benefit balance, the technical arguments about what constitutes pain and suffering and how much is produced versus likely impact on health care delivery very rapidly give way to moral arguments about how these parameters should be valued in the first place.

CASE STUDIES

It is difficult to discuss cost–benefit issues in the abstract which is why so many of the criticisms and defences of animal research resort instead to relating narratives about particular incidents or discoveries. Two case studies have been selected for more detailed discussion here – the discovery and development of insulin, and the development of the polio vaccine. Both have been put forward as examples of triumphs of modern medicine and have subsequently been criticized in animal protection literature. They thus serve as interesting examples of the claims and counter-claims in the animal research debate.

The Discovery of Insulin

The discovery of insulin as a treatment for diabetes mellitus has been described as 'one of the genuine miracles of modern medicine' (Bliss, 1982, p. 11) and the role of animal experimentation in this discovery has received attention from both sides of the debate. A critic, Brandon Reines, claims, 'the animal experiments provided no clear direction, though ultimately the illusion was created that animal experimentation had led to the discovery of insulin' (Reines, undated, p. 11) while Charles Best, co-discoverer of insulin, claims his work to be, 'only one of the many, many thousand series of experiments which testify to the importance of dogs in medical research' (Best, 1974, p. 439). Examining the arguments for and against animal research in the discovery of insulin should help us to judge their coherence and may help us assess what value we might place on at least some of the animal experimentation.

Diabetes is a disease which contradicts the claim that a high standard of living is all that is needed to remain healthy (assuming a well-fed state is one component of good health). As Bliss (1982, p. 21) points out: 'There tended to be more diabetics among people who were prosperous and well-nourished rather than among the poor and lean.' It is also a disease which contradicts Sharpe's claim that 'most disease is self-limiting' (Sharpe, 1988, p. 32) and the juvenile form of the disease cannot yet be prevented although it has been suggested that its incidence might be reduced by appropriate public health initiatives. In addition, it should be noted that the therapeutic benefit of insulin for maturity onset diabetes is more limited than its benefit for the much less prevalent juvenile diabetes. The case of diabetes does, however, address the impact of new research knowledge on the alleviation of morbidity and distress rather than simply dealing with mortality and longevity statistics. For example, Sharpe argues, 'if vivisection were making such an enormous contribution we could confidently expect a massive improvement in health' (Sharpe, 1988, p. 15). Did diabetics experience an improvement in health due to the discovery of insulin and was that discovery a triumph of animal experimentation?

Elizabeth Hughes' life is an excellent example of the life of a juvenile diabetic before the discovery of insulin and her story provides necessary context for those of us living at the end of the twentieth century as to why the discovery of insulin was perceived to be such a miracle. Elizabeth was diagnosed as diabetic in 1919 at the age of 11 or 12. In those days, 'the diagnosis was like knowing a sentence of death had been passed' (Bliss, 1982, p. 43). The only available treatment at that time was a starvation diet developed by Frederick Allen from experiments on dogs which had been rendered mildly diabetic by partial pancreatectomy (thus mimicking human diabetes more closely than complete pancreatectomy). He discovered that undernourishment allowed the diabetic dogs to live symptom free. However, this form of treatment was never easy on the diabetic and required a diet that most patients could not sustain, either physically or mentally. The usual outcome was death by starvation if the patient did not abandon the diet and succumb to diabetic acidosis. Doctors who worked on the diabetic wards before 1920 in the days of starvation treatment were reminded of those wards when pictures of the Nazi concentration camp victims appeared after the Second World War.

Elizabeth Hughes' experience on this diet exemplifies the suffering and discipline required of the patient.

Had she been untreated, Elizabeth Hughes would probably have died in the summer of 1919. With Dr Allen's stern diet, her own discipline, and her sheer strength of character, she carried on very well through the winter of 1919–20. She had a difficult time in the spring of 1920, when colds and tonsillitis threw her out of balance, and was often cut back to a diet of less than 500 calories. But she recovered that summer and fall, and at Christmas 1920 weighed in at 62 1/4 lbs. The winter and spring were bad again, though; by the end of March she was down to 52 lbs. Her diet in April averaged 405 calories. The doctor got her back up to 700 to 900 calories, but her weight was now at a new low plateau, between 52 and 54 lbs. At the age of 13, Elizabeth was a semi-invalid (Bliss, 1982, p. 44).

However, she did not die. Her father had the means to purchase the best medical care and she became one of the first to receive insulin in Toronto. When she arrived, she was five feet tall and weighed 45 lbs but the insulin extracts rapidly cleared the sugar from her blood and within two weeks her diet had been increased from 890 calories to 2400. Elizabeth Hughes could not believe her good fortune and wrote to her mother, 'It is simply too wonderful for words this stuff' (Bliss, 1982, p. 152 – even though the early preparations of insulin quite often produced toxic side effects). In 1929, Elizabeth Hughes graduated from Barnard College and married a young lawyer. She had three children and became prominent in civic affairs in the Detroit area where her husband worked for Ford Motor Company. She died in 1981 from a heart attack after 43 000 insulin injections and a full life rescued from the 'nightmare' years of starvation before insulin.

Elizabeth Hughes is just one example but there have been countless others since then. However, McKeown (1979) argues that the majority of diabetics (who experience the adult onset form of the disease) do not experience the type of miraculous change seen in the smaller group of juvenile diabetics. Nonetheless, insulin therapy has had a significant impact on patients and it now remains to assess what role animals played in the discovery. There are several potentially key discoveries and much spinning of wheels in the insulin story.

Early on diabetes was diagnosed by the sweet taste of the diabetic's urine but knowledge about the etiology of the disease was scant. Reines (undated, p. 9) suggests that the first link between diabetes and the pancreas was demonstrated by Thomas Crawley in 1788 when he discovered multiple calculi in the pancreas of a patient who had died of diabetes. Other autopsy studies on diabetics confirmed Crawley's observation and suggested that the pancreas was the most likely organ affected in this disease. Then, in 1869, Langerhans found two cell populations in the pancreas, one of which secreted the digestive juices but he did not know what the other cells did (these were the beta cells that secreted insulin).

According to Bliss (1982, p. 25) (and contra Reines), evidence connecting the pancreas and diabetes was still tenuous in 1889 when Oskar Minkowski and Joseph von Mering made their discovery. They had removed the pancreas from a dog to see if the pancreatic digestive enzymes were vital to the digestion of fat. Minkowski noticed that the dog was urinating on the laboratory floor even though it was house-trained and tested the urine for sugar (he had been told by his supervisor to test for sugar whenever he saw polyuria). He discovered that the dog had become diabetic. This led the way for other researchers who proved in further experiments on dogs that the pancreas released an internal secretion into the blood stream which controlled the metabolism of carbohydrates (Bliss, 1982).

This discovery unleashed a flurry of research aimed at producing a pancreatic extract that could be used to treat diabetes. The idea of using organ extracts grew out of other work at the time (also involving animal research) that had shown that several diseases (for example goitre and cretinism) could be treated by extracts of the thyroid. In the first few years of the twentieth century, the new field of endocrinology was blossoming and many investigators were searching for the pancreatic extract. However, the initial studies produced conflicting results and many red herrings and experienced researchers learned to be cautious of 'pancreatic extract' effects. With the hindsight of history, Bliss (1982) identifies several researchers who might have been on the right track but it is clear that the evidence did not point clearly in any one direction when Banting approached McLeod in Toronto in 1921 to do his dog experiments.

Reines (undated, p. 3) argues that: 'it is clear from the factual evidence presented in Bliss' book that the animal experimentation which preceded the discovery of insulin was not part of the scientific process that led to the discovery of insulin' and he and others credit a clinical observation for stimulating his dog research. According to a booklet produced by the Australian Association for Humane Research (1988, p. 7): 'the real breakthrough came through the clinical work of an American pathologist, Dr Moses Barron ... who published a paper on a patient with a rare case of pancreatic lithiasis in which the stone blocked the main pancreatic duct'. He reported that, while the acinar cells had atrophied, the islet cells appeared to be intact. This gave Banting the idea that he could obtain healthy islet cells from which to prepare pancreatic extract by ligating the pancreatic duct and waiting for the acinar cells (that were proposed to contain a substance that destroyed the 'active principle' in the pancreas) to atrophy. Hence, the claim that clinical studies led to the discovery (or moment of insight) of insulin.

Another breakthrough in diabetes research that occurred prior to the Toronto team's success and that is part of what made their work successful, was the development of an easy and accurate way to measure sugar in the blood. Bliss (1982, p. 40) states, 'The single most important development in diabetes research, next to Allen's diets, was the rapid improvement between about 1910 and 1920 in techniques for measuring blood sugar.' This development was so important because it permitted the measurement of blood sugar directly rather than the less accurate measure of a reduction of sugar in urine.

Another important ramification of the development of a better technique to measure blood sugar, was that it quite possibly influenced Macleod's decision to encourage and assist Dr Banting with his experimental ideas. Macleod certainly knew that other researchers had failed to isolate a useful pancreatic extract to treat diabetes, but also must have known that: 'almost all experiments done in the past, with pancreatic extracts or by any other method, might show different results now that blood sugar could be tested easily and quickly' (Bliss, 1982, p. 53). So, when Banting approached Macleod with his idea of how to isolate an anti-diabetic substance from the pancreas, Macleod agreed that the experiment was worth trying and agreed to provide Banting with laboratory space, some dogs, an assistant, and guidance.

Banting and Best's research on dogs during the summer of 1921 is well known but Bliss (1982) uses material from the original data books to point out the numerous errors in their research and their reporting of it. However, the results were sufficiently encouraging for McLeod to call on the services of Collip, a biochemist, who started working to purify the pancreatic extracts. One of Collip's key contributions at this stage was to demonstrate that the potency of the pancreatic extract could be readily tested by measuring its blood sugar lowering ability in normal rabbits. He was later responsible for describing the hypoglycemic shock reaction (and associated convulsions) and for showing that it could be reversed by the administration of glucose in his rabbit studies. When it came time to prepare insulin extracts from farm animal pancreases on a commercial basis, an animal convulsion test became a critical part of ensuring that batches of insulin of relatively uniform potency were distributed.

One can question the role of the dog studies done by Banting and Best. For example, it seems clear from Bliss' (1982) analysis that insulin would probably have been discovered within a year or two, even if Banting had not been given space by McLeod, because of such technical developments as a better test for blood sugar. Nonetheless, laboratory animals, especially the early Minkowski and von Mering dog work and the rabbits used by Collip, played a critical role in the identification, successful isolation and standardization of insulin.

The Polio Vaccine Story

The history of the discovery of insulin shares many features with the development of polio vaccine which has also been described in grand terms such as, 'one of the greatest technical and humanistic triumphs of the age' (Paul, 1971, preface). Like diabetes, polio had no satisfactory treatment, could be fatal and children were among those affected (polio primarily affected children). In addition, polio appeared in epidemic form in countries with high standards of hygiene and, thus, did not appear to be preventable by leading a healthful life.

Early attitudes toward polio were dominated by a feeling of hopelessness and mothers would keep their children away from communal places in the summer because of fear of the disease. It has also been suggested that some 'epidemics' might have been caused by mass hysteria, exacerbated by such treatment patterns as putting casts on any limb that appeared to show signs of weakness, rather than actual infection (Paul, 1971, p. 224). When the vaccine was finally developed, the success was due to the efforts of many researchers over a long period of time building on knowledge gained through experiments involving animal and non-animal methods. The animal experiments have also become the focus of criticism from animal activists, probably because polio is often presented as a triumph of animal research.

The major criticism that appears to be leveled at animal research on polio is encapsulated in the statement that: 'Tragically, animal experiments so dominated research that prior to 1937 most scientists rejected the notion that polio is an intestinal disease' (Sharpe, 1993). This claim is usually bolstered by reference to Paul's (1971) magisterial history of the polio story that describes the wrong direction taken by Flexner at the Rockefeller Institute as a result of his reliance on monkey data. However, as Paul also documents, there were many other mis-steps in the search for a therapy for polio, some of which were advanced by clinical investigators.

Polio occurred in epidemics that developed out of a previous endemic condition. The transition of the disease from endemic to epidemic occurred with, and was due to, the development of modern sanitation. With modern sanitation, children were not exposed to polio virus in infancy when the infection is usually silent. Without early exposure children were not naturally immunized and therefore large numbers could be infected at one time, leading to the appearance of the epidemics. In addition, older children are more likely to suffer the associated paralysis (Marten 1981). Therefore, polio epidemics were 'caused' by better public hygiene. With the growth of scientific knowledge about the nature of infection from many different scientific approaches, including epidemiology, clinical studies, animal experimentation and *in vitro* studies, the etiology of polio slowly began to be puzzled out. With such knowledge came a growing hope that there could be a way to prevent or treat the disease (Paul, 1971).

Before the advent of histology, the site of the lesion of polio virus was not agreed upon, and so polio (a name based on the site of the lesion) was usually known as Infantile Paralysis. In 1870, Charcot discovered, through examinations of autopsy specimens (clinical work), that the anatomic location of the lesion was in the anterior horn of the gray matter of the spinal cord, rather than in the muscle or peripheral nerves. Later examinations of the spinal cords of monkeys sacrificed at different stages of the disease (animal research, and studies that could not be done with human polio patients) helped elucidate the degenerative nature of the lesion.

The pathologic organism of polio was also not agreed upon until 1908 when Landsteiner and Popper infected two primates with polio by injecting them with bacteriologically sterile spinal cord samples from a fatal human case of polio (Paul, 1971). The importance of this experiment in leading to an understanding of polio, and in helping explain why the monkey model was chosen time after time by researchers, is expressed by Paul (1971, p. 100) in the following quotation:

> Seldom has the record spoken louder or in a more convincing manner than it did when one of these monkeys 'came down' with paralysis, and louder still when they were shown to have lesions within the spinal cord exactly like those seen in human poliomyelitis.

The monkey model convinced even skeptics that polio was caused by a virus.

Subsequent to Charcot's 1870 discovery of the site of the spinal cord lesion, Rissles, in 1888, pointed out other non-neural lesions of acute polio. His findings led him to the correct conclusion that polio is actually a systemic disease rather than exclusively neurologic. Many years later, in 1912, a team headed by Carl Kling in Stockholm isolated polio virus (by infecting monkeys) from the throat and small intestine of both fatal and acutely ill polio victims. These findings indicated how polio virus might enter and exit the body, and therefore how it is transmitted. One member of Kling's team correctly concluded from epidemiological studies that immunity to polio could be naturally acquired through the process of sub-clinical infection.

However, these data were soon forgotten or ignored as new studies (including both animal and clinical investigations) painted a different view of polio (Paul, 1971).

Paul (1971, p. 108) notes that Flexner of the Rockefeller Institute was so impressed by how closely the primate neurological lesions resembled those in humans that he decided that one could study the disease in either monkeys or humans and he chose monkeys. Unfortunately, the way he conducted his studies on monkeys led him to conclude that polio was a neurogenic infection and his stature in the field caused many to follow this idea. This diverted attention away from the fact that polio might be a systemic infection during the period from 1910 to 1937 when Flexner's ideas held sway.

However, Flexner was not the only person to pursue false leads. Some even stranger theories were proposed including George Draper's 1917 theory of 'constitutional susceptibility', which he formulated through his clinical investigations of children with polio. He concluded that 'large well-nourished children with widely spaced teeth' (Paul, 1971, p. 162) were more susceptible to polio than other children. This conclusion was widely supported for the next 20 years and it was even suggested that, if a prophylactic measure was developed, it should be reserved for those children who qualified as susceptible by Draper's standards (Paul, 1971). Thus, neither clinical research nor animal experimentation were immune from serious error.

In 1931, Burnet and Macnamara made the important discovery that there were serologically different strains of the virus using monkeys (Paul, 1971). Their findings later inspired the 1946 virus typing project (identifying three strains) using large numbers of monkeys that was a key in the development of a vaccine (Paul, 1971). In 1939 Charles Armstrong, and later Max Theiler, succeeded in experimentally infecting cotton rats, and later mice, with the Lansing strain (Type II) which facilitated an expansion of polio research because mice were much cheaper than monkeys. Another important insight from mouse studies was the finding that the virulence of polio virus could be attenuated without losing its ability to immunize (Paul, 1971). This pointed the way to the development of the live-attenuated Sabin polio vaccine.

Another major contribution to polio research came in 1948 with the successful growth of polio virus in cultures of human 'non-nervous' tissue by Enders, Weller, and Robbins (1949). The availability of reliable cell culture technology now made it possible to quantify the amount of virus in a tissue culture sample, and to use tissue culture to replace monkeys in many cases (Paul, 1971). The development of antibiotics to control bacterial overgrowth in tissue culture was an unrelated but very important preliminary step that facilitated the finding by Enders and his colleagues which actually won the Nobel Prize.

The use of animals in polio research and production has declined dramatically (by a factor of one hundred) since hundreds of thousands of monkeys were used annually in the 1950s. This decline can be attributed to improved technology and the implementation of alternatives (see Hendriksen, 1988; LeCornu and Rowan, 1979; Marten, 1981; and Rowan, 1984). For example, steady technical improvements led to dramatic reductions in the annual use of animals in polio vaccine production in The Netherlands from 4500 in 1965 to 30 in 1984 (Hendriksen, 1988, p. 59).

In sum, the polio vaccine story is another illustration of the interdependence of different research approaches, the triumphs and mis-steps, and the way improved technology and changes in societal attitudes led to dramatic reductions in animal use. The polio story can be used to bolster claims for both the utility of animal research and the importance of alternatives but not to prove that one was better than the other. Both the polio and insulin stories demonstrate the difficulty of biomedical research, the sloppiness of some of the work, the frequent blind alleys followed by both clinical and experimental investigators, and the mixture of chance, technique availability, clinical observation and animal experimentation that all play a role in advancing knowledge.

NOTE

1. The research for this paper was supported in part by WARDS (Working for Animals in Research, Drugs and Surgery) of Washington, DC who awarded a summer research studentship, under the supervision of the author, to Cary Dyer of Tufts University School of Veterinary Medicine in 1993. This paper is a reworked and expanded version of Ms Dyer's project report.

Part III: Animal Rights and the Political Process

The success of the animal protection movement will ultimately be judged by the extent to which it can convert the objectives which derive from a convincing moral case into social and political reality. It is this social and political reality with which the final four contributions to this volume are concerned. Goddard Svendsen and Jasper write from a detached perspective on the role played by the European Union in animal welfare and the American animal rights movement respectively, whilst Ryder and Stallwood offer highly personal accounts of the progress of, and the future prospects for, animal protection in Britain and the United States.

All four pieces emphasise to a greater or lesser extent the reliance of the animal protection movement on public campaigning of various kinds. This reliance has two main causes. In the first place, it reflects the fact that, although the stringency of governmental legislation and regulation is obviously a crucial measure of the importance any society attaches to the well-being of animals, such action alone cannot protect animals without a significant shift in cultural values. This is why the animal protection movement is characterised as a 'new social movement' since it seeks more than just mere tinkering with existing government measures and machinery. Secondly, the lack of access accorded to animal protection groups by decision-makers has necessitated a public oriented campaign in order to mobilise public opinion thereby forcing decision-makers to listen. As a result of both of these factors, much effort – as the contributions to this section reveal – has gone into promoting consumer-based lifestyle changes (buying 'cruelty-free' products, encouraging vegetarianism and so forth) which by-pass the conventional political arena altogether.

Animal Welfare Decision-Making

Whilst the cultural changes referred to in the previous paragraph are hugely important, the animal protection movement also needs (and, more to the point, has sought) to enter into conventional pressure group politics. Clearly, it is a bankrupt strategy simply to wait for major cultural changes to somehow miraculously emerge. For one thing, the effect that governmental action can have on social behaviour should not be underestimated. For another, there is much, of course, that can be done to improve the lot of animals short of the major social transformation that is no doubt needed for the achievement

123

of the abolitionist objectives of animal rightists. Furthermore, there is some evidence that the opponents of the animal rights movement (the pharmaceutical companies, the bio-medical community and the meat industry) have mounted a relatively successful counter-mobilisation so that the animal protection movement finds it much more difficult now to gain positive publicity for its campaigns (Jasper & Poulsen, 1983; Elston, 1994).

In the light of this, it is arguably becoming increasingly important that the animal protection turns more of its attention to mainstream lobbying. In this context, the chapter by Richard Ryder provides a fascinating insight into the British movement's attempts to 'Put Animals Into Politics'. One of the key problems Ryder identifies is the fragmented nature of animal welfare decision making in Britain (a problem which occurs even more noticeably in the United States) and one of the objectives of the Political Animal Lobby (a lobbying organisation set up by IFAW) has been to advocate a single Commission with specific responsibility for co-ordinating animal welfare within government. In reality, though, the nature of decision-making in Britain ensures that such a reform is extremely unlikely to occur. In addition, even if a separate Commission or department was created it would find it difficult to wrest control of animal welfare issues from existing centres of influence. Support for this can be garnered from the experience of the Department of the Environment which was set up in 1970 partly at least to co-ordinate environmental policy. Over two decades later, however, significant environmental responsibilities still lie with other parts of government and, moreover, insofar as it existed, the strategy of incorporation has now been abandoned in favour of one which seeks to make each department aware of and act upon the environmental responsibilities relevant to it (Garner, 1996).

Such a negative conclusion is predicated on the assumption that animal welfare policy in the areas of agriculture and experimentation in particular is under the control of distinct 'policy communities' within which those who stand to gain by the continued exploitation of animals are extremely powerful (on the policy community literature see Marsh & Rhodes, 1992). Certainly in the area of agricultural policy, the NFU has had an extremely close relationship with the Ministry of Agriculture, Fisheries and Food. Crucially, this relationship is based not just upon an institutional structure which provides for a privileged position for the NFU but also a shared ideology which has excluded those (such as animal protection and environmental groups) who have sought to challenge the traditional belief in the utility of agricultural intensification (Smith, 1990). Much less work has been done on the institutional and ideological basis of animal experimentation policy but it would seem reasonable to conclude that control has been exercised by a closed policy community consisting of the Home Office together with scientific and pharmaceutical interests. As Mary Ann Elston (1994) has shown, up until the 1970s at least this institutional arrangement was protected by a dominant ideology legitimising vivisection.

Whilst these patterns of policy-making continue to exist, then, Ryder's advocacy of an animal welfare commission is unlikely to succeed or – more to the point – in order to succeed, opposition from powerful interests would have to be overcome and, if this were to happen, then one of the main reasons for the advocacy (to wrest control of animal welfare policy-making from unsympathetic policy communities) would cease to exist.

Challenging Policy Communities

It should not be thought that the preceding discussion is a recipe for despair. One of the interesting developments of the past two decades or so is the way in which the dominant policy communities have had to adapt to the politicisation of animal protection. Thus, both the agricultural and animal experimentation policy communities have had to offer concessions – in the form, for instance, of the 1968 Agricultural (Miscellaneous Provisions) Act and the 1986 Animals (Scientific Procedures) Act – and new forums – such as the Farm Animal Welfare Council and the Animal Procedures Committee – have been created in order to allow for the co-option of animal welfare interests. In addition, as was pointed out earlier, industry groups have had to come out into the open and publicly defend their exploitation of animals. This is important because without an ideological hegemony it is questionable how long the institutional structure of policy communities can survive.

As the articles by Jim Jasper and Kim Stallwood reveal, less has been achieved, at least in a formal legislative sense, in the United States than in Britain. This might be regarded as surprising because the American political system has usually been regarded as more open and pluralistic, thereby allowing for cause groups such as those seeking to protect animals to gain a foothold in the system. In reality, decision-making in America is less open than the formal constitutional structure would suggest and, in addition, although animal protection groups have been quite successful in getting the issue onto the Congressional agenda, the battle still has to be fought out with government agencies and even the courts. Thus, for instance, despite gaining the passage of amendments to the Animal Welfare Act in 1985, opponents have been able to delay and dilute the regulations drawn up to implement it (Garner, 1995b).

It is the politicisation of animal protection, though, which has brought gains in both Britain and the United States. The abuse of animals revealed in the

Taub and Gennarelli cases as documented by Jasper, for instance, did a great deal to place laboratory animal welfare on the political agenda in the United States as did the smoking beagles exposé in Britain. As Richard Ryder explains, too, the campaign starting in the late 1970s to make animal welfare a party political issue has undoubtedly borne fruit. As Richard Crossman, a Labour Cabinet Minister in the 1960s and 1970s, pointed out, the manifesto is often the 'battering ram of change' forcing stable and long-standing alliances between officials and interest groups to change course. A targeting of elections in the United States, advocated by Stallwood, is if anything likely to be more productive in a system where party organisation is weak and where, as a consequence, interest group resources – both financial and numerical – can play a crucial role.

There is no doubt that the animal protection movement can be a more effective campaigning force. Ryder, for instance, points to the constant need for a well-argued and balanced case when seeking to persuade decision-makers and the wider public. In addition, a theme of this book has been the importance of linking animal protection with other issues such as public health and the environment. As Stallwood argues, this would be a means of mobilising the widest possible support. Too often, though, neither of these factors are present. It would be wrong to single out the animal protection movement for exclusive blame here but it is true that the overly moral and confrontational stance of many animal rights campaigns does hinder the development of a case which will be persuasive to the widest number of constituencies.

Jasper's research indicates that this problem is partly caused by the way in which the animal rights movement recruits its members. Whilst many social movements recruit through existing social and political networks, the animal rights movement would seem to be unusual in that most joined after being shocked by something they saw or read. 'Were it not for animal issues', Jasper writes, 'most of today's animal rights activists would probably not be involved in protest activity'. One can see, then, that there is no natural organisational affinity between animal protection and other social movements and, moreover, that animal protection groups may be faced with a conflict between the needs of organisational maintenance, on the one hand, and the need to appeal to the uncommitted and build bridges with other causes, on the other. Nevertheless, Jasper remains optimistic, concluding that: 'If the leaders of animal rights groups can rein in their supporters and expand their own ideological horizons, their movement could join the coalition of mutually supportive causes that has developed over the past 30 years.'

Conclusion – The Spectre of Internationalism

In many ways the most crucial development facing those who seek to protect animals is the increasingly international trend in policy-making. As Rosemary Goddard Svendsen's contribution admirably documents, the role of the European Union in animal welfare is now so substantial that it cannot be ignored. This has both a positive and a negative dimension. On the positive side, as both Goddard Svendsen and Radford, in chapter 4, illustrate, it provides an opportunity to raise animal welfare standards in countries such as Spain and Greece, where the concept is virtually unknown. In addition, Britain's membership has expanded and, to some extent, opened up decision-making arenas providing a new and potentially beneficial focus of activity for the animal protection movement.

On the negative side, the fundamental rationale for the European Union and the general globalisation of the world's economies is the freeing-up of markets. This could yet have devastating implications for animal welfare both in Britain and elsewhere. GATT, as Ryder, Goddard Svendsen and Radford indicate, is already threatening hard-won animal welfare measures and we have seen, in the live exports issue, that British governments are apparently powerless to ban a trade which polls reveal is enormously unpopular amongst the British public. Animal welfare groups will, of course, increase their efforts to be represented on European and world bodies but economic interests have the resources to defend their interests very effectively. The prevailing ideology of free trade would seem, at the moment, to be on their side.

7 The American Animal Rights Movement
James M. Jasper[1]

> Hee doth not forbid mercy or love
> to Beasts or Creatures, but hee
> would not have your love terminated
> in them.
>
> Increase Mather, Seventeenth-Century
> Boston Puritan (Miller, 1967, p. 42)

According to J. Peter Hernance, the United States Department of Agriculture mistreats bees and crickets. Specifically, the USDA developed a technique for attaching microscopic barcodes to the hairs of bees so that they could be monitored during experiments, thereby, in Hernance's words, 'virtually making them our slaves'. Hernance is also outraged that the USDA has experimented with a one-celled microbe that kills Mormon crickets, which destroy crops. Even though the microbe would obviate the need for many pesticides, he feels that the crickets should be 'left alone'. Hernance denounced these practices in the July 1990 *Animal Rights Information and Education Service Newsletter*, of which he is the editor/compiler. He is not alone in his concern for species that normally elude human sympathy. Other American animal rights groups protest the mistreatment of rattlesnakes, bats, even northern California banana slugs, which are slimy and yellow and up to ten inches long. Although the animal rights movement remains primarily concerned with furry, cute mammals, pioneers have extended attention to virtually all species.

The animal rights movement is puzzling. It does not fit easily into the common grids we have for dividing up the political landscape, such as Labor vs. Capital, Left vs. Right, environmental protection vs. economic growth, or human rights vs. dictatorship. Are animal rights activists essentially misanthropes, ignorant cranks who value animals more than humans, as their opponents claim? Are they savvy moral entrepreneurs who opportunistically link their issues with those of other popular movements such as feminism and ecology? Are they do-gooders who are naïve about the power structure of capitalist society? Their growth and visibility since the early 1980s in the United States, Britain and elsewhere prove that they tap into sensibilities widely distributed throughout the advanced industrial world.

Some questions about the American animal rights movement can be answered with confidence, such as who they are, what their beliefs and values are, and what their goals are (although the movement's diversity means that the answers are not always simple). Others are more difficult because speculative: can animal advocates form useful coalitions with other political activists, will they fuse with environmental organizations, will they continue to grow in the coming decade, and is their driving ideology complex enough to involve them in additional political agendas? I want to address, although briefly, both the easy and the hard questions.[2]

A Brief History

More than one hundred years ago, wealthy individuals in the large American cities followed the British lead in expressing their outrage over the treatment of nonhuman species by founding groups devoted to animal protection. The first, the American Society for the Protection of Animals, was created in 1866, and by the turn of the century several hundred others had been formed. Hundreds more groups have appeared in this century. Although many represent the idiosyncratic concerns of their founders, the creation of new groups tends to cluster in waves that reflect widespread changes in public sentiment. The most recent wave of animal protection groups started to appear at the end of the 1970s.

The animal rights movement grew into one of the United States' most visible protest movements of the 1980s, moving from obscurity at the beginning of the decade to the covers of most major news magazines by the end. The issue of fur coats, for example, was raised on popular television shows such as *Designing Women*, *L.A. Law*, and even *Saturday Night Live*. In the early 1980s hundreds of diverse new groups were founded, and later in the decade hundreds of thousands of people enrolled in them. Although the Federal Bureau of Investigation labelled at least one animal rights group 'terrorist' after several destructive raids on research laboratories, most groups were content with the standard tools of contemporary protest: public demonstrations, letter writing, and media coverage. The movement's visibility peaked in June 1990, when almost 30 000 activists came to Washington, DC for a 'March for the Animals'.

The movement brought public attention to a long list of practices in which humans utilize nonhuman species. Some were century-old issues centered on the unnecessary suffering of animals: the beating or starvation of pets by cruel owners; the use of carriage horses in extreme heat; the inadequate anesthetization of animals in scientific experiments; the conditions of animals raised for food. But others were practices in which the animals did not always suffer obvious physical hardship: the keeping of animals in zoos; the use of fully anesthetized animals in research; the performance of animals in circuses; or the sheering of sheep for their wool. Many activists attacked every domestication of animals as an infringement on these beings' deserved autonomy, including the keeping of pets (or 'companion animals', in the phrase of activists more sympathetic to the practice). The aspirations of this new animal rights movement, concerned for the autonomy of nonhuman species, went far beyond those of traditional humane societies, primarily outraged over the animals' physical welfare.

The new movement grew in stages. By the mid-1970s a small network of people around the United States – only several dozen at first – had developed concerns for animals which they felt were not well served by existing animal welfare organizations. Some had participated in other protest movements, especially feminism and environmentalism, and others had been influenced by the ideas of these movements. Environmentalists had emphasized that nature was not ours to destroy at will, that it had moral rights of its own. They had protested against the destruction of endangered species, whether elephants for their ivory or whales for their oil and blubber, as well as against interference with natural balances through practices such as trapping. With these concerns came an appreciation for complex patterns of animal cognition and communication. Feminism contributed a critique of oppressive and instrumental attitudes, as well as a concern for the fragile web of existing relationships between living beings. Feminists insisted that the central institutions of modern society tended to view people, especially women and other vulnerable beings, as means rather than as ends in themselves. Among a small number of Americans, such intuitions and beliefs gelled into an intense concern for animals.

Their compassion for animals did not find satisfying outlets. Whereas many men and women with the same sentiments were content to volunteer at local animal shelters, this small constellation of concerned citizens was dissatisfied with these activities. For one thing, they were concerned about the treatment of animals in laboratories and on modern 'factory' farms, not simply the problem of pet overpopulation. They perceived animal abuse in some of the central institutions of modern society, and not merely as a problem of occasional cruel or thoughtless individuals. And they saw existing humane societies as timid in their protective efforts, more concerned with maintaining the support of wealthy patrons than with extending their activities on behalf of animals, all animals.[3]

At this point, the works of several philosophers provided a language and ideology that seemed to crystallize these new concerns for the treatment of animals. Most influential was Peter Singer's *Animal Liberation* (1975), which denounced 'speciesism' as a bias parallel to racism and sexism, arguing that, because the pains and pleasures of nonhumans were as intense as those of humans, they should not be ignored or discounted. This publication gave a jolt of energy to these scattered citizens, providing them a 'philosophy on which to hang our emotions, feelings, sentimentality – all the things we had thought were bad; it gave us an intellectual hat to put on our heads', as Joyce Tischler, cofounder of the Animal Legal Defense Fund, expressed it (in Jasper & Nelkin, 1992, p. 93). Henry Spira, after taking a course from Singer in New York, organized a successful protest against cat experiments at the American Museum of Natural History in 1976–7. Armed with powerful arguments, this cadre of individuals set out to recruit others to the animal protection movement – soon to be dubbed the animal rights movement, as its demands and tactics outpaced those of existing humane societies.

The animal rights movement differed somewhat from many other causes in the ways early recruits came to the issue. In many protest movements, activists are already politically engaged, and they are drawn to a new cause because it is closely connected to their current ones. For example they see links between civilian nuclear energy, plutonium proliferation, and nuclear weapons, and maybe extend their analyses to include capitalism, imperialism, racism and sexism. At the opposite extreme, some activists come to an issue entirely fresh. Some, for example, become environmental protestors when a hazardous waste dump is proposed for a site near them, or they discover toxic chemicals in their water.[4] These people have a target thrust upon them through a 'moral shock'.[5] The animal rights movement lies somewhere between these two extremes of a logical progression from one cause to the next and the sudden shock of a new issue. In my own surveys of demonstrators in New York and Berkeley, I found that about one third were recruited through pre-existing political and social networks, while most joined when shocked by something they read or saw. Animal protection is partly related to other causes, but in some ways remains unique. The first activists were *inspired* by feminism and environmentalism more than they were directly *extending* them.

Two cases in the early 1980s yielded photographs and videotapes that proved invaluable in recruitment. Soon after helping to found People for the Ethical Treatment of Animals (PETA), Alex Pacheco volunteered to work in the Silver Spring laboratory of Edward Taub, whose neurological experiments involved severing nerves in the limbs of monkeys. Beginning in May 1981, Pacheco kept a diary and took photos of the filthy conditions in which the animals were kept, leading to a public trial and the cessation of Taub's federal funding. In addition, PETA now had a collection of shocking photos and an example of what animal activists could accomplish.

Three years later, at the University of Pennsylvania, five members of the Animal Liberation Front (ALF) broke into Thomas Gennarelli's head-trauma lab, destroying equipment and taking 60 hours of videotapes documenting the experiments. PETA edited the tapes into a short film, *Unnecessary Fuss*, which portrayed researchers in an unfavorable light, joking about the baboons with severe head injuries.

Although acquired by stealth, the evidence from these two labs, spread on television talk shows as well as in brochures, gave an immense boost to the new movement. Of course, these cases also associated the movement closely with a single one of its issues – and not its strongest. Organizationally, PETA and the ALF benefited especially. PETA, through a massive direct-mail effort, grew to be the United States' largest animal rights organization, with several thousand members. In imagery that may have hurt the movement by identifying it with destruction, ALF 'operatives' became a common face (albeit a masked face) in stories about the movement. Other groups also grew rapidly, and even older welfare organizations grew more radical in their rhetoric to keep up with the new groups. By the end of the 1980s, as many as one million Americans contributed to animal rights groups, and millions more to traditional welfare organizations.

Who Are They?

In their demographics and moral values, American animal advocates look similar to participants in other left-liberal protest movements of the past 30 years. The vast majority are white, middle class, well educated, and politically left of center. More than half the respondents to my own limited surveys were unmarried, compared to one third of adults nationwide.[6] Almost all rank-and-file members have pets, although only half of the leaders of animal rights groups do (many of them think that pets, even when called 'companion animals', are necessarily exploited because of their subordinate positions). Two thirds of the participants I surveyed were women, and the proportion is even higher for some groups in the movement. The protestors I surveyed were also similar in their political views to participants in other recent social movements: 34 per cent claimed to be liberal, another 31 per cent progressive or radical left. The movement's main magazine, *The Animals' Agenda*, had identical results – 34 per cent liberal and 32 per cent radical – from its readers (see *The Animals' Agenda*, May–June 1983, p. 26). The majority are also atheists and agnostics. Their ages range widely, but most are in their thirties and forties.

When respondents were asked what other political issues (past or present) had helped involve them in their current cause, 90 people (33 per cent) wrote in other causes and movements. The most commonly mentioned were peace/disarmament (given by 17), civil rights and racism (15), environmentalism (12), the women's movement (10), Vietnam (8), opposition to US military intervention (7), and the antinuclear movement (6). When protestors were also asked what other causes they were *currently* involved in, the most common responses, in descending order, were environmentalism, the women's movement, peace/disarmament, human rights, opposition to US military intervention, and the antinuclear movement.

Responses to these questions undermine two stereotypes of animal rights activists widespread in the United States. One is that they are more concerned with the rights of animals than those of humans. A significant portion of the sample were involved directly in human rights, for example through Amnesty International; others were active in causes such as civil rights, gay rights, women's rights, children's rights, Palestinian rights, and Native American rights. The evidence also casts doubt on the peculiar but common belief that animal rights activists have links to the anti-abortion movement. Only four respondents (one per cent) mentioned the Right-To-Life movement among their other political activities, putting it tenth on the list, and they may belong to the small left wing of the anti-abortion movement rather than the traditional religious wing. Only two respondents mentioned other conservative causes (one active for the Republican Party, the other doing anti-Castro work), and one gave a religious cause (working for the left-liberal Unitarian Church).

What Do They Want?

Animal activists believe that nonhuman species are similar enough to humans that we should take them into account extensively in our moral choices. Many animals, especially mammals, feel pain through central nervous systems similar to ours; they are capable of forming intentions and plans; they are capable of complex mental processes; they communicate with each other and, sometimes, with humans. At the extreme, activists feel that animals have the right not to be interfered with – a right as absolute as that which humans claim. Moderate protestors want, at least, a drastic reduction in the suffering of nonhumans.

In contrast to traditional animal protectionists, who focused on cruelty by humans, animal rights activists analyze the institutional roots of animal suffering and exploitation. The language of the animal rights movement reflects anti-capitalist and anti-instrumental values common to a range of recent protest movements. Activists attack cosmetics companies for putting profits above the lives and the suffering of animals, scientists for pursuing new findings and techniques without regard for their social and ethical implications, and factory farms for the total mechanization of workers and animals. They decry the reduction of the world – humans, animals, and the rest of nature – to a collection of raw materials available for administrative manipulation, as well as the elevation of tools – bureaucracies, technologies, markets – to the status of ends in themselves. The very word 'exploitation' is borrowed from Marxist analyses of capitalism.

Nonetheless, the movement's anti-capitalist rhetoric is rarely used to support workers' rights in more than ideology. Sometimes movement ideologists even portray workers in slaughterhouses and fur ranches as evil (reflecting, to say the least, a lack of sociological insight into economic structures). The political painter Sue Coe, in her series on factory farming, presents the workers as grey, twisted ogres, less victims than perpetrators. In this, animal rightists compare unfavorably to many environmentalists, who persistently try (although with little success) to form ties with workers in the industries they criticize, and to persuade trade unions that environmental programs create jobs. The rhetoric of pro-animal protestors may be more anti-corporate than anti-capitalist, reflecting a – traditionally American – populism that mistrusts big business but lacks a sophisticated analysis of capitalist society.

Animal advocates' evidence and arguments can be surprisingly compelling, though, and many journalists who have written about the movement recount their transformation from skepticism to sympathy (although not conversion). One need not be a sentimental sap to cringe at the crowded conditions of veal calves or chickens on today's farms, or at the use of rabbits as living eyeballs in grisly cosmetics tests. And it is perverse to defend $20 000 sable fur coats as an issue of 'consumer choice'. Scientific experiments undoubtedly used too many animals when, 15 years ago, research animals were inexpensive to procure and maintain. And the ease with which cosmetics companies have reduced their live-animal testing (many, including industry giants, have given it up altogether) indicates that many animals once suffered unnecessarily. As political theorist Jean Bethke Elshtain (1990) wrote: 'We humans do not deserve peace of mind on this issue. Our sleep should be troubled and our days riddled with ethical difficulties as we come to realize the terrible toll one definition of "progress" has taken on our fellow creatures.' Elshtain is hardly a touchy-feely type prone to mushy thinking, but someone who has carefully read the evidence and the arguments.

The protection of animals resonates with popular sensibilities and impulses. Most humans feel some kinship with other species, especially now that, in the advanced industrial societies, we have so little contact with live animals as resources such as food, transportation, or energy. The American movement has packaged its arguments in another popular idiom, rights talk. 'Rights' are the usual way to formulate moral and political demands in the United States, as we have found out from the examples of pornographers, gun owners, and large corporations that insist on their right to free speech in the form of political advertisements and campaign contributions.

Some insist that animals too have absolute rights not to be reduced without consent (which nonhumans cannot give) to the status of someone else's means, regardless of potential benefits to society. The main adherent to this radical rights position (many other animal protection philosophers avoid the word 'rights'), philosopher Tom Regan, argues that mammals are similar to humans in so many ways that they have the same right to lead their own lives. He points to extensive evidence that normal mammals have aspects of complex consciousness – perception, memory, beliefs, desires, intentions, even a sense of the future – that make them 'subjects' of their own lives. It is Regan's language of rights that has been deployed by the American animal protection movement. But granting rights to animals, so that humans could not use them for *any* purposes, goes well beyond the same popular intuitions that favor both animal protection and, when it is applied to humans, rights talk. The same rigid language of rights that has filled animal rights organizations may dampen the appeal of their arguments to other Americans.

Limitations of Rights Talk

The flaw in arguments for absolute animal rights is that all those traits that are supposed to justify rights come in varying degrees, and most humans have more of each trait than most nonhumans. Yet rights do not come in degree: you either have them or you don't. There is no single line to demarcate what species should have the right to live their lives without interference from those that are unaware of what it would mean to live fully. Regan is on shaky ground when he says that, since we don't know how conscious a frog is, we should give it the benefit of the doubt.

Once they adopt the absolute, either/or structure of rights talk, protestors must deny what is obvious to most other Americans: that there are morally significant differences between species (which there are not between different categories of humans). After considering the extensive similarities between humans and nonhumans, one commentator concludes:

> To a surprising degree, other animal species can communicate, choose between alternatives, manipulate signs, recognize themselves in mirrors, and follow rules that allow other species besides their own to live alongside

them. What they do not bring to each of these activities is the ability to attach meaning to a situation by recognizing its uniqueness. [They lack] the capacity not merely to follow rules, but to define for oneself what a rule might mean.[7]

Animal protectionists are most impressed with the long list of similarities; most others insist on the important interpretive consciousness that nonhuman species lack.

Widespread uneasiness with radical animal rights arguments surfaces most clearly over the issue of scientific research. This was the topic that pushed the movement to prominence in the early 1980s, partly because of the photos and videotapes discussed above. To most Americans it seems clear that human lives have been and will be saved by research and techniques developed on other species, and animal advocates make some of their least plausible arguments when they deny this. Popular opinion – reinforced by a concerted countermovement by the biomedical research community – still holds that humans, even if severely damaged or handicapped, should not be experimented upon, although chimpanzees and other nonhumans could be. The intuition is that there are, in the end, morally relevant differences between species.

But differences, even a hierarchy, of species do not mean that we can treat nonhumans any way we wish. We adult humans have most of these same advantages over children of our species, yet we refrain from frying them up for supper or experimenting upon them. One reason is that we love them, or at least certain adults love certain children linked to them by biology or social ties; another is that we feel compassion even for children we do not know. Both reasons also apply to our attitudes toward many nonhuman animals.

This reasoning indicates more solid, because limited, grounds for animal rights arguments (or more properly, now, animal protection arguments). Sympathy, caring, and connectedness are, as feminist psychologist Carol Gilligan (1982) pointed out, just as valid grounds for interpersonal moral guidance as abstract individual rights are. Humans owe something to animals because we live together in the same 'mixed communities' and humans have purposely bred domestic animals which please us and depend on us (imagine a toy poodle living a life on its own without humans). Philosopher Mary Midgley (1983) has elaborated this point in the most interesting book to come out of the animal protection controversy. The argument for better, more caring treatment is strong; that for absolute rights is weak. 'Rights' is a powerful moral and political term, especially in an American tradition of individualism. But it is misleading and self-defeating when applied to nonhumans. Compassion should suffice as a philosophical grounding, and still provide common territory for linking with other protest movements (looking at animals in the context of their relations with humans also allows us to distinguish animals in the wild from domesticated animals, and the policies appropriate to each). But since we are so far from abolishing sheer abuse, the movement has many goals it can attain before these fine philosophical distinctions would matter in practical choices. It would hardly be the first protest movement to use a suspect, unattainable utopia as a rationale for more moderate but reasonable social change.

Taking Midgley's side against Regan, I would distinguish fundamentalists in the animal rights movement from realists. The 'fundis' brook no use of animals no matter what the benefits, while the 'realos' are willing to allow some. The fundis operate by demonizing their opponents as evil, while the realos are willing to negotiate and compromise. Both would attack fur coats, but the realos would allow some research, perhaps some lower species as food, and careful reforms rather than sudden abolition. Realos are more sensitive to the realities of public opinion, political process, and coalition-building.

What about priorities? Even if we agree with the plausibility and desirability of many realo goals, should we devote time and energy to protesting animal abuses when the world's cities are filled with homeless humans, women's reproductive rights are being dismantled, and much of the Third World remains a catastrophe? The question is misleading, for it assumes a zero-sum trade-off between the two causes. We need to ask whether, if they were not protesting on behalf of animals, animal rightists would be working for human causes. And whether they are serious about their anti-capitalist and anti-corporatist talk, and will eventually begin to apply it to cases that do not involve animals.

Were it not for animal issues, most of today's animal rights activists would probably not be involved in protest activity. Most had not been active in other causes prior to the animal rights movement, including most of the movement's leaders. Activity in one cause often leads naturally to participation in others: many men and women moved from environmentalism or feminism into the antinuclear movement, and from there to the peace movement, often with additional stops along the way. But this activist sub-culture needs periodic replenishment; it needs to find issues that attract those not previously active. The abuse of animals – and the photos and many of the actual practices are indeed gruesome – gives many people a sufficient moral shock, a jolt that can move them to their first unconventional political action (in this the animal rights movement is similar to the American anti-abortion movement, which attracted many who had previously been inactive). If we accept that their cause is just, and if inaction is the alternative, then we should see this initiation into political activity as a good thing, an advance in citizenship.

Accomplishments

The American animal rights movement has racked up an impressive list of victories. The movement's biggest success has probably been in cosmetics and substance testing, where alternatives have been perfected that are less expensive than the live-animal tests previously used. By focusing first on cosmetics companies, which could be portrayed as frivolous through slogans such as 'blinding bunnies for one more shade of mascara', activists embarrassed them into donating hundreds of thousands of dollars to research on alternatives. These included cell cultures, tissue cultures, egg membranes, and computer models. Higher organisms could be replaced by lower ones, such as plants, earthworms, and sea urchin eggs. In many areas, the use of live animals for substance testing has been reduced by 80 or 90 per cent; many companies claim to have abandoned live-animal tests altogether.

The movement has also improved the treatment of animals in scientific research in the United States, largely by, in 1985, inspiring amendments to the Animal Welfare Act that specifically deal with laboratory animals. Institutions receiving funds from the National Institutes of Health are now required to establish Animal Care and Use Committees to review research proposals in order to reduce the use of live animals and minimize their pain, as well as to provide advice about painkillers, anesthetics and animal handling. The entire controversy has made all researchers acutely conscious of their animal use and the possibility of suffering. And fear, if not genuine awareness of animal suffering, has reduced egregious cases of mistreatment.

In science and testing, activists were able to change the rules of large organizations, but their appeals to individual consumers have been less successful. The one exception is fur coat sales, which have declined over the last ten years. But meat eating and the use of leather products continues with little apparent effect from the animal rights movement. Zoos and circuses are still popular entertainments. And those who believe that keeping pets is a form of oppression have made no headway at all – even within their own movement.

Certain animal issues will gain more support than others. With 1500 brands of hair shampoo already on the market, we probably do not need to kill animals to create one more. Hunting, trapping, live bird shoots: these are marginal activities for all but a few subsistence groups such as the Inuit (today only seven per cent of Americans hunt; the percentage is even smaller in other advanced industrial countries). Animal protectionist critiques of science and technology have deep resonance in a society barraged with scientific embarrassments: Nobel laureate David Baltimore's arrogant reaction to accusations of impropriety on his research team; the dubious expenses incurred by Stanford President Donald Kennedy and charged to federal research grants (the luxury items purchased were more shocking than who was charged); the dehumanizing treatment of the sick in our hospitals. If animal rightists would go too far in banning all vivisection, the biomedical community is just as extreme in its arrogant defense of any and all uses of animals. Yet *how* to limit science and technology is a crucial question too long ignored by socialists and other critics of modern society: citizens and animal protectionists have a common enemy in technocracy.

Future Directions

My final question is where animal activism will lead those newly recruited to activism, and here the evidence is not yet available. Many movement leaders are trying hard to make ideological links with other left-liberal issues. The group Feminists for Animal Rights makes this explicit. The movement's central magazine, *The Animals' Agenda*, vigilantly promotes alliances with environmental groups. It changed its subtitle to 'The International Magazine of Animal Rights and Ecology' then to 'Helping Animals and the Earth'. Philosophers and other writers associated with the movement insist that there are important logical connections with other ideologies: that animals are exploited, disregarded, even exterminated in the ways that African-Americans, German Jews, women, workers, children, and other humans have been, and that the same group – white males in positions of institutional power – is responsible for all these abuses. Some of the movement's hyperbole in linking these issues is no doubt opportunistic and occasionally insensitive (comparisons to the Nazi holocaust have been especially controversial), but I believe that the majority of these beliefs are sincerely held.

Political naïveté pervades the animal rights movement, and there is much educational work to be done. There is little concern for democratic procedures at group meetings. The all-white movement exhibits occasional insensitivity to people of color, as in the California campaign against home slaughter of animals, which some Asian-American groups found racist and xenophobic. Many women in the movement complain of sexism. I cannot predict with confidence whether large numbers of animal protectionists will adopt broader left-liberal positions or will remain exclusively concerned with animals. But if environmental and leftist groups shun them, it is almost certain that animal rightists will not expand their concerns. If animal protection remains an isolated, single-issue cause, this will allow the fundis to set the tone of the movement.

There are a few irreducible tensions between animal rights and the goals of other progressive movements, especially environmentalism. For example, environmentalists sometimes embrace the culling of nonhuman populations – anathema to animal activists – in order to maintain an ecological balance. They also tend to admire groups that claim to hunt, fish, or trap for subsistence or traditional, indigenous ways of life – claims that animal activists often dismiss as 'just another excuse to kill animals'. Policies that maintain natural habitats and those designed to aid domesticated animals have little overlap; perhaps animal activists would do well to concentrate on the latter, leaving the former to environmentalists.

If the animal rights movement tries to build alliances with feminists, environmentalists, socialists and others, I hope they are met partway. Animal rightists would learn a great deal; those on the left might too. If the leaders of animal rights groups can rein in their supporters and expand their own ideological horizons, their movement could join the coalition of mutually supportive causes that has developed over the past 30 years. Such a coalition would be useful to the left as well as to the animal rights movement. This new movement is testing the borders of acceptable protest behavior in its disregard for the American veneration for private property. Since the movement first appeared in the United States at the end of the 1970s, lab break-ins to free animals, often accompanied by vandalism, have been part of its repertory. Sabotage and vandalism have been a less legitimate political tactic in the United States than in Britain and many other countries. Mainstream public opinion in the States still disapproves, but the left could use this opportunity to contemplate the use of property destruction – always to be distinguished from personal violence – as a legitimate protest device. As the left has always maintained, the American aura of private property should at least be questioned.

I am arguing less for the public to embrace the animal rights movement than to pay attention to it. Dialogue with it might lead to coalitions, or might not; but no coalitions will occur *without* dialogue. Animal activists are doubtless wrong about certain issues, but right about others, and the questions they raise are often more intriguing than their answers. Animal protection is an unusual but nonetheless valid entry point into serious, universal questions of compassion, domination, and instrumentalism. The animal rights movement may not be the vanguard of emancipatory politics, but it should not be dismissed as reactionary or as merely a lunatic fringe.

NOTES

1. The author would like to thank Andrew N. Rowan for comments on an earlier draft of this chapter.
2. For additional details from my own research, the reader may consult Jasper & Nelkin (1992) and Jasper & Poulson (1993).
3. In recent decades a handful of animal activists had already founded groups whose activities and concerns extended beyond those of existing humane societies: Ellen Thurston's American Fund for Alternatives to Animal Research, Helen Jones' International Society for Animal Rights, Alice Hetherington's Friends of Animals, and Cleveland Amory's Fund for Animals. But these isolated groups, usually animated by one person, failed to blossom into a visible protest movement.
4. Edward J. Walsh (1981) has described the 'suddenly imposed grievance' of the 1979 nuclear accident at Three Mile Island, which politicized many in the surrounding communities.
5. I elaborate on the sources and dynamics of moral shocks in Jasper (forthcoming).
6. With the help of several students, I surveyed participants at two animal rights demonstrations in April 1988: a rally of roughly 1000 people protesting an experiment using monkeys at New York University, and a rally of 100 people opposed to animal experimentation at the University of California at Berkeley. In New York 270 surveys were completed at the protest. At Berkeley, 35 surveys were mailed in. Thus, at both protests roughly one third of the demonstrators completed surveys. The activities at the protests were similar: speeches (Berkeley) or chanting and picketing (New York), after which small groups of protestors began offering themselves for arrest by blocking roads or entrances. I combine these two samples in my discussion. Other data about movement participants reported in this chapter come from these, plus several surveys conducted of *The Animals' Agenda* readers: see Greanville & Moss (1985). For confirmation, see Jamison & Lunch (1992).
7. Wolfe (1990), p. 631. Wolfe's search for defining differences is somewhat beside the point; the shared traits help explain the sympathy most humans feel for other species, but sympathy cannot be decisively claimed or refuted on the basis of philosophical arguments like his.

8 Animal Welfare and the European Union
Rosemary Goddard Svendsen

The protection of animals on the farm, in the laboratory, in international trade, and in nature is today a matter for European legislation. European Community laws now govern the keeping of pigs, calves, and battery hens. They set conditions for the humane slaughter of farm animals, and for the transportation of all kinds of animals. They control the use of animals in experimentation. They ban commercial trade in endangered species. From the northernmost to the southernmost borders of the European Union, they give the same basic protection both to wild birds and animals, and to the habitats they depend upon. All this is so in principle at least, since implementation of Community laws is dependent on the individual Member States.

Animal protection does not figure explicitly among the stated objectives of the Treaty of Rome. Neither has its validity as a Community concern gone unchallenged by legislators. At the same time, national animal welfare organisations have often felt that the Community's influence was, like the curate's egg, excellent in some parts only. On the one hand, although very much aware of the problems of getting Community law equally well implemented in all Member States, animal welfare groups do acknowledge that European lawmaking offers an unparallelled opportunity to ensure that all EU countries enact reasonable animal welfare standards. On the other hand, animal welfare organisations in countries with well-developed legislation, such as the United Kingdom, see the norms set by the Community as a threat to their own relatively high national standards. This view is mainly held in connection with farm animal welfare, where Community legislation is based on the concept of setting minimum standards. Those set by the Directive on veal calves are the most strongly criticised in animal welfare circles, as being both extremely minimal and, in places, self-contradictory.

Certainly, Community farm animal welfare standards in general do fall short of the best examples of Member States' own laws, although they also represent an improvement over the worst. They set a baseline in countries whose own law previously made no detailed provision for farm animal welfare at all, and are welcomed by animal welfare groups in such countries as a useful step forward. Minimum standards laws all provide for review and amendment, and therefore can reasonably be seen as a starting point for raising the overall standard of farm animal welfare in the long term. In the meantime, individual countries can and do apply higher welfare standards on their own territory. Use of veal calf crates is, for example, permitted by Community law but banned in Denmark and the UK and restricted in Germany. However, no Member State can refuse to trade with other Community countries that simply stick to the minimum, with the result that in the case of veal calves, welfare problems are simply exported, along with the animals, to those States operating only the minimum standards.

The fear of some animal welfare organisations that the influence of Community standards would prove negative has been accompanied to some extent by uncertainty over the future ability of member countries to legislate individually. Critics point to Denmark and the Netherlands, for example, where recent general animal welfare law reform has been accompanied by a mixture of legal strictures and government statements to the effect that the future development of farm animal welfare will depend on joint Community action, rather than isolated national initiatives. However, these are national policies. That they are based on Community trade rules restricting the improvement of farm animal welfare in individual countries is an impression often formed by misunderstanding. The negative influence on national improvements comes mainly from competition in agricultural exports, and the strength and attitudes of sectional farming interests in these and other countries. The introduction of Community welfare laws, based on the Community's responsibility to ensure fair trade within its borders, reinforces the right to maintain and extend existing national legislation by conferring implicit recognition on the need to provide for animal welfare within the framework of Community agricultural policies.

The need to take account of animal welfare in the Community context, as well as the national, was acknowledged explicitly at the highest government level in 1991, when a *Declaration on the protection of animals* was agreed by heads of government meeting at the European Council and attached to the Maastricht Treaty on European Union. Greeted at first with some scepticism as to its practical effect, the Declaration was nonetheless a welcome reassurance to animal welfare organisations. Yet, no more than a year later, Member State governments began to question the declared necessity of taking Community action on animal protection. They did so as part of a wider, ongoing debate on the extent of European institutional powers. This triggered a review of current and proposed Community legislation on many issues. Animal welfare laws were among those examined in connection with the so-called subsidiarity principle, which is set out in the Treaty on European Union as a guide to when and how far the Community, rather than the Member States, should legislate. Community farm animal welfare legislation was initially threatened by the review, but the need for it was subsequently reasserted by the Commission, the European

Parliament, and national governments. However, binding legislation in the form of a proposed Directive for the welfare of zoo animals was downgraded to the non-binding status of a Recommendation. This appears to place zoo animal welfare on the borderline of Community lawmaking competence, even though the proposed Directive had originally been drafted as a support measure for the Community's legislation controlling wildlife trade.

Community animal welfare law development has certainly been held back by the process of determining the relative powers of the EU's constituent parts. At the same time, the cynical invocation of subsidiarity, when some Member States foresee bothersome Community legislation in the offing, is an unwelcome element of the present political climate with which animal welfare interests have to contend. Although not wholly unscathed, animal welfare has emerged from the debate over the extent of Community versus national powers as an acknowledged subject for collective action, wherever it touches the implementation of Community policies. At the same time, despite all the uncertainties, animal welfare organisations have come to recognise the positive aspects of Community influence and have advanced their understanding of how to exploit the way the legislative system works. As a result, they are showing themselves much more aware of the need to carry the development of animal protection legislation forward in the framework of the European Union.

The European Union (EU) itself was created by a Treaty which came into force in 1993.[1] It is based principally on the old European Economic Community (EEC), which is now known as the European Community (EC) and has become the lawmaking pillar of the Union. The European Community first began to legislate for animal protection in 1974 with a Directive on the slaughter of food animals. Since then, it has enacted some 13 major animal welfare and conservation laws, and has set in train a number of useful animal protection initiatives.

The importance of Community animal protection legislation is based on two things. First of all, Community law takes precedence over the national law of the Member States on any point where the two conflict. Secondly, the creation in 1993 of the single, internal market between EU member countries has required the application of common trade rules, including common production and marketing standards. Animal welfare requirements are part of national production and marketing rules in the farm and food industry, and in the animal testing of chemicals sold for industrial or household use. They therefore fall into the category of activities where legislation is enacted at Community level in order to 'harmonize' existing national laws. The aim is to ensure that the internal market functions without the distortion of competition which might arise if national rules differed too widely. Wildlife trade also falls into the category of activities for which common rules are required.

Areas of Community activity with the potential to affect animal welfare are clearly identified in the 1991 *Declaration on the protection of animals* referred to earlier. They are: the common agricultural policy, transport, the internal market and research. These very broad areas of activity also have the potential to impinge on the natural environment. However, environmental protection now has a clear place in the common objectives defined by the European Union treaty system. Environmental policy is now required to be 'integrated into the definition and implementation of other Community policies',[2] whereas animal welfare and protection, except in relation to nature preservation, is still dealt with largely as a secondary consideration – a spin-off from the need to ensure the smooth functioning of trade within the Community. This linkage to essentially economic, rather than ethical, considerations makes Community measures unique in animal welfare legislation.

The basis of Community lawmaking becomes clearer still if one looks at the aspects of animal protection which the Community does *not* cover, and the areas of overlap between Community and national competence. Issues dealt with by the Member States individually include general welfare legislation. This would cover acts of cruelty which fall outside the scope of Community laws dealing with the handling of animals on farms, at slaughter and in the laboratory. The use of animals in traditional festivals and bullfights is viewed as part of folkloric culture, and is therefore an area in which the Community does not interfere. Yet while Community legislation on slaughter does not cover the death of the bull in the bullring, it would not allow apprentice bullfighters to practise killing with swords in an ordinary slaughterhouse, as allegedly takes place in parts of Spain. Field sports and angling are also generally looked at as traditional pursuits governed by national rules. However, the Community has a recognised role in promoting environmental protection. Therefore, in the interests of wildlife conservation, it bans non-selective or large-scale capture and killing methods, limits hunting seasons, and requires that hunting be prohibited in areas where protected species would be vulnerable to disturbance. Ancillary aspects such as health controls on trading in commercially reared game species are also a matter for Community regulations.

A similar split between Community and national competence exists on the use of animals in sports such as racing. The Community lays down rules covering protection during transport along with health requirements for animals travelling between Member States. Otherwise, the basic welfare of the animals is dealt with under national laws. The welfare of pet animals is also a matter for individual Member States. However, the Community is expected to propose a common system of health certification for pet dogs and cats travelling with their owners from one Member State to another. This will certainly have implications for dog and cat identification and registration at national level, as the Community's objective of facilitating the free movement of peoples comes to imply free movement of their pets as well.

Who Makes Community Law?

To understand the way animal welfare organisations lobbying the Community have to work, not to mention the complexity of the task facing them, it is helpful to take a look at the official bodies with which they have to deal. The lawmaking institutions of the European Community, and thus of the Union, are the European Parliament, the Council of Ministers, and the Commission. Once made, Community laws are upheld and interpreted by the Court of Justice, which can be asked to give its opinion as a kind of constitutional court, although it more usually gives judgement in disputes between individuals, companies and countries over the implementation of Community law.

As far as animal protection is concerned, there are now a number of Court judgments dealing with the implementation of the Community's *Directive on the conservation of wild birds*. As the Community's earliest piece of nature protection law, introduced when the concept of common action on the environment was in its infancy and not yet enshrined in the Treaty system, it may have suffered from the initial reluctance of some Member States to accept the political and legal basis for Community action on environmental matters – hence the number of Court cases, many of which are still pending. However, the resulting body of case law, by virtue of being interpretive, can be said to be part of the *lawmaking* as well as the *law-enforcing* process.

Law enforcement is itself crucial to the improvement of animal protection standards in the EU, and is a central concern of the animal welfare lobby. The process of complaint to the Commission, which can then take a Member State government to Court, is used by animal welfare organisations from time to time. The lodging of such complaints backed by strong and valid evidence is not only a means to get justice. It is also a valuable weapon in the battle to publicise issues where improvements to the law are sought.

New laws must go through a long and complicated process before they are finally passed. As experience shows, this can take, on average, between one and four years. First of all, whenever a new Community law is proposed, the Council of Ministers and the Commission may ask for opinions from two committees. The older of the two, the Economic and Social Committee

(ESC), was expanded to 220 members following the entry of Austria, Finland and Sweden to the EU. Nominated by their national governments, the members represent employers and employees from industry and agriculture, and also consumers. The ESC's opinion on proposals for new Community legislation is required in almost all circumstances, although in practice it has at best a degree of influence, rather than any real power. However, the ESC has produced opinions on all animal welfare legislation proposed so far. In fact it was the scene of heated arguments and much lobbying from the fur industry, indigenous peoples and animal welfare, when the Community's Regulation on the leghold trap and wild animal fur imports was under discussion in 1989–90.

The newer advisory body, the Committee of the Regions, was only established in 1993. The same size as the ESC, it consists of representatives of local and regional authorities nominated by their national governments. It may be consulted on certain issues, some of which could concern aspects of animal protection in the future. Membership of the Committee of the Regions has also expanded to include representatives from the new EU Member States.

The Commission

The Commission of the European Union, as it is now officially called, is the executive arm of the system and guardian of the EU Treaties. As a target for lobbying, its importance is more or less equal to that of the European Parliament, and its staff are reasonably accessible for consultation – often more so than some national civil servants. The Commission's job is to implement Community policies, and to ensure that Community rules and the principles of the internal market are respected. It is the main initiator of new Community laws.

It currently consists of 20 members, called Commissioners. These are nominated by their national governments. The five largest countries (France, Germany, Italy, Spain and the UK) are allowed to nominate two Commissioners, while smaller countries may nominate only one. Nowadays, most Commissioners are political figures in their own countries and may have served in the European Parliament or on the staff of a previous Commissioner in the past. A fair proportion of those nominated for the five-year term from January 1995 to December 2000 have served as government ministers. They are, however, supposed to put aside their national views and act on behalf of the EU once they take office.

Each Commissioner is responsible for a Directorate General (DG) covering a specific area of activity, although major Commission decisions are actually taken jointly. New legislation drafted by one Commissioner's staff must be approved by the whole college of Commissioners before it is presented to the Council of Ministers and referred on to the Parliament. As far as animal protection is concerned, the two most important sections of the Commission are the Directorate General for Agriculture and the Directorate General for the Environment.

The Directorate General for Agriculture, now led by Franz Fischler from Austria, administers the Common Agricultural Policy, which accounted in 1995 for 49 per cent of the Community's budgeted expenditure. It also deals, as might be expected, with all aspects of farm animal use and farm animal welfare, including transportation and slaughter. It disposes of funds to aid research into methods of farm animal husbandry. It is responsible for drafting new farm animal legislation.

Despite the rather small size of its veterinary inspectorate, the Directorate General for Agriculture is responsible for ensuring that Community legislation on farm animal welfare is properly implemented by the Member States. Its ability to do so in practice is questionable, however. The Commission's veterinary inspectorate is, for example, technically obliged to carry out inspections under the Community's Directive on the keeping of battery hens, in force since 1987. In fact, it had not carried out a single inspection by the end of 1991, and is not thought to have done any since. Its staff do manage to inspect slaughterhouses, where their work also involves meat hygiene and chemical residue checks, both within the Community and in the numerous countries from which meat is imported. Within the Community, these inspections are meant to supplement the work of the national authorities. They are made in connection with licensing, as random checks, or in response to complaints. However, more recent Directives on the keeping of pigs and calves and a draft Directive on general farm welfare also provide for periodic inspection by the Commission. Therefore the veterinary inspectorate's workload can only increase and there must be doubts as to whether it can fulfil its enforcement and advisory role effectively without more resources.

The Directorate General for the Environment is now in the hands of the Danish Commissioner, Ritt Bjerregaard, a Social Democrat and former environment minister. It is responsible for a wide range of issues including nuclear safety, combating pollution, and monitoring the environmental impact of development. Its brief also includes nature protection and conservation, wildlife trade, and, interestingly, the protection of animals used for scientific and experimental purposes. It is responsible for drafting and implementing legislation in all these areas, as well as following up the

Community's obligations under a string of international wildlife protection agreements.

Furthermore, within its remit, it provides funds for projects of European interest, from which animal welfare has benefited. One such project aimed to promote better understanding of the Community Directive controlling animal experimentation, in force since 1989, and helped spur implementation of the law in countries where progress had been slow. The Environment Directorate is responsible for encouraging the development and use of technologies which will reduce or replace the use of animals in experimentation. This is being done mainly through the European Centre for the Validation of Alternative Methods (ECVAM), which is based in Ispra, Italy, at one of the five joint research centres in the Community. The centres are operated by the Commission's Directorate General for Research. This Directorate stands behind the European Primate Resources Network (EURPREN), which is attempting to co-ordinate the supply of primates captive-bred for research in Europe. At the same time, EURPREN advises on ways of reducing the use of primates in medical research and is seeking to develop ethical standards for experimental primate use. In 1993, the Research Directorate set up the complementary Primate Vaccine Evaluation Network (PVEN), which now inspects primate breeding centres in 69 countries and requires that they meet strict criteria, at least for health. Both these initiatives are related to the Community's policy of moving towards use of captive bred, rather than wild, primates for laboratory research. The policy is based on the requirements of the Directive on animal experimentation, firstly that captive bred animals should be used in preference to those taken from the wild, and secondly, that endangered species, such as chimpanzees, should only be used in work which either benefits the species itself, or which is carried out for essential biomedical purposes for which no other species could be used. The policy is obviously only in the very early stages of implementation.

The Directorates General for Agriculture and Environment predominate in animal welfare matters, but as the activities of the Research Directorate show, their work overlaps with other sections of the Commission, which therefore also merit lobbying attention. For example, although the Agriculture Directorate is responsible for legislating on the conditions of transport for live animals, the defining of design standards for commercial vehicles carrying live animals falls under the remit of the Directorate General on Transport.

Similarly, although the protection of animals used in experimentation is the responsibility of the Environment Directorate, recent legislation on the marketing of cosmetic products, including the use of animals in safety testing, involved Commission staff responsible for internal market rules and consumer protection. There is also some overlap between Environment and the Directorates General responsible for Community aid to Eastern Europe, Asia and Africa.

The Directorate General for Environment is concerned with protection of marine mammals and sea birds, which are covered by a Directive on wildlife and habitats, a Regulation on wildlife trade, and the Directive on the conservation of wild birds, but legislation restricting purse seine and driftnetting is the responsibility of the fisheries section of the Commission. Fisheries has usually been a subdivision of either the Agriculture or the Environment Directorate, but sometimes has the status of a separate Directorate with its own Commissioner.

The European Parliament

The European Parliament has always had influence on the development of new Community legislation, not least where animal welfare is concerned. Its Members have privileged access to the Commission, to representatives of the Council of Ministers, and to national governments. Thanks to the updating of the Treaty of Rome in 1986 and 1992, the Parliament has now begun to acquire more real power as well.[3] One of its new powers is the ability to initiate legislation, as well as to reject it or have it annulled if Members believe they were not properly consulted. Members can also demand and get answers from the Commission and Council of Ministers by tabling written and oral questions. At the same time, the new Treaty rules have made it harder for the Council of Ministers to reject Parliament's recommendations for amendments to draft legislation. The entry of new Member States in January 1995 increased the Parliament's membership to 625. Elections to the Parliament are held simultaneously in all Member States every five years. The next are due in 1999.

Political Groups

Members of the European Parliament (MEPs) arrange themselves in cross-national political groups, of which the smaller ones tend to vary in title and composition following elections. The two largest are the Party of European Socialists, which consists of the mainstream social democratic and labour parties, and the European People's Party, which is drawn from the Christian Democrat and Conservative ranks. In the present Parliament, the others are, in order of size, the Liberal Democratic and Reformist Party (assorted liberals), the Confederal Group of the United Left (current and former

Communists), Forza Europa (Italian MEPs of a centrist persuasion), European Democratic Alliance (Gaullists and right of centre), the Green Group (Greens of various nationalities), the European Radical Alliance (progressive left and pro-federal grouping containing Scottish nationalists and Italian and Spanish regionalists), and the Europe of Nations Group (anti-federalists). There are also a number of Independents, currently consisting of one Unionist from Northern Ireland and 26 representatives of the extreme right who have failed to form their own group. Altogether, more than 70 national and regional political parties are represented in the European Parliament's political groups.

The Political Groups are important because they control the business of the Parliament to a large extent. Their leaders sit alongside the President of the Parliament and the 14 Vice-Presidents in the so-called Enlarged Bureau, which runs the Parliament. Seats on the Bureau and on the Parliament's permanent committees and various *ad hoc* committees, including chairmanships and vice-chairmanships, are allocated between the Political Groups on the basis of proportional representation. Additionally, each Group appoints its own spokesmen and co-ordinators for particular policy areas, and maintains a permanent secretariat of officials.

Animal protection has benefited from the ability of senior MEPs to generate support among their fellow Political Group members. Animal welfare issues regularly figure in Group manifestos. However, there have also been one or two nasty moments, as in 1988, when a Report on banning the leghold trap was badly mauled in the environment committee due to a wholly unrelated conflict between members of the Conservative and socialist groupings. Fortunately it was possible to repair the damage later when the Report was debated by the full Parliament.

Specialist Committees

After elections, the Parliament establishes a number of specialist standing and temporary committees to deal with the legislative proposals and motions for resolution on which it must report. Currently there are 20 standing committees and one temporary committee. Each has between 18 and 50 full members, plus an equal number of subsititute members. Moreover, the Parliament now has the power to set up a committee of inquiry into breaches and maladministration of Community laws by the Member States.[4] The operational framework for such committees of inquiry is currently being thrashed out between the Parliament, the Commission and the Council of Ministers.

When proposals for new Community legislation have been drafted by the Commission, they are formally referred to the Parliament by the Council of

Ministers. They will first be examined by MEPs sitting on the appropriate specialist committee. The committee's meetings will be attended by Commission representatives involved with the legislation, who will often take an active part in discussing and formulating amendments. This was the case, for example, during recent environment committee discussion of the new Regulation on wildlife trade. The two most important Parliamentary committees for animal protection are, as one might expect, those on agriculture and environment. With the recent advent of marine protection laws, the fisheries committee has also come to play a part.

Although responsibility for a proposal is always referred to one particular committee, additional opinions may be requested from others. So for example, the proposal which led to the Community's present framework Directive on the protection of animals during transport was referred to the agriculture committee, with supplementary opinions requested from the committees on environment, budgets and transport. The proposal for a Regulation banning the leghold trap and imports of certain wild animal furs, which took effect in 1995, went to the environment committee with a second opinion from the committee on external economic relations.

When a committee receives a legislative proposal, it appoints a rapporteur if it is the main committee, or a draftsman if it is giving a supplementary opinion. The rapporteur's job is to draw up a report and resolution stating the opinion and amendments which the committee considers Parliament should put forward. If the Parliament's adopted views differ from those of the Commission or the Council of Ministers, then the rapporteur will play a key role in any subsequent negotiations. This negotiating role has been enhanced by the new conciliation procedure introduced by the Treaty on European Union. In May 1994, the conciliation procedure was invoked over the draft *Directive on the legal protection of biotechnological inventions* – a law consistently opposed by animal welfare organisations because it allows the patenting of live animals. Disagreement between Parliament and the Council of Ministers arose partly over the question of whether farmers should be asked to pay 'royalties' in order to breed from genetically engineered livestock.

Rapporteurs and draftsmen are usually appointed on a party basis, with the Political Groups taking it in turns to nominate members in each committee. The power of the Political Group is a factor, and is taken into account, alongside the importance of the subject and the workload of individuals, in the process of allocating tasks to rapporteurs. In the case of an own-initiative report, that is a report reacting to a motion for resolution tabled in the Parliament instead of to the referral of a legislative proposal, a committee member may volunteer to act as rapporteur. Own-initiative reports well supported in the Parliament have, by moral pressure, played a part in generating legislation on the leghold trap and in the establishment of the European Centre for the Validation of Alternative Test Methods.

Animal protection has been fortunate in its ability to attract sympathetic rapporteurs on a good many issues, although this does not in itself guarantee success. If amendments to legislation are to have a chance of getting into the final text, they must be adopted by a majority of the whole Parliament, at least at the second reading. At the end of a long session, only a small number of Members may turn up for lower priority votes. Then a majority is good enough to approve legislation, but not to amend or reject it. Indeed, in exactly such circumstances, useful, and previously well supported, amendments to bird protection legislation were lost at second reading just before the 1994 elections. Broad support from at least one of the larger Political Groups is crucially important to the success of amendments at this stage, when the lobbyist's task is to persuade the Group leaderships to call out their troops. All previous efforts are wasted unless MEPs are motivated to take the subject seriously enough to turn up and vote.

The Council of Ministers

The final role in the lawmaking process is played by the Council of Ministers. To influence the Council, lobbying must focus on the Member States. To succeed, it must involve national input in most, if not all, countries, co-ordinated with input to the Community institutions. At this stage, the strengths and weaknesses of national support become crucial to the outcome of legislation. It is certainly noticeable that governments with the least enthusiasm for higher animal welfare standards are usually from countries where national animal welfare legislation is modest and support for animal protection is most weakly voiced and mobilised. Cultural differences between Community countries in the way that they view animal welfare are frequently cited as a problem in this context. There are also differences, just as important and often overlooked, in the political cultures and general circumstances under which animal welfare and other interest groups operate. For instance, interest group activity on environmental matters is a fairly recent development in the three EU Member States which were governed by dictatorships until the early 1970s. Similarly, the interaction of interest groups and politicians, as it is known in the British Parliament, does not take place in quite the same way elsewhere. In addition, the relative economic weakness and poverty in certain Member States still tend to inhibit the development of the voluntary societies which are both the infrastructure and the basis of public support for the environmental and animal welfare lobbies. Finally, the potential economic impact of new legislation, which varies according to the circumstances of each country, very much affects government responses to proposals for animal welfare reform. If there is no effective counter-pressure, the economic impact may be the only aspect seriously considered.

Member State governments take it in turns to chair the Council of Ministers. This 'Presidency of the Community' changes every six months. Although the holder country is obliged to work for consensus, and so cannot push its own views too strongly, it can nonetheless set the agenda so as to give priority to issues it wishes to see settled. Not that the ability to set priorities necessarily means that settlement will be easily or satisfactorily achieved. In the second half of 1994, the German government gave priority to finalising special rules for the transport of animals to slaughter, only to find that the viewpoints of its fellow member governments diverged radically, with the Southern European States lined up on one side and the North Europeans on the other. This geographic division of opinion was also economically based.

Adding to the complexity, the Council of Ministers is really several different Councils, as the national government ministers responsible for the relevant area of activity make up the Council which takes the decision in each case. So, new farming laws will be agreed by a Council of Agriculture Ministers. New nature protection laws will be agreed by a Council of Environment Ministers. Internal market issues will be decided by a Council of Trade and Industry Ministers. A super Council – the European Council, consisting of heads of government – meets twice a year. Otherwise, each ministerial council generally meets every six to eight weeks, depending on its workload. Draft legislation is presented to the appropriate Council of Ministers when it is first published by the Commission, and returns to the Council later on, along with the advisory committees' opinions, Parliament's recommended amendments, and any revisions the Commission might want to make.

The preparation for Council meetings is made by Brussels-based civil servants from the national governments, known as the Committee of Permanent Representatives (COREPER). These officials play a key mediating role between the national administrations. They also co-ordinate the working parties of the Council, whose members are civil servants or other experts seconded from the Member States to deal with particular pieces of legislation. These working parties compare draft Community laws with existing national measures and policies. On straightforward issues they will resolve differences and recommend a final position to the Council. If differences are substantial, then Ministers will have to discuss them more fully. The Council working parties now usually meet in parallel with the

European Parliament's committees, and there is considerable unofficial interchange of documents between them. At the same time, proposed Community legislation will receive parallel consideration by the specialist committees of national parliaments. Given that the power to make final decisions on Community legislation rests with the Council of Ministers and its working groups, it is obvious that contact with national government ministries and members of national parliaments, together with national public support, is a vital component of lobbying success at European level.

Foundations of the European Animal Protection Lobby

Although the European Community has only been legislating for animal protection for the last 20 years, animal protection has in fact been a part of the European political scene since the mid-1950s. At that time, the European Community was only just being formed by the original six member countries.[5] Until the mid-1970s, therefore, animal welfare concerns were voiced through another international grouping, the Council of Europe, which had been set up in 1949. This body, which is a forum for the promotion of European unity, parliamentary democracy, and human rights and values, initially brought together Members of Parliament and government representatives from the democracies of Western Europe. The Council of Europe does not make laws, but it does negotiate agreements, or Conventions. Member countries may sign these if they wish, but are not obliged to put them into law unless they also ratify them. It was with the Council of Europe that the European animal protection lobby first began, although at first it was not truly 'European', since individual animal welfare societies mostly worked separately.

The main international animal welfare concern of those days was the appalling long-distance transport conditions endured by horses and cattle sent for slaughter. Pressure for action was exerted both through representations to the institutions of the Council of Europe and through national parliamentarians appointed to its Parliamentary Assembly. This led to the drafting of the *European Convention for the Protection of Animals during International Transport* (1968). It also set in train the Council of Europe's work on four other European Conventions on animal welfare. These Conventions, which have been supplemented by Recommendations over the years and are still being developed today, are now open to the new democracies of Eastern Europe. Furthermore, despite inherent weaknesses, such as the general nature of their content and varying national attitudes to implementation, they have also served as a starting point for some of the European Community's present legislation. Direct input by non-governmental organisations to the extension of the Conventions is now made through the leading European grouping of animal welfare societies, Eurogroup for Animal Welfare, and the World Society for the Protection of Animals, both of which hold observer status with the Council of Europe.

Although the picture has changed since the 1950s, transport conditions for slaughter animals remain a major welfare concern in Europe today. This does not mean that nothing has been gained in the intervening years, but it does show the persistence of the problem, beset as it is by the need to reconcile powerful interests where jobs will be affected by the outcome. For issues like this there can be no quick fixes.

Indeed, as a subject for legislation, the transport of farm animals exemplifies the kind of problem increasingly faced by animal protection organisations working in Europe; namely, that which cannot be dealt with on a purely national basis. Transport of live animals is a trading activity carried out in several countries and across borders. It involves other major industries – in this case, farming and slaughter – which also operate under differing national animal welfare standards, and differing national emphases on the importance of such standards. Improvement of animal transport conditions therefore calls for collective legislation of some kind. The only European body that can deliver binding transnational legislation founded on common basic standards is the European Community.

During the 1970s, the European Community's membership expanded to nine with the entry of Great Britain, Denmark and Ireland. By the end of that decade, animal welfare organisations in most of the EC member countries had begun to realise that the influence of the Community was growing, and that EC legislation was a potentially powerful instrument which might, for good or ill, determine the future of their national animal protection standards. It was also becoming clearer that 'one country' legislative solutions to animal welfare problems involving intracommunity trade were either of limited effect or would be unworkable in the framework of the Treaty of Rome.[6] Moreover, few national organisations had the resources to lobby individually for legislation at EC level, whilst at the same time it was essential to involve groups from all EC Member countries if the necessary support at both European and national level was to be mobilised for Community action. Indeed, to obtain a hearing at European level, it is more or less compulsory to be organised on a Europe-wide basis. Community institutions such as the Commission give preference to lobbies organised at Community level due to the impossibility of consulting individual interested parties from each member country on every single issue.

The formation of Eurogroup for Animal Welfare was motivated by just these considerations. Eurogroup is the Brussels-based lobbying association which today groups together the main national animal welfare organisations from each EU Member State. Its membership also includes the London-based World Society for the Protection of Animals (WSPA). It enjoys co-operative links with the International Fund for Animal Welfare (IFAW) and the larger conservation organisations, as well as with a number of smaller specialist or 'single issue' national groups.

The Interest Groups

The key player in the European animal protection lobby, then, is Eurogroup for Animal Welfare. Eurogroup was established in 1980, largely at the initiative of the British Royal Society for the Prevention of Cruelty to Animals (RSPCA), which provided its first office and staff. Eurogroup was constituted in its present form in 1986, and established its permanent office in Brussels a year later. Its membership consists of the leading, broad-based, general animal welfare organisation in each EU Member State. Its central lobbying position rests on two things. Firstly, it links the mainstream animal welfare societies in all EU Member States with each other and also with those in most Council of Europe countries outside the EU, although the latter cannot be full members. Secondly, it acts as secretariat to the European Parliament's Intergroup on the Welfare and Conservation of Animals.

The Intergroup was set up in 1983 by Members of the European Parliament as a way of helping to deal with the animal protection questions raised by the voters they represented. Some MEPs have calculated that around 10 per cent of all the mail they receive from the public concerns animal protection in one way or another. The Intergroup meets monthly during parliamentary sessions, and is open to MEPs from all political groups and nationalities. Its work programme is planned, in co-operation with the Eurogroup secretariat, by its President, currently Hanja Maij-Weggen of the Netherlands, its seven Vice-Presidents, who are drawn mainly from the two largest Political Groups and represent six nationalities between them, and its Honorary Secretary. They are elected at two-year intervals from among the MEPs most closely involved. On average, the Intergroup's meetings are attended by 20–25 MEPs, with 20 or so assistants coming on behalf of MEPs unable to attend in person. Between 20 per cent and 40 per cent of all Parliament Members receive information regularly on the Intergroup and Community animal protection developments at their own request. The figure varies over the lifetime of a Parliament and from one election to the next. It indicates a comforting reservoir of potential support, although individual MEPs cannot be expected to back the animal welfare viewpoint on every issue.

Representatives of the Commission are often present at Intergroup meetings as observers, as are representatives of the Council of Europe and of national animal welfare and conservation groups. Attendance by these groups is not limited to the membership of Eurogroup, but must be by invitation. They may be asked to speak during meetings. Intergroup meetings are also attended by observers from lobbying consultancies representing industry and from organisations concerned with field sports, the fur trade, and other aspects of wildlife exploitation. It is perhaps worth mentioning at this point that all the major commercial and consumer interest groups with which animal protection must contend are organised on a European basis, with representation in Brussels and Strasbourg. The MEPs involved with the Intergroup believe that each issue deserves fair and open discussion with input from all sides. Furthermore, in the shifting patterns of alliances between differing interests there is always the possibility of establishing common ground on a given issue. The breadth of Intergroup participation is therefore both an opportunity for dialogue and for studying the opposition.

Parliamentary intergroups, of which there are many, are essentially lobby groups for the lobbied. That is, they exist, sometimes on a temporary basis, and sometimes permanently, for the purpose of exerting internal parliamentary pressure on specific issues. The numerous 'intergroups', or informal cross-party discussion groups, within the Parliament, reflect Members' personal interests in everything from European integration to the problems of the elderly. The Intergroup on Animal Welfare and Conservation is generally considered to be one of the most effective, and certainly the best organised, in the Parliament. This is a compliment to individual MEPs and to Eurogroup, as secretariat. A forum for exploration of issues and the exchange of views, the Intergroup on the Welfare and Conservation of Animals is also a springboard for legislative initiatives.

Although the Parliament's role in lawmaking is essentially based on response to proposals produced by the Commission, Reports and Resolutions drawn up at the Parliament's own initiative had influenced the production of animal welfare law long before its right to initiate legislation was confirmed by the Maastricht Treaty on European Union in 1992. One example of this is the 1987 Report on farm animal welfare policy, drawn up on behalf of the Parliament's agriculture committee. The Report's demands that the Community take action to improve the welfare of calves and pigs in intensive farming, and of all animals during transportation, led to the drafting of present legislation in these areas. However, the earliest example of Parliamentary influence on the initiation of animal welfare law is the Community import ban on skins from hooded and harp seal pups. This piece of legislation came about in 1983 as a direct response to parliamentary demands supported by public pressure across Europe. It was in the wake of this successful effort that the Intergroup on the Welfare and Conservation of Animals was formally established. Since then, MEPs involved with the Intergroup have actively promoted the farm animal welfare measures already mentioned, and many others, helping to generate a level of parliamentary support for each case which the Commission and Council of Ministers could not ignore, even if the resulting legislation was not always as strong as Parliament intended.

The role of Eurogroup for Animal Welfare in providing information to parliamentarians, whether involved with the Intergroup or not, and in helping to shape the Intergroup's agenda, presents the animal protection lobby with a strong – indeed, unique – opportunity to put its case at the European parliamentary level.

Constitutionally, Eurogroup is structured to be as representative as possible of mainstream animal welfare support in each EU country, although it must be said that its member organisations vary considerably in size and resources, and occasionally in philosophical approach. They range from the RSPCA, which employs approximately 1000 full-time staff, to societies which have only recently been able to take on their first paid assistants to administer their offices, animal refuges and other activities. In all cases, however, the role of volunteer workers and supporters among the wider public remains central to the nature of the organisations and vital to their work. Neither does lack of professional staff automatically imply that the smaller societies lack skills, since voluntary workers bring with them knowledge and experience gained in other aspects of their lives. However, even the best of volunteers cannot devote as much time to the work of their society as full-time employees, while financial resources place the greatest limitations on what steps an organisation can take to achieve its goals. This is particularly obvious in campaigning, where an imaginative approach to generating interest and publicity, along with such practical support as may be available from other sources, has to make up for lack of cash.

Eurogroup itself is a lobbying, rather than a campaigning association. As such, it leaves campaigning squarely in the hands of its member organisations. Its business is to keep in touch with Community developments and the legislators responsible for them, instigating and fostering action where it can. Its role in relation to campaigning is therefore to provide the information its members need in order to plan their own national activities in support of their collective European legislative demands. Given the uneven campaigning resources of its members, however, Eurogroup also arranges joint planning meetings, and acts as a medium through which practical aid can flow, courtesy of its larger member organisations. National campaign efforts are supplemented by the central issue of press releases from Brussels.

In its capacity as secretariat to the Intergroup in the European Parliament, Eurogroup undertakes to bring the widest possible range of views to MEPs, and to spread information about Community activities as broadly as possible. It attempts to achieve this aim of broad representation firstly through the work of its national member organisations and their contacts with other groups, and secondly by the dissemination of information on Community developments through its own bulletin and other publications.

Eurogroup's policy and lobbying priorities are developed in part reactively, since they depend to a great extent on the plans and timetables of the Community institutions. However, its fundamental aims and objectives are developed on a more long term, consensus basis through regular meetings of its member organisations. Its plenary and campaign meetings are also open to participation by animal welfare organisations from non-EU countries belonging to the Council of Europe, and, by invitation, to other groups. Eurogroup is staffed by its Director, David Wilkins, and five assistants, and can call on its member organisations and other contacts for particular expertise which may be required for specific tasks. It is mainly funded by its member organisations, which contribute according to their means, but also receives donations from other bodies which benefit from its lobbying work. Its activities are supervised by an executive committee made up of representatives from the member organisations.

The bringing together of national groups for joint campaign activity at European level has been emulated in a looser and more subject-specific way by other animal welfare and conservation groups in recent years. For example, the British Royal Society for the Protection of Birds (RSPB) formed a temporary grouping of national bird protection societies from other EU countries in order to oppose the international trade in wild birds more effectively. Eurogroup for Animal Welfare worked together with the bird protection societies on what became a joint campaign.

Subsequently, the British Union for the Abolition of Vivisection, supported by the International Fund for Animal Welfare, formed the European Coalition of societies from EU and other countries in order to campaign for a ban on the use of animals to test cosmetics. Eurogroup for Animal Welfare was already actively engaged in discussions on the subject with the Commission and MEPs, as a result of the Commission's plan to update existing Community marketing rules. Had the Commission's original intentions gone unchallenged, they might have led to an increase in animal testing of cosmetic ingredients, in contravention of the Community's stated policy of reducing animal use in experimentation generally. The European Coalition, which involved Eurogroup member organisations as well as groups specialising in animal experimentation issues, helped to attract media attention to the question of animal use in cosmetic testing, and to demonstrate the widespread public distaste for using animals in toxicity testing where alternatives could be found. More recently, the European Coalition has, in conjunction with Eurogroup for Animal Welfare, been pressing for a ban on the taking of nonhuman primates from the wild for laboratory use. The Community's policy on this issue is only just beginning to move into practice, and does not specify any deadline for an end to the use of wild caught animals.

Other organisations also extend their activities to European level at times. The British-based Compassion in World Farming has been involved in protesting the extention of European patent Convention rules to include genetically modified animals. It is also vocal on farming issues, particularly transport and slaughter, and has opened branches in Ireland and France during the mid-1990s. American animal welfare organisations, such as the Humane Society of the United States, sometimes attend meetings of both Eurogroup and the Intergroup on Animal Welfare and Conservation, where marine mammal protection and wildlife trade are issues of transatlantic interest. A wide range of national and international organisations joined forces with Eurogroup to work for a ban on the leghold trap between 1987 and 1991.

Among interest groups representing particular professions, the European Federation of Veterinarians (FVE) is one that takes a lively interest in Community animal health and welfare developments, and has issued a number of statements supporting tougher rules for the transport of slaughter animals. There has for some years been a useful dialogue between the FVE and Eurogroup for Animal Welfare on a range of issues.

Returning to the parliamentary level, a relatively recent addition to the European environmental interest group community is GLOBE. Founded at the end of the 1980s with support from the International Fund for Animal Welfare, GLOBE (Global Legislators' Organisation for a Balanced Environment) is a pressure group for parliamentarians on a broad scale. Subdivided into four world regions based on the EU, USA, Japan and Russia, it aims to foster the exchange of information between parliamentarians interested in the environment, to harness and initiate legislation, and to co-ordinate action in response to specific problems. Its European activities are divided between the EU section, whose membership consists of 64 MEPS under the chairmanship of Carlos Pimenta, and GLOBE-Europe, also administered from Brussels, which links national parliamentarians in Western and Eastern Europe. Although not centrally concerned with animal protection, GLOBE may from time to time make common cause with Eurogroup and the Intergroup on the Welfare and Conservation of Animals.

Looking Forward

The future of animal protection in the Community holds a mixture of opportunities and challenges. The EU has just increased its membership. Concentration on ensuring that Norway would, had she joined, be bound by Community rules protecting whales and other marine mammals from commercial exploitation has to some extent overshadowed consideration of what positive influence the arrival of Finland and Sweden might have on the development of Community animal protection legislation. The new Nordic members come to the Community with reasonably good animal welfare laws of their own, and strong environmental credentials in general. Their leading animal welfare organisations already have long-established links with Eurogroup for Animal Welfare.

On the farming front, Community Directives on the keeping of pigs and calves are due for review in 1997. New rules on housing systems for laying hens are in the pipeline, together with a Directive on general farm welfare. Additional rules on the slaughter of poultry are expected. At the same time, general reform of the Common Agricultural Policy includes moves towards a greater emphasis on environmental considerations. Small though this shift is at present, promotion of less intensive farming methods and the special provisions for farming in Environmentally Sensitive Areas may bring further openings for animal protection initiatives.

On the wider international scene, there are question marks over the effect that participation in the World Trade Organisation will have on Community and national animal protection law. There is nothing to prevent countries or blocs of countries, such as the EU, from enacting legislation to protect animals and the environment within their own territory, or to protect animals at international level, in connection with the *Convention on International Trade in Endangered Species* or other multinational nature protection agreements. It is unilateral actions to impose import bans in pursuit of environmental objectives, like the American legislation to protect dolphins in the yellowfin tuna fishery, which may need to be drafted and justified more carefully in future. In the meantime, Canada has already initiated an appeal through GATT as a last-ditch rearguard action against the introduction of a Community ban on imports of fur obtained from certain wild animals. The ban will not bite until 1996 and will not affect countries which have prohibited use of the leghold trap, as the Community itself already has. Some foresee other difficulties under GATT if the Community eventually refuses to follow America and license use of the BST growth hormone to increase milk yields in dairy cattle. At present the Community has imposed a moratorium while it evaluates the problem.

Within the EU, there are almost certainly further institutional changes to come. Most national parliaments already subject Community law proposals to committee scrutiny, but among the possibilities to be floated at the next round of Intergovernmental Conferences in 1996 is the idea of giving national parliaments a more defined role in the development of Community legislation, as well as pressure for increasing the powers of the European Parliament. If the national parliaments are given a greater say, then national lobbying in pursuit of European objectives will become even more important for animal protection organisations in future. At the same time, a more powerful European Parliament will merit even more careful attention. It is unclear whether these moves, separately or together, would entirely remove the frustrations caused by the way the Council of Ministers sometimes cobbles together its compromises on new legislation.

Another issue likely to be raised in 1996 is the implementation and enforcement of Community legislation. Differences between the administrative systems in the Member States may be a factor in poor implementation, together with under-resourcing of both national agencies and the Commission. Animal welfare problems resulting from the flagrant violation of transport and slaughter rules in a number of Member States represent one small corner of this broad and thorny issue. At present the United Kingdom is preparing new legislation which will allow it to prosecute UK-based carriers for animal transport offences committed in other Member States. Such 'long-arm' laws are not without precedent elsewhere, so part of the solution to the enforcement problem on animal transport, and perhaps wildlife trade, could be for other governments to follow suit. Scepticism among animal welfare organisations about the value of Community legislation has been partly motivated by poor enforcement in some Member States, coupled with uncertainty over how best to confront the problem in general and to exert more pressure in those countries where animal welfare interests are, for the time being, least strongly represented.

Finally, although the validity of animal protection as an area for Community, as well as Member State action now appears beyond doubt, and is given practical effect by a very substantial body of legislation and administrative initiatives, there is still a case to be made for consolidating this position through amendment of the Treaty of Rome. Animal welfare organisations have campaigned for the inclusion of specific references to animal protection in the Treaty since 1984. In this, they have been supported by Members of the European Parliament and successive German governments. The animal welfare organisations' efforts have been motivated by two concerns. The first is the wish to ensure that legislation for animal protection can be straightforwardly enacted at Community level whenever necessary, and that steps can be taken to avoid unnecessary negative effects on animal welfare due to other Community activities. The second is the need to ensure effective implementation and enforcement of Community animal protection legislation. Specific reference to animal protection among the Community's stated environmental objectives would raise the status of legislation concerning animals and might therefore help to achieve both optimum provision and better implementation. The closest the animal welfare lobby has come to achieving this goal is the *Declaration on the protection of animals*, which was agreed by heads of government during the last round of Intergovernmental Conferences in 1991. Yet this was not, by itself, enough to place the Community's role in animal protection beyond doubt during the subsequent subsidiarity debate. Neither has it effectively emphasised that implementation of Community legislation on animal welfare, as on any other subject, is an obligation for all Member States under the Treaty of Rome.

Currently, animal protection is in much the same position as general environmental protection was before it was formally included among the Community's objectives by Treaty amendments made in 1986 and 1992. Perhaps 1996 will be the year in which animal protection also receives political recognition within the treaty system to underpin the many practical steps which the Community has already found it necessary to take.

NOTES

1. The Treaty on European Union was signed at Maastricht on 7 February 1992. The Union was established for the closer union of European peoples through economic and social progress, common citizenship, and the pursuit of common aims in foreign policy, security, home affairs and justice. It is founded on and comprises the original European Community, the European Coal and Steel Community, and the European Atomic Energy Community, all formed in the 1950s as steps towards European integration.
2. Title XVI, Article 130r, Treaty on European Union, signed 2 February 1992.
3. The Parliament's powers were increased by amendments contained in the Single European Act of 1986 and the Treaty on European Union, signed in 1992 and in force since 1993.
4. New EC Treaty Article 138c, Title XVII, Treaty on European Union, 7 February 1992.
5. France, Germany, Italy, Belgium, Luxembourg and the Netherlands.
6. Article 36 of the Treaty of Rome, which established the Community in 1957, allows a Member State to impose trade restrictions on certain grounds, including protection of the health and life of animals. However, it is difficult to invoke in cases where harmonised legislation exists, as is the case with farm animal welfare, and its invocation must not constitute a disguised barrier to trade.

9 Putting Animals Into Politics
Richard D. Ryder

This chapter is a largely autobiographical account of attempts over the last quarter of a century to 'put animals into politics'. As a social scientist I make every effort to order and analyse my experiences in a manner which will provide some useful insights for others. My approach is historical and its emphasis is upon contacts with politicians and not upon descriptions of direct action or publicity campaigns; these have been described elsewhere (Ryder, 1989).

The Ethical Foundations for Reform

The animal welfare reform movement is based upon a set of moral principles. As Robert Garner (1993a) has pointed out its philosophical foundation is, for a reform movement, unusually well established, having, as earlier chapters have shown, been the subject of international debate among philosophers for some years. Whereas laws protecting humans tend already to be based upon a 'rights' position which protects the individual human from exploitation absolutely (for example it is a crime to murder another human regardless of the material benefit to the murderer), most laws protecting nonhumans are utilitarian in that they prohibit the infliction of pain or distress only unless such pain is considered 'necessary' for some greater (usually human) advantage. In other words, the current basis of our law is speciesist. Humans receive first class protection while nonhumans, if they have any legal protection at all, receive only second class (that is utilitarian) treatment. I consider that this is wrong and that human and animal welfare laws should be harmonised.

Animal Welfare or Animal Rights

For some people the distinction between 'animal welfare' and 'animal rights' is considered important. This is surely true if it is equated with the distinction between the utilitarian and rights positions. Often, however, it is used merely to indicate traditional or moderate versus modern or radical. The media in Britain attach connotations of sabotage and violence to the phrases 'animal rights' and 'animal liberation' and, for this reason, these phrases tend to be eschewed by British politicians. This is not true in every country where, in Australia for example, these labels cause little political embarrassment. No political party in Britain has yet chosen to adopt them to describe their spokespeople or policies (although all are prepared to use the phrase 'human rights' when occasion arises). The phrase 'animal protection', however, is used as a compromise, sounding to the British political ear rather more modern than 'animal welfare' while not so revolutionary as 'animal rights'. The concept of protection may also suggest a connection with certain more politically established notions such as the protection of habitats, conservation and the protection of the environment generally.

For some, there is resistance to the concept of 'rights' in general; it is still viewed rather as Jeremy Bentham viewed it as 'nonsense upon stilts' or is interpreted less in the sense of moral rights than as legal rights, that is to say, the granting of powers. According to this view, moral concern centres upon the agent rather than upon the victim and so the preferred words are 'duties' and 'responsibilities'. For those brought up in the American philosophical tradition, however, and for most younger British people, the use of the word 'rights' (in its passive sense) is preferred. Perhaps this is especially true of those who themselves feel vulnerable and who thus tend to identify with victims generally.

Maybe the fashion for preferring 'duties' to 'rights' will return. But it is only a fashion. The distinction between 'rights' language and 'duties' language is more psychological than material. Rights and duties are two sides of the same ethical coin. Neither rights nor duties exist on their own. Both are human creations.

Animal welfare can be seen as part of the 'new politics'. But it has never been the exclusive property of the political Left. Indeed, the far Left has often shunned it. Some Marxists, for example, have argued that there is a gulf between the human and other animals based upon the human capacity to plan consciously; such speciesism forgets, of course, that there are some humans, such as babies, who cannot plan, and, even more fundamentally, fails to explain why planning bestows superior moral status. Nevertheless, some Marxists reject the whole business of animal welfare; they tend to regard morality itself as a bourgeois defence of the status quo and the concern for animals as a distraction from the class struggle (The Critical Lawyers Group, University of Kent: Debate, 9 March 1994). Animal welfarists in Eastern Europe have confirmed that during the Communist era this latter criticism was the official one and that animal welfare organisations were discouraged. Lenin, however, posed with his cat – a portrait used as a defence by Russian animal welfare workers during totalitarian times (personal communication, Tatyana Pavlova, November 1994). In the 1990s we have seen a remarkable resurgence of interest in animals in the ex-Communist States.

Animal welfare also tends to divide the political far Right. Some contemptuously dismiss a concern for animals as decadent and sentimental while others, and I suspect particularly those whose right wing views stem from their difficulty in forming good relationships with members of their own species, display a special regard for nonhumans. British far Right groups produced leaflets in the 1970s and 1980s which attacked certain forms of animal experimentation. Hitler was photographed with his dogs.

The Political Campaign: a Personal View

From early 1969 I began campaigning by writing letters (see *Daily Telegraph*, 7 April & 3 May 1969), leaflets (Ryder, 1970, 1972, 1974a, 1974b) and a book (Ryder, 1975) attacking animal experimentation (of which I had had some experience as an experimental psychologist), generating as much media interest as I could and organising street protests and demonstrations against experimentation and also against hare coursing and otter hunting (which was outlawed successfully in 1978).

My letters in the press attracted the attention of the writer Brigid Brophy who invited me to join her on what I believe was the first-ever televised animal rights programme[1] in December 1969. She also put me in touch with others in Oxford who were beginning to revive philosophical interest in the subject. This culminated in the publication of a collection of our essays entitled 'Animals, Men and Morals' (1973). None of these essays, however, addressed the politics of the issue.

Although my main interest was in the fate of farm, wild and laboratory animals, my first direct contact with Parliament was concerned with pets when Ruth Plant, the pioneer of the modern concept of the educative Dog Warden, invited me to explain this idea to a group of MPs in the House of Commons. It was my first public speech and turned out to be a baptism of fire. Two of the Members present began a heated exchange of insults which ended only when one angry old backbencher stormed out of the Committee Room.

I learned several things from that meeting. One was that MPs are extremely busy; although many had been invited only three turned up. By the end of the meeting only one remained and he, so it turned out, was really in no position to help us. I had also discovered the hard way that elderly men do not always relish being told what to do by younger ones! Yet I remained obstinately convinced that if only I could find the right MPs they would hold the power to reform the law controlling animal experiments and to ban bloodsports. It took me several years to realise that backbenchers have little influence over the legislative programme.

Some Historical Considerations

There is always a tendency for campaigners to believe that before we arrived on the scene nothing was happening. This is not only natural egotism but also an important incentive which helps us to believe that whatever is happening is due to us! However, in 1985 I sent a questionnaire to a score of the older generation of animal welfarists asking them about their memories of previous decades. A strong consensus emerged from this exercise to the effect that the animal welfare movement in Europe had been fairly moribund since the end of the Second World War and until its British revival in the early 1970s. Good people had continued throughout this period rescuing dogs and cats but in the 1970s the character of the movement changed in several ways. Firstly, it gained intellectual respectability with the various publications of the informal Oxford Group.[2] Secondly, it changed its image from being middle class, female and elderly into being classless and youthful. Thirdly, it started to campaign actively, using direct action and publicity. Fourthly, it concentrated upon the institutionalised cruelties such as factory farming, wildlife exploitation and animal experimentation rather than upon the treatment of domestic pets. Finally, it became increasingly political.

It should not be overlooked that there had been revivals before. In 1776 Dr Johnson had remarked that there was 'much talk of the misery which we cause the brute creation' and there were a number of important publications at this time (Ryder, 1989, pp. 59–80). This flowering of intellectual concern had preceded the first parliamentary legislation in this field of 1822 and the foundation of the future RSPCA in 1824. In the 1870s there were another 40 years of revival, focusing initially upon anti-vivisection, and culminating first in the passage of the Cruelty to Animals Act in 1876 and finally with the Protection of Animals Act in 1911. All these campaigns could be called 'political' but, with the exception of some of the protests centred on the Brown Dog Affair (1903–10), they involved only a politicised middle and upper class minority. The revival of the 1960s and 1970s, on the other hand, permeated virtually the whole of British society.

Wars have tended to put an end to reform campaigns and, after both World Wars, the movement had slumped. Yet, despite a relative lack of media interest and the absence of mass protest following 1945, four official enquiries were instituted: the Scott-Henderson enquiry into bloodsports (1951), the Balfour enquiry into live exports (1957), the Brambell enquiry into modern farming (1965) and the Littlewood enquiry into animal experimentation (1965). All four were set up largely at the instigation of influential individuals who felt a genuine concern (see, in particular, Harrison, 1964). All four produced careful research but very moderate recommendations for change.

And all failed to ignite decisive government reforms. In the opinion of some later campaigners these enquiries served one purpose only – to take the heat off government.

The outstanding efforts of Muriel Lady Dowding in establishing the organisation Beauty Without Cruelty and in reviving the National Anti-Vivisection Society (NAVS) also took place in the 1960s. For some years the NAVS had been lobbying Parliament in order to amend or scrap the Cruelty to Animals Act of 1876. Like the League Against Cruel Sports (LACS), which attempted to outlaw hare coursing and other cruel sports at this time, they did so by lobbying backbench MPs. The favoured technique was to persuade sympathetic MPs to introduce Private Members Bills – which they did on several occasions. The RSPCA, believing that its charitable status was at risk if it lobbied, and preoccupied as it then was with largely parochial issues, did little in the political field from about 1940 until the mid 1970s.

Outstanding MPs of this early period included Rafton Pounder, Kenneth Lomas, Bill Price, Sir Bernard Braine, Arthur Latham, Marcus Lipton, Ivor Stanbrook, Hugh Jenkins and Richard Body. Later came Janet Fookes, Alan Clark, Robin Corbett, Peter Bottomley, Ron Davies, Elliot Morley, Simon Hughes, Roger Gale, Andrew Bowden, Teddy Taylor, Steve Norris, Tony Banks and many others. Sir Richard Body went on to be the Parliamentarian chiefly responsible in 1990 for obtaining the government's agreement to phase out the use of veal crates and sow stalls and tethers.[3]

It is worth noting that these MPs, all prominent as animal welfare campaigners, cover the whole political spectrum. The same all-party situation has applied in the Lords where leading supporters have included the Earl of Selkirk, Lord Houghton, Viscount Massereene and Ferrard, Baroness Wharton and Lord (Ted) Willis.

The Political Revival of the 1970s and 1980s

It was at a dinner held by the NAVS in Westminster in 1972 that I first met the redoubtable Douglas Houghton. He was by far the biggest 'catch' of the NAVS as he was at the time Chairman of the Parliamentary Labour Party and a recent Cabinet Minister. Although he had held no post in Government which was directly responsible for animal matters (such as in the Home Office or the Ministry of Agriculture), he had indicated an interest in the subject and had accepted the NAVS's invitation. For some reason I was seated next to him at dinner and used the opportunity to pour out my ideas as to why animal welfare was an important moral issue which politicians should address more seriously. A few months later he retired from the House of Commons and joined me as a member of the RSPCA's brand new Animal Experimentation Committee. In 1974 he became a Life Peer and, together with Clive Hollands and myself, began to break entirely new ground in the development of animal welfare as a political subject (Hollands, 1980). Houghton's main achievement at this time was to deflect our attentions away from backbench MPs and onto the Government itself. An analysis of the Parliamentary record will show how few Private Members Bills ever reach the statute book and our own attempts to legislate in this way in the early 1970s had, quite typically, failed. Houghton taught us that, in the United Kingdom, it is *governments* which introduce legislation and that without government support no Bill is likely to succeed. Moreover, Houghton managed to effect several meetings with old colleagues who were again in office after the Labour election victories of 1974.

The first Ministerial meeting to discuss amendments to the Cruelty to Animals Act 1876 was, however, rather a disaster. Such was the high respect for science and medicine at the time that a deputation consisting of Lord Houghton, Lord Platt (a previous President of the Royal College of Physicians), Clive Hollands, Dr Kit Pedler, Bill Jordan and myself was received very frostily indeed by the Home Office Minister, Dr Shirley Summerskill in 1976. We were made to feel as if we were subversives. Houghton and Platt were furious at this reception and said so. The next four meetings of this sort were upgraded to the level of Secretary of State – three with Merlyn Rees and one, after the Conservative victory of 1979, with William Whitelaw. All these were amicable and led, eventually, to the replacement of the 1876 Act with the Animals (Scientific Procedures) Act of 1986. This did not meet all our demands and, although I felt strongly at the time that greater efforts should have been made to press for these, David Mellor, as Parliamentary Under Secretary of State, introduced a law that has, on balance, turned out to be an improvement.

Several points can be learned from the campaign to reform the animal experimentation law between 1969 and 1986. At least three ingredients were required for success: a high level of public concern, a well argued case and direct contact with Ministers. I will consider each in further detail.

Public Concern

Public awareness over animal experimentation was at a fairly low level in the 1960s and the media carried few stories on the subject. The conventional view was that all experiments were for valid and important medical research and involved little suffering. However, my experiences in psychology laboratories in Britain and America had taught me otherwise and, from 1969,

I set about trying to re-educate the British public. I was fortunate that the eventual publication of my book *Victims of Science* in 1975 achieved an extraordinarily high level of publicity. Before the end of the year the book had not only been reviewed by periodicals (such as the *New Scientist*, the *Spectator*, the *New Statesman* and *The Economist*) and the serious daily papers but had also been featured in most of the tabloid press and on some 12 nationwide radio and television shows. Why did the book achieve so much attention? Partly because it was the first serious scientific critique of the status quo and it made what the media like to describe as 'revelations' by an insider of what was going on behind locked doors. To this extent it was something new. But it also coincided with a tabloid story about the ICI Smoking Beagles which I had helped to set up with reporters from the *Sunday People* (26 January 1975). The beagles had been forced by ICI to smoke tobacco substitute in a series of experiments, and photographs of this caused a major stir. The two publications, one rather sensational and the other sober, complemented each other, and the issue rapidly became a national controversy. One important by-product was that the media rediscovered that their readers were extremely receptive to stories of this sort. In consequence, newspapers and television quite suddenly began to adopt a more tolerant attitude towards animal welfare. Previously, reporters had either ignored stories or published them in mocking tones. Despite the activities of the hunt saboteurs the prevailing press stereotype of animal welfarists until the early 1970s remained the Edwardian image of old ladies in hats. However, the new proponents of reform, such as Houghton, Hollands and myself, could hardly be fitted into this stereotype, nor could the growing numbers of young activists.

It sounds strange now but in 1970 it was quite a novel idea to urge animal welfare activists to write letters to Ministers, MPs and the media. This is what we did with increasing vigour throughout the decade with the result that the genuine revival of interest was certainly brought home to the politicians. By the mid 1970s many MPs were saying they received more letters on animal welfare than on any other topic and this has remained the position. During the 1970s, as a result of this pressure from constituents, Parliamentary Questions and Early Day Motions on the topic of animal experimentation escalated, debates were held in Parliament and Ministers became increasingly involved. Several speeches in Parliament at this time referred to the greatly increased public interest in the subject.

A Well Argued Case

Secondly, the case against animal experimentation began to be argued in a manner that was less easy for governments to ignore. Campaigners began to call for reforms rather than for immediate and total abolition. We tried to argue our case logically and with supporting evidence. Several of us were rebels from the scientific and medical communities – initially myself, then Dr Kit Pedler, Lord Platt, Bill Jordan (the RSPCA's Deputy Chief Veterinary Surgeon), Dr Harold Hewitt (a cancer researcher) and Angela Walder (a senior laboratory technician). The RSPCA had established its Animal Experimentation Advisory Committee which was, by 1976, chaired by Pedler (an ophthalmic scientist), and which included in its ranks Dr Elliot Slater, a distinguished psychiatrist. The Committee's secretary was Bill Jordan. Houghton dominated the Committee's political thinking and, in order to shake off the restrictions we experienced as being part of a charity, we established the Committee for the Reform of Animal Experimentation (CRAE) in 1978, composed of almost exactly the same people and with Clive Hollands as secretary. Our scientific and parliamentary gravitas lent new and considerable credibility to the political campaign. The Houghton-Platt Memorandum of 1976 called for reforms in Houghton's characteristic tones of no-nonsense common sense. He spoke as an elder statesman to government ministers who were 10–20 years his junior. My own tone in *Victims of Science* also tried to be objective and scientific and thus, to a very large extent, avoided the standard charges of being emotional or ill-informed. In the response which I sent to hundreds of members of the public who wrote to me in the weeks following publication, I called for five immediate reforms – the complete reform of the Home Office Advisory Committee, strengthening of the Inspectorate, government funding for the development of humane alternatives, increasing information to the public and new legislation including the introduction of licence fees. By 1986 all these, to an extent, had been achieved.

The chief tactical lesson to be learned from all this appears to be that governments are more likely to listen to calls for reform that are (a) moderate, (b) scientific and well reasoned, and (c) argued by experienced and qualified people. Once moderate reforms are achieved, the next steps towards a complete cessation to the abuse of animals can then be taken.

Meetings with Ministers

Our campaign probably would not have achieved the success that it did had we not been able to meet Ministers face to face. In the 1970s this was quite new for the modern animal welfare movement and was due almost entirely to the influence of Houghton. It is never easy to persuade a busy Minister to hold a meeting – especially when, as in the 1970s, it involved a subject that was not yet recognised by the Minister's officials as a usual issue for such high level action and on which they themselves were not particularly well briefed. It is still true that a meeting will rarely be agreed unless there is some advantage in it for the Minister in terms of obtaining good publicity, reducing pressure, or gaining information. As regards publicity, a ministerial meeting gives the media a 'peg' on which to hang their story and, as Ministers usually cannot give reformers everything they demand at a meeting they therefore risk generating bad instead of good publicity – 'Minister refuses to stop cruelty' is the sort of headline no politician needs. Furthermore, by yielding to requests for a meeting Ministers may generate more pressure rather than less; other campaigning groups may get the idea and may also start clamouring for meetings. For these reasons it is more likely that Ministers will agree to meetings if they can be reassured that the resultant publicity and pressure will swing the desired way. The submission of factually accurate and scientifically sound advice is clearly a good tactic and this can be a genuine plus for a Minister. The other possible advantages for a Minister include pleasing Cabinet colleagues, increasing electoral popularity or attracting party donations. Finally, of course, there is the Minister's personal sympathy for the cause and there is little doubt that without this commodity in the cases of both Merlyn Rees and David Mellor little would have been achieved in our case.

By the mid 1970s the increased publicity given to animal experimentation had created a reaction from the scientific establishment. Two organisations based in London, the Research Defence Society (RDS) and Animals in Medical Research Information Centre (AMRIC), became more outspoken in their defence of research. Both emphasised the medical argument that animal experiments are essential for human health. This, in turn, spawned a response from a new generation of animal welfarists who began, in the 1980s, to revive the old counter-argument that not only were such experiments of little scientific value but were actually dangerous to human well-being; they cited examples of drugs which had been found safe in animal tests but which turned out to have occasional although serious side-effects in humans. Furthermore, they argued that the great reductions in infectious diseases (which had been used as an argument to promote animal research in the early years of the century) had in fact been caused not by the development of vaccines based on animal research but by dietary and sanitary improvements (Sharpe, 1988). To every political action there is a reaction.

The Scottish Seals and the Export of Livestock

During the years 1970 to 1986 the revived animal protection movement in Britain was somewhat dominated at the political level by the animal experimentation question. But other issues were also rising on the agenda. Some became chronic issues which dragged on inconclusively year after year (such as the campaign to stop the export of live food animals from the shores of Britain) (Stevenson, 1994) and some were quite abrupt. An example of the latter – and one which stands as a paradigm for successful one-off campaigns – is the Scottish Seals issue of 1978 where Greenpeace confronted the Norwegian sealers in Scotland, thus creating a news story. The International Fund for Animal Welfare (IFAW) placed full-page advertisements in the British national press simply saying 'write to the Prime Minister' and the RSPCA asked for insider meetings with the Government which supplied the Secretary of State for Scotland with a good scientific reason (and a useful face-saver) for calling off the slaughter. James Callaghan, the British Prime Minister, received 17 000 letters in one week – more than had ever been received on any topic before – and eased the way for his Secretary of State's retreat. This successful operation was a model of co-operation between organisations (each doing what it was good at doing), the creation of media interest, the focusing of public outrage upon the Prime Minister and insider negotiations on a scientific basis (Ryder, 1989, pp. 199–200).

The General Election of 1979

Shortly after the conclusion of the Scottish Seals campaign came the general election of 1979. Houghton, Hollands and I formed a new group to prepare for this event. We called it the General Election Co-ordinating Committee for Animal Protection (GECCAP). Its overall aim was, in Houghton's words, to 'put animals into politics' by persuading the main parties to publish animal welfare policies in their election manifestos. Houghton approached the Labour Party, I was charged with approaching the Conservatives and Hollands and myself dealt with the Liberals. As expected, the Conservatives proved the hardest to convince, not least because communications between two of their key figures, William Whitelaw and the Chairman, Lord Thorneycroft, were strained. The upshot, however, was that all three parties did, for the first time, publish some commitments in this field (Ryder, 1989, p. 201). Although the Conservative commitments to animals were not as much as we had hoped for, the Party pledged to 'update' the legislation on live animal experimentation. This led to the Animals (Scientific Procedures) Act of 1986.

The GECCAP campaign also started animal welfare lobbying at Party Conferences which has now become traditional in the UK. These annual get-togethers of the party faithful give pressure groups a chance to distribute their literature, rent stalls promoting their points of view and to hold fringe meetings. Some lobbyists feel this is important. But other than cementing old acquaintances and possibly making some new ones, it is doubtful whether much is really achieved on such occasions. In those parties, however, where policies are determined to an extent by Conference decisions (not the Conservatives) then there certainly is a chance for the party grassroots to influence policy. In other words, party animal welfare groups (such as the Liberal Democrat Animal Protection Group and the Labour Animal Welfare Society) probably have a greater opportunity to achieve something at Conferences than do independent pressure groups.

The year 1979 was not only the year in which animals entered politics in a manifesto sense; it was also the year in which activists were told to lobby their election candidates. They did so in large numbers. Prior to 1979 one would often hear British politicians say – 'I receive scores of letters about animals' and follow this type of comment with a wry smile or a cynical laugh which meant – 'but I don't take them seriously'. After 1979 such sneers were less frequent. Labour politicians, too, had often seemed quite hostile to the idea of animal welfare in the early 1970s, seeing it as a distraction from more important human issues or as a form of middle class (Conservative) sentimentality. In the 1980s the Labour Party began to take the issue more seriously and, by the early 1990s, was challenging the Liberal Democrats as the leaders in this field. The Liberals had begun discussing animal welfare measures at their Conferences in the mid 1970s and this interest culminated in their adoption of a major and comprehensive policy document *A Matter of Conscience* (the production of which was assisted by the Political Animal Lobby (PAL)) at their Harrogate Conference in 1992. Only at Blackpool in 1994 did Labour finally debate the issue at a Conference, passing unanimously a composite motion calling for an enhanced status for animals under the European Treaty, the phasing out of hen batteries over five years, protection for wild mammals against cruelty (including hunting), a maximum journey time of eight hours for animals going to slaughter and a ban on animal cosmetics tests.

Outside Britain

One of the more successful developments of the 1980s was the creation of Eurogroup for Animal Welfare. This derived from my RSPCA initiative in 1978 to set up a European political operation to work for legislative advances in the European Community (Ryder, 1989, p. 198). This was quite far-sighted of the RSPCA Council for, at the time, many British institutions failed entirely to anticipate the Community's relevance. This early action thus assisted in the building of a body of European law on some of the major areas of animal exploitation before the opposition was similarly organised (see chapter 8). Edward Seymour-Rouse, under RSPCA direction, set up Eurogroup as a federal organisation on which was represented the principal established animal welfare organisation from each Member State. Seymour-Rouse created good personal links with members of the European Parliament and with officials of the Commission in Brussels. Little progress was made, however, with the Council of Ministers and this third part of the legislative machinery time and again was allowed to frustrate progress.

It was Brian Davies who definitively put animal welfare on the European political map when, in 1982, IFAW launched a massive letter writing campaign to stop the importation of seal products into the European Community and, under Ian McPhail's direction, lobbied MEPs in Strasbourg. This hugely flattered the neonatal European Parliament as its members at that moment found themselves, more than on any previous occasion, the centre of media attention in their home countries (Ryder, 1989, p. 228). Led largely by British MEPs such as Stanley Johnson, they rose to the occasion, banning baby seal imports in 1983. Those of us who campaigned found MEPs genuinely fired by this experience. They had discovered the value of animal welfare in terms of media attention and electoral popularity in their own constituencies.

The lobbying of the European institutions has continued during the 1990s although a clear distinction has emerged between the northern and southern states, with the former appearing to have better organised pressure groups and governments more inclined to respect the welfare position.

Some Perennial Questions

An interesting question is whether campaigning using high levels of publicity is as effective as quiet behind-the-scenes influence. In the 20 years since the movement went high profile in America, has there been more legislative advance than in the previous 20 years? Doubtfully. There has certainly been increased public awareness of the issues but are the animals significantly better off? Perhaps, if there had *not* been the explosion of public interest, they might have become *worse off* as the commercial and technological aspects of animal exploitation were developed and refined in intensive farming systems, laboratories and elsewhere. It is certainly true that, over time, the easier reforms are achieved first, making it increasingly difficult to achieve further progress. This is especially true in 'lead' countries where trade with less regulated states can act as a drag on progress.

There are several perennial questions which are constantly raised. Is it most effective to press for revolution or reform? To use direct or constitutional action? To hit governments and exploiters with maximum negative publicity or to negotiate quietly? Do groups which have a low public profile tend to have greater 'insider' influence? Fortunately, the animal welfare movement is so unstoppably diverse that it seems that all these options will continue to be in the field simultaneously. Indeed, this is probably the most successful approach. Often the more moderate, the more constitutional and the more discreet actually benefit from the antics of their more extreme colleagues. Without the extremists the moderates might not be admitted to the centres of influence. Occasionally it happens the other way around and, for a while, exploiters and governments have some success in claiming that the extremists have discredited the moderates. But not for long. One may conclude that there should be some tolerance of diversity within any movement which seeks to be effective.

Insiders and Outsiders

Much depends upon the character of the component parts of the movement. An extremely well-known and 'established' body like the RSPCA is widely reported in the media and respected by government. A small shift in position by such an organisation can often be of greater influence than the strident shouts of extremists. Yet both need each other. On the other hand, dedicated individual campaigners can often do more on their own than whole organisations – especially when the latter become bureaucratised or complacent. Some individuals have founded their own groups while others, such as myself in the cases of the RSPCA and BUAV, have struggled to modernise and galvanise existing organisations. Mark Glover of Lynx played a significant role, for example, in the disappearance of fur coats from British streets in the late 1980s. Clare Druce of Chickens Lib helped to put the battery hen on the political map. Virginia McKenna and her son Will Travers did likewise for the elephant. Stefan Ormrod helped to do so for zoos. Penny Lewis for exported British livestock. Richard Body, Peter Roberts, Peter Stevenson and Joyce D'Silva for farm animals generally. And there have been many others, ploughing a narrow furrow, who have achieved exceptional results through publicity and determination; their close political contacts have tended to be with backbenchers rather than with ministers. Others have done good work by being experts, advisers and diplomats, naturally working through consultation rather than confrontation. Although the relationship between the two groups – the dedicated and the professional – has often been embittered, both have played complementary roles in the political process. The dedicated individual has often provided the drive while the professionals have supplied the detail. The former are shakers while the latter are smoothers. The shakers are prepared to defy the tide of events while the smoothers are content to float along with it. Seldom are the shakers allowed insider status by the political establishment, but without them little progress would be made. Only rarely, it seems, are radical drive and insider diplomatic skills combined in the same person. PAL has tried to be both, never evading publicity and yet never seeking it.

The Political Animal Lobby (PAL)

In 1989 Brian Davies discussed with me his idea of setting up a new sort of pressure group: one that would be more direct in its dealings with politicians. The Political Animal Lobby (PAL) was established as a limited company in December 1990 to 'energise greater consideration of animal welfare issues'. Because electoral law in Britain does not allow the funding or promotion of individual party candidates at elections (except with their agents' approval and up to the maximum financial limits imposed by the law), Davies proposed that the new body should raise funds from the public and donate them to the national parties. This proposal was put to some 300 000 IFAW supporters early in 1991 and raised the remarkable sum of £216 000. Davies asked donors to indicate whether they wished their donations to go to a particular named party or whether they wished to give him discretion. The upshot was that in the run-up to the general election of April 1992 I handed over cheques on PAL's behalf totalling £20 000 to the Liberal Democrats, £68 000 to the Conservative Party and £100 000 to the Labour Party. This was breaking new ground and caused some surprise among the politicians; at least one party hesitated before accepting our money. There are, of course, good arguments against allowing parties or individual politicians to accept funds from external sources and for believing that all such funding should come from the state itself. However, we have to deal with the situation as it is. The fact is that parties in Britain, under present arrangements, have to accept outside funding in order to meet their own administrative costs, and for decades they have received donations from a variety of sources including business interests, idealistic as well as self-seeking individuals, and groups campaigning to achieve results for a cause.

In our case we knew that some of our opponents who exploited animals for commercial reasons had been among the largest donors to parties. By making sizeable donations ourselves we considered that we might help somewhat to redress the balance. Furthermore, we raised funds from the public specifically for this purpose. Unlike a company whose board decides to donate to a party with minimal assent from their shareholders, we went to the public and offered them the clear choice – to give or not to give us some money for this purpose. We acted upon two further principles: firstly, to donate fairly to each of the main parties thus avoiding the charge of political bias and secondly, not to attach any strings at all to our donations. In the latter case I felt we were on the horns of an ethical dilemma, considering that we had a duty on one hand not to use a donation to steer a party's policy but, on the other, that we had duties to our supporters and to the animals to spend the money in a way which maximised the benefits for the animals' welfare. The course of action we adopted was to hand over the donations without any accompanying policy pressure of any kind; to wait for a week or two and then to ask for meetings with party leaders. Somehow we had to engage the serious attention of leading politicians. We had to persuade them and their closest advisers to give the subject of animal welfare a few minutes of their undivided attention. We were not asking them to take specific policy decisions but merely to address the issue seriously.

There proved to be little difficulty in gaining this access to the leaders of the opposition parties, Paddy Ashdown and Neil Kinnock. The Conservative Party, however, explaining that it was in a special position as the party of government, at first demurred, offering us merely a meeting with its Chairman, Chris Patten. Eventually, however, we were invited also to meet John Major, the Prime Minister, and were thus – probably – the first animal welfare group to be invited to Downing Street. At all these meetings we decided to demand nothing until the politician asked us what we sought. In the event, all parties did ask us what we wanted. In each case our reply was the same: we wanted animal welfare to be put far higher on the political agenda, for it to be given the serious attention it now merited in view of the obvious public concern, and for this to be reflected in election manifestos. We also suggested that governments should service the subject with improved administrative machinery.

The Machinery of Government

PAL has taken the line that the Government should reorganise its machinery dealing with animal issues in order to provide better forward planning and improved co-ordination between ministries. Instead of asking for an Animal Welfare Minister we suggested an Animal Protection Commission providing an analogous service to that provided by the Health and Safety Commission. It would co-ordinate between ministries, enforce existing legislation, publish reports and advise Government, through a Cabinet Minister, on the need for new legislation. We felt that the proposal for a Commission made better sense than the idea of a special Minister. Clearly no Minister for Animal Welfare would be given Cabinet status unless there were also similarly senior ministers for children and women. And if the Minister was not in the Cabinet he or she would have little power to influence the big Departments which might have strong reasons for wanting to continue the exploitation of farm animals, laboratory animals or wildlife. As several pressure groups were already asking for ministers for their own ends, the Commission proposal seemed altogether more politically sophisticated and more practical.

We pursued the Commission idea with Downing Street, the Cabinet Office and with various Ministers for several years and, although the matter was discussed between officials at MAFF and the Home Office, few obvious changes emerged; except, perhaps, that the administrators began to think about the topic a little more carefully than previously and a few modest improvements were made within the existing machinery. The Home Office operation, for example, was divided into two sections in 1993 (see below).

When 'new' subjects such as environmental protection, women's rights, safety at work or animal welfare begin to climb the ladder of political recognition, they pose certain problems for the bureaucracy. Where to fit them in? What status to give them? In recent decades the tendency has been to set up new QUANGOS, such as permanent commissions, rather than create new government departments. In the case of animal welfare the subject has now spread right across Whitehall and into almost every major Department. The Home Office and MAFF are the most involved, the latter dealing with the welfare of farm animals on farms, in transport and at markets and the former with the basic laws against cruelty (mainly the Protection of Animals Act 1911), animal experimentation under the Animals (Scientific Procedures) Act 1986, the conservation of seals, the dangerous dogs issue, the protection of badgers, horses and captive wildlife. The Department of the Environment is concerned with other aspects of wildlife such as its transportation between countries (for example the Convention on the International Trade in Endangered Species) and with environmental pollution, while the Department of Trade and Industry is concerned with trade in animal products and with the use of animals for some commercial purposes (for example, in cosmetics testing). The 'territorial' Ministries for Scotland, Wales and Northern Ireland also have special animal welfare responsibilities for their own territories. In answer to a Parliamentary Question in 1992 the Prime Minister revealed that the Foreign & Commonwealth Office, too, now recognises a responsibility for animal welfare.

Two Junior Ministers have had a listed responsibility; the Parliamentary Secretary at MAFF was described in 1992 as having responsibility for 'food science, animal health, animal medicines, meat hygiene and animal welfare' along with five other quite different duties, and the Parliamentary Under Secretary of State at the Home Office is listed as being concerned with 'animals' among eight other responsibilities. These labels are surely a strong indication of the low and confused status still given to the subject by Whitehall generally.

Both the Home Office and MAFF each have about 30 staff dealing with animal welfare full time. The Animal Welfare Division of MAFF is headed by a Grade 5 Civil Servant who also supervises the work of the Secretariat of the Farm Animal Welfare Council. At a separate establishment of MAFF the Animal Health and Veterinary Group is headed by a Chief Veterinary Officer who is at the superior Grade 3. At the Home Office, the two animal welfare sections (until 1993 there was only one section) come under E Division (one of some 40 divisions in the Home Office) which also deals with unconnected issues such as equal opportunities and coroners and is headed by a Grade 5. The Chief Inspector under the 1986 Animals (Scientific Procedures) Act is a Grade 4 and so is senior to the head of the Division with which he serves. Nearly all of the Home Office officials concerned with animal welfare are working on the 1986 Act. In practice the regular civil servants appear to have less influence than the 21 Home Office Inspectors.

Public Concern

The MAFF and the Home Office in 1994 reported each receiving an average of about a 1000 letters a week on animal protection and, when a campaign is peaking, this can increase to 3000 a day. MAFF received about half as many letters during the 1980s. Few other political subjects can match this level of public interest. A MORI poll commissioned by the RSPCA in the summer of 1993 revealed that animals were the subject on which MPs, in several years (for example, in 1991), had received most letters from the public. British European MEPs said likewise. In 1992, however, approaches to British MPs about animals (animal welfare and hunting together with dog registration) were slightly exceeded by those concerned with housing. The ratio was housing 73, animal welfare/hunting 60, dog registration 8, environment/pollution 23, inflation 2, health service 50, education 39, nuclear disarmament 4, unemployment 20.

An earlier MORI survey conducted for the RSPCA in 1991 found that 64 per cent of Conservative voters 'thought that animal welfare should be higher up the political agenda', and 74 per cent of Labour voters and 73 per cent of Liberal Democrats thought likewise. Support for various issues varied somewhat between the parties: a ban on experimentation on live animals for testing cosmetics for example, had the support of 93 per cent of

Liberal Democrats, 87 per cent of Labour and 82 per cent of Conservative voters; a ban on the transportation for more than eight hours of live animals for slaughter was supported by 81 per cent of Liberal Democrats, 66 per cent of Conservatives, and 63 per cent of Labour voters; a ban on hunting with hounds was supported by 65 per cent of Liberal Democrats, 64 per cent of Labour and 48 per cent of Conservatives (within two years the support for these reforms increased). About 20 per cent of the electorate can be regarded as floating voters, and the research suggests that over a million of these rated animal welfare as one of their 'top three or four election issues' in 1991.

In January 1995, a NOP opinion survey carried out for IFAW showed that 95 per cent of a representative sample of adults in Britain believed that *all* British wildlife should be protected from deliberate cruelty, 97 per cent wanted snares controlled, 87 per cent considered foxhunting, deerhunting and hare coursing to be cruel, 92 per cent considered it important that their MP supported the McFall Bill (aimed at banning cruelty to wild mammals) and 42 per cent said they were less likely to support their MP at the next general election if their MP did not support the Bill.

In view of these high levels of public interest, Whitehall's arrangements for dealing with the subject appear to be entirely inadequate. The MAFF machinery was set up in the mid 1960s by a sympathetic Permanent Secretary, Sir John Winnifrith, and has not substantially altered since then, although its name evolved from Animal Health Division II to Animal Welfare Division in 1988. The attitude of MAFF officials towards the subject noticeably improved during the 1980s and, in particular, while John Gummer was Minister. Indeed, officials sometimes have been accused by commercial interests of siding with the animal protectionists (*Observer*, 18 December 1994). Partly responsible for the more sympathetic attitudes was the strengthening of the Government Advisory Committee in 1979 as a result of our campaigns and its renaming as the Farm Animal Welfare Council (FAWC).[4]

While British law has become somewhat ossified, attitudes have continued to improve. Although the RSPCA's annual statistics reveal a high level of convictions for cruelty over the years, it is probable that this in part reflects the size and efficiency of the Society's inspectorate. In general, over the last two decades public opposition to the institutionalised cruelties (such as intensive farming, hunting, whaling, sealing and non-medical animal experimentation) has grown considerably. As we have noted, some of the greatest opposition among the British public has been towards cosmetics testing on animals and live food animal exports, with cruelty towards whales, seals and other wildlife following closely, along with hostility towards various forms of factory farming. Fur trapping and bull fighting, too, are extremely unpopular with the British public. Surveys in the 1970s indicated overall population opposition levels to various forms of cruelty ranging from 60–75 per cent, whereas in the 1990s, similar surveys suggest that overall opposition to the same cruelties ranges from 65–85 per cent. Those most opposed to animal cruelty tend to be female, under 40 and middle class. British children showed, in a survey of their interest in all world events (not just environmental), a special concern for animals; their top five concerns in 1993 were found to be the killing of whales, seals and dolphins, hunting and animal testing (*The Sunday Times*, 10 April 1993). Further, surveys commissioned by the LACS reveal that the disapproval of fox hunting in 1992 was also highest among younger age groups, running at 83 per cent for ages 16 to 24, 84 per cent for ages 25 to 34 and 66 per cent for ages 65 and over.

How does this extremely high level of public interest affect voting behaviour? The fact that people often feel emotional about animal welfare suggests that it is an issue that *could* alter voting. Consumer research indicates that just over half of British consumers (51 per cent) say they buy household domestic or toiletry products that have not been tested on animals. One would expect that the greater the emotion in an issue the more likely it is to change habitual behaviour patterns, whether buying or voting. In 1992 hunting became a strong issue, and after the election, psephological analysis revealed that around 200 voters in marginal constituencies had actually shifted their party support as a result of the anti-hunting campaign waged by the LACS and IFAW. None switched to the Conservatives and it is likely that most switched to Labour (the Liberal Democrats' position on hunting became ambiguous at this time). According to MORI, four seats were probably won by Labour on the strength of the party's clear stand against hunting. Some 200 voters in each marginal constituency apparently shifted their party support as a direct result of the anti-hunting advertising campaign run during the election (MORI Memorandum, 21 April 1992). In 1992, even Conservative voters, by a ratio of nearly five to one, indicated their support for a ban on fox hunting with hounds, with six to one opposed to stag hunting.

Europe

With the growing influence of the European Union the power of British Ministers appears to be dwindling as sovereignty is ceded to Brussels and to various supranational bodies. At least the European Union has some semblance of democracy but, as I write, the threat of the World Trade Organisation looms, and far less democratically.

One of the promising aspects of the Intergovernmental Conference at Maastricht in December 1991 was the attachment to the Treaty of European Union of a Declaration on the Protection of Animals. This followed campaigns in Germany and in Britain, the latter involving Peter Roberts, Joyce D'Silva and Peter Stevenson of CIWF, myself and others. The Declaration, which has political rather than legal effect, reads :

> The Conference calls upon the European Parliament, the Council and the Commission, as well as the Member States, when drafting and implementing Community legislation on the common agricultural policy, transport, the internal market and research, to pay full regard to the welfare requirements of animals.

Following Maastricht, the politically-minded UK animal welfare groups – which in practice then meant RSPCA, CIWF, BUAV, IFAW, WSPA and PAL – lobbied against animal welfare becoming decentralised from Brussels and returned to the control of individual states. We considered that such 'subsidiarity' would mean a few short term gains for animals in Britain but a long term disadvantage as the lower standards of Southern Europe began to undermine the rest. In the production of meat, for example, it is theoretically less expensive to produce it cruelly than humanely; this would soon create demands for the lowering of welfare standards from producers in states with high animal welfare regulations when faced with the competition of cheap meat from less animal welfare-minded countries.

This was a campaign we partially won. Although animal welfare was listed by the Edinburgh Summit of December 1992 as a subject fit for subsidiarity, the British Government, among others, agreed not to allow this to happen, and the European Commission eventually complied. The proposed EU legislation on zoos, however, was made a sacrifice to the subsidiarity principle.

Some Failures and Successes

PAL has failed, so far, with its long campaign to persuade the British Government to restructure its machinery dealing with animals, only the Liberal Democrats explicitly agreeing with our proposals. We also failed in our campaign for a regular official progress-audit in animal welfare. At Brian Davies' initiative, the British Government was asked to establish an annual audit and to meet regularly with the representatives of the major animal welfare groups to discuss this. After researching the subject of progress-auditing with Coopers & Lybrand I submitted papers to Downing Street and to the Cabinet Office in 1993, but to no avail. Perhaps the

Government considered there would be no advantage for them in such a system; an audit would only serve to reveal publicly its own failures in this field. Under pressure from states less advanced in animal protection and blocked by the votes of Ministers from such states in the EU, the British Government was finding that progress was hardly possible and Ministers privately told us this, urging us to step up the pressure in the European Union, particularly upon the Southern European countries.

Although PAL has had its failures it has also had some successes. Our request to the parties to increase the animal welfare content in their election manifestos in 1992 resulted in a remarkable result: compared with the contents of 1987 the Liberal Democrats' increased by 44 per cent, the Conservatives' by 405 per cent and Labour's by 533 per cent. Counting the number of words on the subject, although exact, may be a crude way of measuring changes in policy. However, all three parties also made more manifesto promises about animals than at the previous election – Labour made eight, the Liberal Democrats made 11 and the Conservatives (admittedly rather less radical in content) made 12 promises. These can be compared with the number they made in their 1987 manifestos which were respectively one, two and one. So, the total number of manifesto pledges on animal welfare made by the three main parties increased from only 4 in 1987 to 31 in 1992 – an increase of 675 per cent!

Another spectacular but unpublicised success shared by IFAW and PAL occurred over Christmas 1993 when Brian Davies received news of the EU Commission's intention to drop proposed EU legislation relating to the protection of wildlife. At PAL's request John Smith, the then leader of the British Labour Party, wrote a strong letter to fellow socialist Jacques Delors (Commission President) expressing opposition to this proposal and stating the importance he attached to the subject of animal welfare generally. Davies meanwhile mobilised support from two previous Environment Commissioners, Lord Clinton-Davis and Carlo Ripa di Meano, who both travelled to Brussels and expressed their opposition. Davies and I also met with British Environment Minister, John Gummer. Quickly and quietly the offending proposal was shelved.

There are, at any one time, over 70 animal protection issues which are the subject of political campaigning in Britain. Clearly no one person or organisation can keep up the pressure on all these simultaneously. In general, it is better to hit the softer targets first and those where individual animals suffer most seriously. Although dealing with specific issues as they arose (for example dangerous dogs, snaring, the transportation of live food animals, cosmetics testing on animals, whales, seals, eco-labelling, bloodsports, the importation and use of nonhuman primates in research), PAL began, after the 1992 election, to carve out for itself a special niche in being the organisation which handled the structural or systemic problems (Vines, 1994). The machinery of government issue was the first. Then came subsidiarity and progress-auditing. We then helped to revive the question of the legal status of animals under the European Treaty and met regularly with CIWF, RSPCA, Eurogroup and IFAW to discuss amendments to be proposed at the 1996 Intergovernmental Conference so as to create a separate status for live animals, distinguishing them from all other items of trade on the grounds of their painience. The problem of lobbying the Council of Ministers was also considered. Nearer home, and specifically within PAL's United Kingdom ambit, was the question of how the subject was being handled by the British parties. PAL offered to fund party researchers in animal welfare in the three main parties. Two parties accepted this offer and one demurred. Once these researchers were in place we found that the subject began to gain internal credibility, papers from internal party sources often being regarded by politicians as having greater authority than those emanating from an external pressure group. Liaison with the parties consequently improved, and policy positions became better informed and more detailed. PAL asked the parties to list animal welfare as an official subject on their internal documents and to appoint spokespeople. The Labour Party did so, appointing Elliot Morley MP as Party spokesperson on animal welfare with a sympathetic contact within the Shadow Cabinet in the person of Ron Davies MP. The Liberal Democrats followed by appointing Matthew Taylor MP as their animal welfare spokesperson in 1994.

PAL also helped financially and technically with the research and production of party leaflets on animal welfare (Liberal Democratic Party, 1992; Labour Party, 1992; Conservative Political Centre, 1994). These leaflets were found to be extremely popular with party members, and that produced by the Conservatives for the European Parliamentary Election in 1994 included an introduction written by Prime Minister John Major in which he acknowledged one of PAL's main claims that 'animal welfare is no longer a fringe issue'. Always careful to make even-handed offers to the three main parties, PAL also helped to finance the meetings of the party grassroots animal welfare bodies and to assist in any way it could to enhance the standing of these bodies (the Liberal Animal Welfare Group had been set up by Basil Goldstone in 1980, the Labour Animal Welfare Society by Wally Burley and Alison Chapman in 1992 and the Conservative group by Roger Gale in 1995). PAL had a hand in establishing the last two.

Most recently, PAL has concerned itself with the threat to animal protection legislation posed by the GATT World Trade Organisation (WTO), alerting politicians to this problem and helping to arrange meetings with MPs and

MEPs to discuss this. I had been made aware of this threat by Professor Tim Laing whose main interest was in food safety. At my invitation he addressed the Scientific, Technical and Academic Committee of the RSPCA in February 1994 and Stuart Harrop, the Society's Director of Legal Affairs, was consequently put in charge of the Society's GATT team. Wearing my PAL hat I had attended the GATT Conference on Trade and the Environment held in Geneva in June and there had met US lawyer Leesteffy Jenkins who had confirmed the WTO danger to animal protection laws. Unable to rouse other bodies to action PAL warned all British MEPs. Elements in the environmental organisation GLOBE had succeeded in persuading GATT to take on board the threat to environmental law but, sadly, had excluded the animal welfare organisations. At the instigation of Cindy Milburn of the World Society for the Protection of Animals (WSPA) we set about trying to remedy the situation. We hurriedly set up a coalition entitled GATT Animal Protection (GAP) and the employment of Chris Fisher was jointly funded by IFAW, RSPCA and WSPA. GAP succeeded in drawing the attention of the EU Commission and MEPs to the new WTO threat. PAL secured a meeting with Pauline Green MEP, the leader of the Socialist group in the European Parliament (EP) and IFAW arranged contacts with Lord Plumb and Commissioner Leon Brittan. We found the European politicians strangely unaware of the implications of the WTO as regards EU sovereignty. Jan Creamer, the Director of the National Anti-Vivisection Society (NAVS) asked members to write letters to the British Government. When the European Parliament finally gave its assent to the new WTO in December 1994, Commissioner Brittan pronounced a public undertaking that animal protection would be included in the WTO's considerations. We had achieved a little but, as so often happens, it was a question of too little and too late. The alarm bells, which should have sounded several years earlier, had failed to go off.

The Live Exports Debate 1994–5

Chronic issues can make sudden advances after years of stagnation. In the summer of 1994 the media turned its attention again to the transportation of live animals and, using televised images obtained by the RSPCA and Compassion in World Farming (CIWF), animal welfare groups (including PAL and IFAW) succeeded in persuading the main ferry companies to stop the carriage of live food animals across the English Channel. Campaigning against this trade had been continuous since the early 1970s and had reached a high level of interest in 1978. Little had been achieved other than a temporary ban. But in 1994, public opinion, directed at the ferry companies at a time when two ferry disasters and the opening of the Channel Tunnel made them vulnerable to loss of customers, was finally successful. This campaign worked because it proved possible to remobilise media interest during the summer months when other political news was, as usual, at a low ebb.

The live exports issue and the legislative attempt by John McFall MP to protect wild animals from cruelty continued to raise animal rights to a new high on the political and media agendas early in 1995. No less than five MPs in the top 20 ballot chose to introduce Private Members Bills on animal welfare topics. Both the Prime Minister and the Foreign Secretary were obliged to make statements (*Daily Express*, 29 January 1995; *Financial Times*, 18 January 1995). The year began to resemble 1975. The media interest provoked ordinary citizens to take to the streets and to join peaceful protests at ports and airports. In turn, these demonstrations maintained media coverage. This largely self-sustaining cycle was energised by occasional episodes of violence: the breaking of a transporter lorry's windscreen at Shoreham, for example; the far more serious violence exercised by riot police upon respectable middle-class demonstrators; and the tragic death of a protester, Jill Phipps, who was crushed to death by a lorry carrying calves outside Coventry airport (*Daily Telegraph*, 2 February 1995; *Independent*, 3 February 1995). Initially, the media angle was to assert that the protesters were 'rent-a-crowd' extremists and the *Spectator* went as far as to equate them with the IRA (*The Times*, 19 January 1995). But truth eventually overcame fantasy and the press, for a while, abandoned the terrorism theme. Those who had instigated the revived campaign in 1994 – Mark Glover of Respect for Animals, CIWF, three celebrities (Joanna Lumley, Carla Lane and Celia Hammond) and, above all, the investigative journalist Penny Lewis – had the satisfaction of seeing local communities spontaneously take over the business of campaigning. Protesters seemed to consist of a complete cross-section of society, with the middle classes well represented. Towards the end of January, French, Dutch and Belgian activists began to stage sympathetic protests in Belgium and elsewhere (Helm, 1995) and support came from the German Government (Brown, 1995).

While ports were forced to cease the trade, not least due to the escalating costs of policing, the Government itself, unwilling to upset vested interests, refused to use Article 36 of the Treaty of Rome to stop the exports entirely. A significant analysis by the *Guardian* (Erlichman, Vidal & Keeble, 1995) precipitated some further media curiosity into why the Government had failed to take seriously the public interest in animal welfare generally. This was a point echoed by the eight Conservative 'Euro rebels' – a group which included two well known animal sympathisers – Sir Richard Body and Sir

Teddy Taylor – who used it as a stick with which to attack the European Union. These were not the only right-wingers involved; Alan Clark, too, was revealed as an eloquent advocate of reform (*The Times*, 12 January 1995). The Labour Party issued a strong statement calling for a total ban on live exports and their spokesperson, Elliot Morley, argued the case in Parliament. Paul Tyler, the Liberal Democrat MP, however, appeared to side with the dairy industry.

In British media terms, live exports in 1994–5 reached an all-time high for any animal welfare issue. The previous peak had been in 1975 over animal experimentation. Seal issues had reached somewhat lower peaks in 1978 (Scottish seals), and in 1982–3 (the EC ban on seal pup imports). Television and radio, although more superficial and capricious than in the 1970s, were generally sympathetic to the animals. Reporters seemed more sensational- istic and less serious than in the 1970s and, although constantly looking for new angles rather than answers, they nevertheless gave the subject an enhanced status. Editorials, too, began to recognise the political importance of the subject (see *The Economist*, 21 January 1995).

Under this pressure, the British Government pleaded that the EU prevented them from stopping the trade and several Conservative MPs read out parts of encyclopedias and a telephone directory in order to talk out a Private Members Bill to stop veal calf exports introduced by Labour MP Eric Martlew on 3 February.

Those of us caught up in the media excitement were often confronted with the same questions and it is worth considering the replies to them which can be made. Why is it only the British who care about animals? Answer: this is not true – the Germans, Austrians, Swedes, Danes and, to an extent, the Dutch, have laws which are, in some respects, better than ours and they show tremendous concern for animals. Why do people demonstrate in the streets for animals but not on behalf of cruelly treated children and other humans? Answer: the cruelties to farm animals are organised and deliberate rather than isolated cases; the law provides protection for children but allows the massive exploitation of nonhumans; cruelties such as rearing veal calves in crates and then killing them are even greater and starker than most cruelties towards humans in our society; animals cannot speak for themselves. Why do the protesters only care about animals and not people? Answer: historically this is not true. William Wilberforce and Thomas Fowell Buxton who stopped the slave trade, also founded the RSPCA; Lord Shaftesbury, possibly the greatest of all social reformers in the nineteenth century, also led the anti- vivisection movement; the RSPCA helped to found the NSPCC. Society is not divided into animal lovers versus those who care for people, but between those who care for all suffering things and those who care only for themselves.

Why does this campaign require so much activism? Answer: because the Government is not listening; it is out of touch with public feeling. Democracy seems to be breaking down. The politicians are marginalising themselves by endlessly arguing obscure points of economics, just as mediaeval theologians used to debate how many angels could stand on the point of a pin. Few people understand or care about such issues. But animal welfare, and environmental protection, are issues which they can understand and about which they feel strongly. Furthermore, many people no longer consider that the difference in species is morally relevant.

William Waldegrave, the British Agricultural Minister, managed to give the impression that while he did very little to stop live exports, he nevertheless sided with the welfarists. He actively encouraged the demonstrations on the continent of Europe which had been instigated by IFAW and, at meetings of the Council of Ministers in Brussels, IFAW protesters were joined by supporters of the RSPCA and CIWF as well as growing numbers of protesters from other countries. On 27 March 1995, some 600 demonstrators in Brussels were addressed by Brigitte Bardot. At this demonstration, for the first time, the German and French speakers far outnumbered the British.

Meanwhile, PAL, IFAW and the RSPCA, co-ordinated by Stanley Johnson, the ex MEP, had sought legal advice, arguing that the UK had powers to stop exports under the 'animal health' and 'public morality' provisions of Article 36 of the Treaty of Rome and that the EU itself, as a signatory, had an obligation to bring its laws into line with the Council of Europe Convention on the Protection of Farm Animals (*Guardian*, 23 March 1995). This view was supported by the legal opinion of Gerald Barling QC published jointly by IFAW and the RSPCA on 30 March (*Daily Telegraph*, 31 March 1995).

Conclusions

Regarded as a rather right wing issue by some socialists in the 1960s, animal welfare was considered definitely left wing by some Conservatives of the Thatcher era. Alan Clark had experienced such an attitude in Mrs Thatcher herself (Clark, 1993, pp. 213–17). Except on the subject of bloodsports, where a vociferous minority of some 60 Conservative MPs have held their party to ransom, there has nevertheless remained an all-party consensus at Westminster typified by the continuation of the All Party Parliamentary Animal Welfare Group which meets monthly in the Palace of Westminster, during the 1990s under the chairmanship of Roger Gale MP (Conservative) with Vice Chairmen from the other parties.

Perhaps because the UK has animal welfare legislation which is highly developed in comparison with that of many other countries it has become harder to effect further improvements, especially at a time when the autonomy of nation states is being undermined by powerful supranational bodies such as OECD, NAFTA, the EU, GATT/WTO and the transnational corporations, and we see consequent pressures to drop standards to the lowest level. In the early 1990s international commercial pressures increased and the tide turned against social issues generally. For these reasons we now find ourselves sometimes being obliged to campaign hard to stay in the same place. Within the field of animal welfare the confrontational relationships between British animal welfare reformers and exploiters, common in the 1970s, have become less noticeable in the 1990s as the younger generations of farmers and scientists have accepted some of the animal protection arguments. The media must take much of the credit for these significant attitude changes. Younger farmers and biologists rarely assert publicly, as once they did, their belief in the right of humans to exploit nonhumans almost without restraint. Such blatant speciesism has become far less obvious among the advocates of exploitation today.

The animal welfare movement, too, has moved. The activists' attitude of almost total hostility towards animal-users has softened, making dialogue possible. For example, PAL's approach has been to meet face to face with politicians, officials and users, rather than to continue the 'megaphone diplomacy' of earlier years. Meeting someone over a meal may well allow animal users and politicians to begin to accept that change is necessary. Liking someone is a way to the mellowing of stereotypes and, eventually, to the changing of attitudes. PAL can claim to be one of the few such groups to have entertained Cabinet Ministers to dinner. The fear that animal welfarists will, by such tactics, compromise their principles, should not deter the civilised approach if it is accepted that changes in farming, scientific and commercial practices usually must come gradually or not at all. Compromises become possible when viewed as progress rather than as a betrayal of a cause. The weapons of public opinion, technical advice and appeals to compassion can seldom instantly overcome the powerful financial facts of life. Gradual change, with firm dates for the phasing out of unacceptable practices agreed well in advance so that major capital expenditure for new farming and laboratory equipment can come at a natural pace (allowing, for example, for old equipment to run down and be discarded), is a far better way to secure lasting change than demanding immediate and too costly bans. The latter can stiffen resistance. Changing over as wide a geographical area as possible is also highly desirable. Legislation on a Europe-wide basis rather than on the level of individual countries, will prevent, for example, one country's farmers resisting improvements because they feel unfairly handicapped as regards their competitors in other states who are less constrained by welfare standards. The acceptance of the need to secure changes on such planned schedules, and on as wide a geographical basis as practicable, becomes increasingly important as the world enters an era of relative free trade.

Animal rights, along with environmental protection, diet and aspects of human rights, are late-twentieth-century concerns which have not yet reached their deserved priority on the political agenda. The subject means a great deal to the electors and the body politic needs to wake up to this. For many voters animals are a far more stirring matter than are important but dull aspects of the economy. This new agenda needs political recognition. Speciesism needs to be acknowledged as being as serious a subject as racism or sexism. Britain may have led the world in interest in animal welfare but British governments have also led the world in resistance to change. It was perhaps hardly a surprise that a survey in 1995 showed that 68 per cent of the British public considered that it was acceptable to break the law on such issues (*Daily Telegraph*, 3 June 1995).

I believe that the human feeling of compassion for the suffering of other painient creatures, once these sufferings have been revealed, is almost universal, and that we are witnessing this compassion being gradually converted into a greater recognition of the rights of nonhuman animals at the political and legislative levels.

NOTES

1. The programme was 'The Lion's Share' shown on Scottish Television in December 1969. Brigid Brophy published her article 'The Rights of Animals' in *The Sunday Times*, 10 October 1965. Her importance as a pioneer of the modern movement cannot easily be overestimated. Disablement, sadly, ended her ability to campaign actively.
2. My own leaflet on speciesism was published in Oxford in 1970 and I mention this concept in my contribution to Godlovitch, Godlovitch and Harris (1973). Other outstanding Oxford authors in this field at this time were Stephen Clark, Andrew Linzey and, a little later, Peter Singer.
3. The Welfare of Calves regulations came into force in 1990 and in 1991 the British Government introduced regulations requiring the phasing out of all sow stalls and tethers by 1999. Much credit goes to CIWF for this latter advance.
4. I owe this information to officials within government departments and to Sir Richard Body MP.

10 Utopian Visions and Pragmatic Politics: Challenging the Foundations of Speciesism and Misothery[1]
Kim Stallwood

Americans share their homes and, in many cases, their lives with 57 million cats, 52.5 million dogs, 45 million fish, 12 million caged birds, and untold numbers of hamsters, gerbils, snakes, guinea pigs, iguanas, and other assorted animals. In 1993 Americans spent $2.9 billion on pet supplies and accessories (Packaged Facts, 1994). Yet despite this devotion to companion animals, their frequent mistreatment in their homes and the relentless exploitation of animals in commercial enterprises – not to mention people's willingness to feed on some species while fawning over others – reveals an ambivalence in America's attitude toward animals. Thus, the American Humane Association (1992) reports that roughly 12 million unwanted cats and dogs are euthanized annually. According to various government and industry sources, 93 million pigs were slaughtered for consumption in the United States in 1993, as were 33.3 million steers, heifers, calves, and dairy and beef cows; 5.2 million sheep and lambs; and 7 billion chickens. An additional 20 million animals, by conservative estimate, are sacrificed annually in research laboratories (Stephens, 1994). Moreover, countless other animals suffer and die in zoos and roadside animal displays, in the hunting fields, circuses, rodeos, classrooms, marine mammal exhibitions, various forms of 'entertainment', and in a myriad of other uses. Even 'purebred' dogs, arguably the apotheosis of America's fascination with animals, are subject to more than 300 genetically transmitted abnormalities.

The enormous number of animals consumed or sacrificed annually taxes the ability of the mind to attach meaning to strings of zeros. Nor is it easy to comprehend the enormity of the suffering and cruelty that the individual animals represented by those numbers are forced to endure. What is equally astonishing is humankind's seemingly unlimited creativity in devising ever different ways to exploit animals, an ingenuity matched only by the human ability to implement those ideas. That proficiency was depicted by Isaac Bashevis Singer, who wrote: 'All other creatures were created merely to provide [man] with food, pelts, to be tormented, exterminated. In relation to [animals], all people are Nazis; for the animals it is an eternal Treblinka' (quoted in Wynne-Tyson, 1985).

Those with a financial interest in the commercial exploitation of animals avoid acknowledging – or else they rigorously deny – that cruelty to animals occurs. What's more, they attempt to scare others into believing that people are more healthy for eating animals and that cures for diseases can be discovered only through animal-based research. This is the politics of animal exploitation as practiced by the animal-abuse industry. It is a transparent policy, as British author and animal rights advocate Brigid Brophy noted in *Unlived Life – a Manifesto Against Factory Farming*: 'Whenever people say "We mustn't be sentimental", you can take it they are about to do something cruel. And if they add "We must be realistic", they mean they are going to make money out of it' (see Wynne-Tyson, 1985, pp. 26–30). Brophy maintains that the same rationalizations were employed by generations of slave traders, ruthless industrialists, and contractors who found that the most economical method of cleaning a chimney was to force a small child to climb it. This ideology is 'passed on, like an heirloom', from factory farmers and others whose livelihood depends on 'livestock'.

Because of our species' relentless domination of them, most animals lead a life unworthy of life. Rendered in German as lebensunwerts Leben, a life unworthy of life was Nazi Germany's philosophy toward Jews, gays, and others not considered worthy of membership in the master race (Lifton, 1986, p. 25). With few exceptions today members of our species practice a philosophy of lebensunwerts Leben toward animals.

The dominant culture's attitude toward animals also is similar to the attitude toward women described by Simone de Beauvoir in *The Second Sex* (1983). Nonhuman animals are the 'Other'. They are other than humans, nonhumans, things, no-things, or, simply, nothing. Nonhuman animals are thoroughly objectified – even down to the way they commonly are referred to in the abstract as 'it' rather than 'he' or 'she'. They are reduced to the status of economic units of production, sources of entertainment or adornment, or objects to be manipulated for human ends.

The basis for this domination is the social construction of speciesism, which is based on the assumed superiority of Homo sapiens and which segregates nonhuman from human animals. This segregation, in turn, licenses a hatred of animals. Animal activist Jim Mason, writing in *An Unnatural Order* (1993), calls that hatred *misothery* and explains that it gives humans license to exempt the labor of nonhuman animals from moral consideration. Consequently, in every human society, whether communist, capitalist, or developing world, the labor of nonhuman animals is used without any moral consideration to provide services and to produce commodities for human consumption.

The foundation for speciesism is reflected not only in the personal value systems of individuals but also in the values of the society they have constructed: a patriarchal, capitalist society whose spirituality is provided by monotheistic religions and materialist science, a society that views animals as property. Therefore, it is just about impossible to avoid in any investigation of the mistreatment of animals the questioning of society's values and the cultural and economic traditions that hide animal suffering from public view. As Gary Francione, professor of law at Rutgers University, makes clear: Property rights in modern society are among the most important of all human rights, and animals are property in the eyes of the law. As he points out (1994):

> Even if [in an effort to secure better treatment for animals] we increase the weight attached to animal interests, human property rights cannot be abrogated without a compelling justification; and as long as animals are considered the property of their owners, no animal interest is likely to be regarded as compelling. Nor is any form of animal welfare [legislation] likely to be successful as long as all animal interests may be sacrificed for consequential reasons alone and there are no absolute prohibitions on any form of animal exploitation.

The dominance of speciesism and misothery dictates a two-fold mission for animal advocates: to challenge and to refute the ingrained justifications for speciesism and to expose the sham of misothery as the basis for exploiting animal labor. In addition, animal advocates must effect a social and political revolution that brings about the inclusion of nonhuman animals into the community of equals.

Mobilizing Public Opinion

1995 marked the 20th anniversary of the publication of Peter Singer's *Animal Liberation*. When this book appeared, Gerald Ford was in the White House, *Jaws* was in the movie theaters, and Americans were in the dark regarding the plight of animals; but as a 1993 *Los Angeles Times* survey (25 December 1993) demonstrated, the animal advocacy movement has compiled an impressive list of laurels since Singer's book was published. The movement has wrung pledges from many segments of the cosmetics industry to stop using animals in product testing. The movement has advanced the cause of vegetarianism, an advance that can be measured by the increase in the number of vegetarians and in the number of restaurants that offer vegetarian entrees. The movement has stigmatized the consumption of veal and the wearing of fur, ivory, and exotic leathers. The movement has pushed hunters closer to the social margins, challenged and to some extent reduced the traditional reliance on animals in scientific experiments and educational settings, forced the tuna industry to spare the lives of dolphins and caused many individuals, especially young people, to see the cruelty inherent in circuses, rodeos, zoos, horse racing, dog racing and high school biology labs.

Equally important, the animal advocacy movement has changed the way many Americans perceive animals. Twenty years ago no one would have thought to conduct a public opinion poll to gauge society's attitudes toward animals, but in the *Times* survey 47 per cent of the respondents believed that animals 'are just like humans in all important ways'. For persons between the ages of 18 and 29 this figure rose to 61 per cent.

For all its accomplishments, however, the animal advocacy movement did not march as far during its first 20 years as other movements for social change had marched during theirs. The animal advocacy movement has not effected anywhere near the amount of federal or state legislation promoting its agenda as the women's and the civil rights movements have for theirs. Although Singer, Tom Regan and others have legitimized the moral status of animals as a topic worthy of philosophical discussion, concern for animals has yet to be established as an accepted discipline in the academic catalogue, as women's and African-American studies have been. There is no animal viewpoint in literature, as there are women's, black, and, increasingly so, gay and lesbian viewpoints. There is no animal rights caucus in Congress with the leverage of the black and women's caucuses. There is no animal advocacy magazine with the circulation and the influence of women's and black publications.

Although cruelty to animals occurs throughout the United States with surprising and disturbing frequency, it generally does not receive media coverage unless it is particularly monstrous. The media tends to focus instead on the cute-animal story (a baby animal born at the local zoo), the dramatic account (an elephant runs amuck at a circus), on situations that pose a risk to human life (California mountain lions preying on joggers), on conflicts of interests between humans and animals or among humans, the environment, and animals (the debate regarding the reauthorization of the Endangered Species Act), or when the exploitation of animals becomes completely invisible (reporting on the latest findings of medical research).

Liberating animals from human tyranny is not a mainstream concept, nor is it an issue that the mainstream media believes to be important and worthy of serious consideration (although the annual Genesis Awards indicate that the mainstream media's serious coverage of animal issues is increasing, albeit slowly). What's more, the media's approach to animal-related news does not represent accurately the complexities of animals' plight in this country. For example, when Tyke the elephant killed her trainer and seriously injured her groom while performing with Circus International in Honolulu, Hawaii, the media failed to investigate the reasons why performing elephants frequently injure and kill trainers as well as circus-goers (*Animals' Agenda*, Vol. 14, 5, 1994, pp. 34–5).

Seeking to counter the lack of media coverage on cruelty-to-animal issues, some animal advocacy organizations discovered that the media became interested in animal causes when celebrities were involved in promoting those causes or when an outrageous stunt was contrived to dramatize a situation. These activities have resulted in a significant increase in coverage in popular-media venues like Music Television (MTV) and on tabloid television news shows such as 'Hard Copy' and 'Entertainment Tonight' and, to a lesser extent, in the mainstream media, that is, *Newsweek* and the *New York Times*. In his noteworthy commentary on the relationship between the Students for a Democratic Society (SDS), the new left, and the mass media, Todd Gitlin, associate professor of sociology and director of the mass communications programme at the University of California, Berkeley, also represented the dynamic between the animal advocacy movement and the media. The SDS, the new left, and the media 'discovered and acted on each other', wrote Gitlin, 'they worked out the terms with which they would recognize and work on the other; they developed a grammar of interaction' (Gitlin, 1980).

The net effect of using celebrities or outrageous stunts to call attention to animal suffering, however, is that the media tends to view the animal advocacy movement narrowly – and to rely upon it exclusively – as a source of limited (and easy) copy involving celebrities or publicity stunts. There may be differing perspectives on whether there is such a thing as bad press, but there is no denying that news stories based on the attraction of celebrities or on an outrageous act tend inevitably to trivialize the issue for which the movement is seeking to gain attention. Often these confrontational and oppositional situations are constructed artificially or exaggerated by the media to make good copy and soundbites. For example, the reintroduction of wolves into Yellowstone National Park was framed by the media as a confrontation featuring wolves and environmentalists on one side and cattle ranchers who would shoot the wolves to protect the sheep produced for meat consumption on the other side.

The media's business is to make, produce, and distribute to consumers a product called news, which is composed of 'media frames'. Gitlin describes media frames as 'persistent patterns of cognition, interpretation, and presentation, of selection, emphasis, and exclusion, by which symbol-handlers routinely organize discourse, whether verbal or visual' (p. 7). Whether a 15-second soundbite or a seven-page cover story in the magazine section of Sunday's *New York Times*, a news frame as constructed by the media presents a complex set of events, situations, and individuals that constitutes a story. News is deployed into column inches or minutes of air space not occupied by advertising. The vehicle of the media itself influences how people receive and interpret the news. For example, CNN's live broadcast of images of starving people in Mogadishu prompted George Bush to send troops to Africa.

The mainstream media also certifies the movement's leaders and then converts them into celebrities. Moreover, the news establishment – in order to satisfy its need for product (news) – defines a movement as good copy when it is flamboyant. This requires the presence of media-certified leaders and celebrities to fit whatever frame the newsmakers have constructed to be 'the story' at a given time. Although people appear to have access to an abundant choice of diverse media, there are only minor degrees of difference in analysis and commentary among the mainstream media. By its very being the mainstream media must reflect the dominant culture's myths, values, symbols, and information. Every media image reflects these biases plus those of the publishers, editors, journalists, and advertisers who construct or influence news reporting.

The independent media, however, offers alternative viewpoints and analysis to those presented by its mainstream counterpart. 'Independent media' includes public radio and television and publications ranging from *Ms.* and the *Utne Reader* to *E MAGAZINE* and *The Animals' Agenda*. These media, which are rich in diversity, challenge mainstream thinking from a number of different perspectives – political, social, economic, and philosophical.

There is much in the independent media with which a person may disagree, but the independent media is an insightful source of information, commentary, and analysis that the mainstream media consistently fails to provide. Furthermore, the independent media is not beholden to the budgets of national advertising campaigns upon which the established media rely. Many of these advertising campaigns are funded by powerful institutions that exploit animals and considerably outspend the animal advocacy movement in public relations campaigns. Because the animal liberation movement's limited resources restrict its efforts to reach a wide audience, activists have no choice but to interest all media in animal protection, to co-opt, as it were, the media's ability to communicate in order to influence public opinion.

During the last 20 years in the United States, the scale and range of actions for animals ensured that animal liberation became newsworthy, but in the process animal advocates implicitly submitted themselves to the rules of newsmaking by conforming to journalistic notions of what constitutes a story, an event, and a protest. As a result, the processed, news-food image of animal activists protesting outside a laboratory became the symbol by which the movement was perceived by the public because most people do not have access to the movement's publications or to the alternative media. Another example of the movement playing by the media's rules is the speak-out on fur. This conflict between animal activists and fur-wearers on city streets, in airport terminals, and other public places provides the necessary ingredients – verbal attacks and the display of graphic posters – to guarantee a successful media frame. That frame comprises confrontation, opposing viewpoints, individual rights of fur wearers versus animal interests, and so on. As a result the public does not receive any image other than the mainstream media's protesters-confront-fur-wearers, pictures-at-eleven minireport. Thus, when the animal advocacy movement is being challenged in the media, what is being opposed is in large part a set of mass-media images.

The media also likes to construct oppositional situations with a protester on one side and a medical doctor on the other. Such confrontations represent the clash between fringe animal advocates dedicated to stopping 'valuable' animal research and medical practitioners who represent the established viewpoint and the authority on the subject.

The perils and the profits of playing by the media's rules were revealed in the *Los Angeles Times* poll mentioned above, wherein 47 per cent of the respondents said that animals 'are just like humans in all important ways'. If this is true, why is membership in the animal rights movement not larger than it is? There are, according to the Census Bureau, 203 452 000 persons 21 years of age or older in the United States. 47 per cent of 203 452 000 is 95.6 million people who believe that animals 'are like humans in all important ways'. There are, according to the generous but self-serving estimates of the movement's opponents, 10 million people who support a variety of animal advocacy organizations (Strand, 1993). Where are the other 85.6 million folks who said that animals 'are just like humans in all important ways'? Why have they not come forward yet to be counted? Why are their voices not yet raised with ours in protest of the treatment of animals?

Is it because people who believe in animal rights do not believe in them strongly enough to accept being viewed by their families, friends, and colleagues as animal rights activists – just as some people who believed in women's rights did not want to be labeled 'bra-burning' feminists in the 1970s? Is it because when push comes to experiment, most people who say that animals are just like us believe, nevertheless, that causing animal suffering is acceptable in the interest of preventing human suffering – as long as the animal suffering occurs within humane guidelines? Is it because some people have been influenced by the media's portrayal of animal rights activists as placard-waving zealots whose neck muscles are permanently bulging in self-righteous, full-throated indignation? Is it because many people do not feel knowledgeable enough about animal issues and, therefore, do not want to expose themselves to being trumped in a discussion with animal-use supporters? Is it because people tell pollsters what they (the people themselves) want to hear? Is it because some people do not find it easy to admit to, much less share, strong emotions about animals for fear of being called wimps, or, Heaven forbid, bunny huggers? Is it because of the perversity of human nature? Is it because some people are unwilling to make a commitment to animal rights because they are unable to adopt a cruelty-free, vegetarian lifestyle? Is it because the stridency and boorishness of some animal rights activists make people uncomfortable about identifying themselves with such behavior?

Groucho Marx is reputed to have said, 'I wouldn't want to belong to any club that would have me as a member'. Could it be that some fledgling animal advocates, looking at an animal rights group roiling with dissension, say to themselves, 'I wouldn't want to belong to any movement that would have those people as members'?

The Challenges of the Animal Advocacy Movement

The task of the animal advocacy movement is to challenge the cultural, political, and scientific assumptions of speciesism through the pursuit of a strategy that balances a utopian vision of animal liberation with a pragmatic political agenda for achieving rights for animals. If successful, this strategy will achieve two goals: The community of [human] equals will be extended to include all nonhuman animals, and nonhuman animals will be accorded under the law the right to life, the protection of individual liberty, and the prohibition of torture.

To meet this goal the animal rights movement must overcome the following seven challenges:

1. to establish unity and professionalism within the animal rights movement by forming a professional association of animal advocacy organizations;
2. to develop a complementary programme of political objectives and public educational campaigns – from the international to the grass-roots levels – that establishes animal advocacy as a legitimate political issue;
3. to demonstrate the connection between human suffering and nonhuman animal exploitation;
4. to oppose unequivocally acts of violence toward humans and animals, even when those acts are committed in the name of animal rights;

5.   to develop a positive relationship with the media;
6.   to promote international cooperation among animal rights groups;
7.   to articulate a vision of a new society that extends the community of
     [human] equals to include all nonhuman animals and to make people
     aware of the practical, everyday actions they can take toward this end.

A Professional Association of Animal Advocacy Organizations

Animal advocates are a diverse group of people with wide-ranging ideas and
convictions about ethics, strategies, tactics, and even animals themselves.
Consequently the animal rights movement has become an eclectic
confederation of local groups, national societies, and unaffiliated individuals.
Cooperation among these elements is not as universal as it should be. Until
it is, the movement is at constant risk of losing the momentum provided by
growing public support for animals and, even worse, of allowing the powerful
vested interests opposing animal rights to define the movement as one driven
by anti-human, anti-scientific zealotry.

    To avoid this fatal conclusion the animal advocacy movement must form
a professional association of national organizations, local groups, and
individuals – the US Federation of Animal Advocacy Organizations
(USFAAO), perhaps – that represents the animal rights movement by
presenting a united voice for animals. The USFAAO would articulate a
clearly defined animal rights mission; it would incorporate a legislative and
public education program that would amplify the voice of the animal rights
movement to the public, the media, and local, state, and federal lawmakers;
it would establish a network for sharing expertise and resources; it would
promote codes of professional conduct and ethics; and it would provide a
framework for mediating disagreements between individual animal rights
groups. Members of this umbrella group would continue to operate as
individual organizations, but by its very existence the USFAAO would
emphasize the unity, and hence the strength, of the animal rights movement.

    Perhaps the USFAAO might grow out of the annual meeting of the Summit
for the Animals attended by leaders of animal rights groups throughout the
United States. Indeed, the progress toward unity that has been made in
recent summit meetings is an example of the progress that needs to be made
in the movement as a whole.

A Programme of Political Objectives and Public Educational Campaigns

The failure of the animal rights movement to establish itself as a strong
lobbying presence in Washington DC is no small hindrance to attaining

movement goals. Holly Hazard and Sara Amundson of the Doris Day Animal League argue that the animal rights movement has to become more directly involved with the political process. They believe that animal rights advocates must become active participants in the political parties to help further the agenda for animal rights. This participation, they suggest, can take the form of standing for elected office within the party, becoming a delegate to party conventions, or standing for public office. They also recommend that the animal rights movement establish its own political action committees at the state and federal levels (Hazard & Amundson, 1994).

Animal advocates in the United States would do well to use the British campaign 'Putting Animals into Politics' as a model (see Ryder in this volume). Started in 1977, this campaign successfully established animal protection as a legitimate political issue. This was accomplished through the formation of the General Election Coordinating Committee for Animal Protection (GECCAP), a committee of representatives from national organizations and individual animal experts. GECCAP founding members included the League Against Cruel Sports (LACS) and Compassion In World Farming (CIWF).

The GECCAP campaign promoted a platform that consisted of a general mission statement, four areas of concern (companion animals, farm animals, laboratory animals, and wildlife), and a list of priorities (the abolition of the battery cage, the banning of all hunting with dogs, and so on). The campaign was based on two simple premises: firstly, political candidates and elected representatives care about votes and campaign contributions; and secondly, political candidates and elected representatives will care about animal rights when they are linked to votes and campaign contributions. Proceeding from these assumptions, the animal rights movement in the UK succeeded in demonstrating a significant fact to the three major political parties: a sufficient number of voters would be influenced by a party's or a candidate's position on animal rights – and by a party's or a candidate's record on animal rights issues.

During the 1979 and the 1983 general elections, the platform of the GECCAP was advanced by committee members who attended the political parties' annual conventions and lobbied for its adoption. GECCAP's approach combined national and local action focused on the same program. This program was nonpartisan, and although its ultimate goals were abolitionist, no positive action for animals was derided – or worse still, rejected – because it was considered unworthy of some philosophically or politically correct theory. As a result, the major political parties accepted animal protection as a legitimate political issue, one that was included in their manifestos for the first time in the 1979 general election. This acceptance came about after GECCAP had convinced politicians that their positions regarding animals could gain or could lose them votes.

In the 18 years since the original election committee was formed, other coalitions have carried on its work and have further established animal protection as a political issue. Thus, veal crates are now banned in England, the single-sow stall will become illegal in 1999, many county and town councils have banned not only hunting with dogs but also circuses with performing animal acts from their land. In addition, the Wild Mammals (Protection) Bill, which will outlaw the hunting of foxes and other wild mammals with packs of dogs, stands a good chance of passage should the Labour party win the next general election.

Politicians' increasing concern with animal rights issues has been matched by – and to a certain extent has contributed to – the public's growing participation in this arena. There has been unprecedented public outrage over – and media coverage of – the protests against the live export of food animals from Britain to the European mainland. People who would never identify themselves as animal rights activists have been joining demonstrations at the ports from which animals are shipped. When the *Independent* discussed the live export of calves and sheep for slaughter in Europe it also editorialized its support for the campaign to outlaw the trade and acknowledged that the 'political discourse has changed ... The new battle is over ethics and morality' (21 January 1995). Moreover, the *Guardian* editorialized that 'Hunting is cruel to animals' and should be outlawed like 'slavery, child prostitution, female circumcision, duelling and bear-baiting' (3 March 1995). The weekly news magazine, *New Statesman & Society* published details of a recent public opinion poll about hunting and other forms of cruelty to animals. The poll's findings revealed that 69 per cent of respondents favored a ban on fox hunting and hare coursing, with 70 per cent agreeing that the Conservative government should support the Wild Mammals (Protection) Bill introduced by John McFall MP (21 April 1995).

The abolition of hunting and the ban on the live export of food animals were part of GECCAP's original campaign in the 1979 general election. There are tremendous obstacles still to be overcome in the campaigns to abolish these inhumane practices, but the tenacity of the animal advocates involved in those campaigns ensures their eventual success.

Political campaigns, of course, will not provide the answers to all challenges animal activists currently face. There is reason to believe, however, that if activists were to launch a coordinated campaign in the United States, the movement would be in a far stronger position to influence the nation's decision-making process than it is today.

Demonstrating the Connection Between Human Suffering and Nonhuman Animal Exploitation

Many nineteenth-century social reformers exposed the link between the exploitation of animals and the social movements of the time, most notably the anti-slavery movement, the suffragette movement, and the campaign for children's welfare. One example of that linkage is the American Humane Association's (AHA) dual commitment to protecting children and animals from 'cruelty, neglect, abuse, and exploitation'. That mission, articulated when AHA was founded in 1877, is reflected today in AHA's efforts to focus attention on violence toward children and animals.

For the animal liberation movement to succeed it must build bridges with those who are disadvantaged by animal suffering. There is a unity of oppression between the workers exploited by the poultry industry and the chickens slaughtered for human consumption, between the workers exploited on the backstretch of every racetrack and the systematic disregard of the welfare of racehorses, between the suffering of animals in the research laboratory and the suffering of people who take drugs that were not as safe as animal tests had certified them to be.

We live in such violent times that the finger on the pulse of the nation is often someone's trigger finger. We should not be surprised, then, that the dominant culture with its make-my-day mentality fails to see the killing and consuming of a chicken for the act of violence it is. It is true, nevertheless, that animal abuse is a human problem. Animals do not cause their own suffering. Humans cause it, and in doing so, they bring down suffering on themselves. We consume animal products to the detriment of our health and the environment, as well as to the detriment of those countries where famine threatens. We waste money on animal-based biomedical research to the detriment of the nation's healthcare. In order to demonstrate the link between animal and human suffering we must build alliances with healthcare reformers to oppose biomedical research and to support increased public-health and disease-prevention measures.

Opposing Acts of Violence Toward Humans and Animals

The animal rights movement is a life-affirming campaign for animals that opposes individual and institutional violence toward them. No one in the movement would deny that animal advocates also oppose violence to humans because, like animals, humans are sentient beings, too. Advocates must be more articulate, however, in their opposition to any acts of violence toward humans and animals, even when those acts are committed in the name of animal rights.

Developing a Positive Relationship With the Media

While not sacrificing our ability to attract popular and mainstream media coverage – and while still acknowledging that confrontational tactics and civil disobedience are legitimate forms of protest – we must increase our capacity for commanding attention from the serious media by presenting a united, professional front to the world. Meeting that challenge will, in large measure, be a natural consequence of meeting the first four challenges facing animal rights advocates: establishing greater unity and professionalism in the movement, making animal advocacy a legitimate political issue, exposing the link between animal exploitation and human suffering, and opposing all violence to living beings.

Promoting International Cooperation Among Animal Rights Groups

As trade agreements and tariffs break down the barriers between nations, the commercial exploitation of animals will become increasingly international in scope. To combat this trend, animal advocacy groups around the world must communicate more frequently, sharing strategies and expertise and raising standards of animal care to match the highest common denominator instead of the lowest. Mexican activists, for example, could seek help in raising standards for tuna fishing to match those of the United States, and the United States, in turn, could seek help in raising its standards regarding the use of growth hormones in milk production. The increasing number of persons with Internet access should facilitate increased cooperation among activists; but we must remember that what we say and do in New York may not always work in Missoula, Montana, or Sydney, Australia.

Articulating a Vision of a New Society

Ken Shapiro (1994), the president of the board of directors of the Animal Rights Network, Inc., which publishes *The Animals' Agenda*, describes animal advocates as 'caring sleuths' – a hybrid of Mother Teresa and Sherlock Holmes. As caring sleuths we see the invisible animal suffering. We not only see it, we also seek it out; and as we seek out the invisible animal suffering, it permeates our lives and influences how we live and what we think. We are outraged that others cannot see what is clearly visible to us. We become the unwelcome guest who points out that the food the host is serving was once a living individual.

During the last 20 years or so the animal rights movement was society's unwelcome guest. Nevertheless, we fought hard to be noticed and to be heard. There is no denying that progress has been made, albeit painfully slow and pitifully meager at times. The good news is that animal rights has arrived and is now being recognized. We have become the vegetarian guest for whom the host must cater. Our next goal is to persuade the host to prepare a vegetarian dinner for all the guests. And then for the host to become vegetarian and, eventually, vegan.

In our one-on-one personal dealings with people we need to gain their respect before they will allow themselves to agree with us. So, too, the animal liberation movement must gain the respect of society before society embraces animal liberation. The movement can make a start with the media that it produces. In newsletters, magazines, flyers, and, indeed, in its activities, the movement must be accurate, honest, and professional. Advocates need to balance their passion and anger – and the compassion they feel for animals – with rational argument, facts, figures and quality investigative reporting.

Conclusion

Countless numbers of animals suffer and die in the United States and throughout the rest of the world each year in order to fulfill human 'needs'. Within the last 20 years, however, a growing movement has emerged dedicated to improving the moral status of animals. Individual organizations and activists have increased public awareness of animal suffering. They have been successful in establishing 'cruelty-free living' and vegetarianism as credible alternatives to a lifestyle based on animal consumption; but the animal advocacy movement has yet to transform this growing support into meaningful legal protection for animals. What's more, the animal advocacy movement faces enormous challenges because any investigation of the mistreatment of animals must involve a questioning of society's values and the cultural and economic traditions that hide animal suffering from public view. There are also powerful economic and political interests that benefit greatly from animal exploitation. From an individual's viewpoint, these challenges are further exacerbated by the seemingly impossible task of helping billions of animals by the mere personal action of adopting a vegetarian and cruelty-free lifestyle.

Not the least of the movement's challenges is finding a way to accommodate the philosophical differences among its members. Ours is a complex movement predicated on different philosophies and different approaches to achieving our goals. The movement sometimes works together but oftentimes does not because each organization has its own set of priorities and methods for achieving its aims. Currently, there is a crisis in leadership at both the local and national levels of the US animal advocacy movement. This crisis manifests itself in the movement's inability to articulate a long-term plan to accomplish specific objectives. Even if it were possible to articulate a long-term strategy, it is quite probable that the movement's leadership crisis would undermine the ability to discuss it because virtually every discussion about the movement's future degenerates into a battle triggered by egos and the desire to protect organizational turf.

Eventually animal advocates must realize that success in the animal advocacy movement is not a question of deciding which is a more effective vehicle for change: a national society or a local organization. They are both essential. Success is not a question of competition between national organizations and grass-roots groups. Each has a responsibility to help the other. Nor is success a question of whether incremental measures that improve the welfare of animals are inimical to the preferred goal of abolition based on the rights of animals. No one has ever proven that a small step obviates a larger one. Success in animal rights is, however, a question of the mind-numbing quantities of individual animals whose suffering cries out to those who hear them. In order to hear those cries more clearly, the animal advocates must reject the artificial constructions and selfishness that divide their movement. They must unite around a long-term strategy that balances our utopian vision with pragmatic politics.

NOTE

1. I would like to recognize Phil Maggitti, copy-editor of *The Animals' Agenda*, for his singularly important contribution to the presentation of my viewpoints contained in this chapter.

Bibliography

Adams, C. (1990) *The Sexual Politics of Meat: A Feminist Vegetarian Critical Theory*, New York: Continuum.

Agriculture Select Committee (1980–1) *Animal Welfare in Poultry, Pig and Veal Calf Production – first report*, London: HC 406.

Alternatives Report (1990) *Statistics on the 3R's*, 2, 2.

Alternatives Report (1992) *Animal Research and Alternatives in the Netherlands*, 4, 5.

American Humane Association (1992) *1992 Shelter Reporting Study*, Englewood, CO.: AHA.

Australian Association for Humane Research (1988) *Exploding a Myth*, Sydney.

Barnes, D. (December 1994) 'The Dangers of Elitism', *Bulletin of the National Anti-Vivisection Society*.

Barrett, P.H. *et al.* (eds) (1987) *Charles Darwin's Notebooks 1836–1846*, Cambridge: Cambridge University Press.

Bentham, J. (1948) *The Principles of Morals and Legislation*, New York: Hafner.

Benton, T. (1993) *Natural Relations: Ecology, Animal Rights and Social Justice*, London: Verso.

Best, C. (1974) 'A Short Essay on the Importance of Dogs in Medical Research', *The Physiologist*, 17, 4, pp. 437–40.

Bethke Elshtain, J. (1990) 'Why Worry About the Animals', *The Progressive*, March, p. 23.

Bliss, M. (1982) *The Discovery of Insulin*, Chicago: University of Chicago Press.

Botting, J.H. (1991a) 'Penicillin: Myth and Fact', *Research Defence Society Newsletter*, June, pp. 8–9.

Botting, J.H. (1991b) 'The Conquest of Polio and the Contribution of Animal Experiments', *Research Defence Society Newsletter*, October, pp. 4–5.

Botting, J.H. (1993a) 'Smallpox and After', *Research Defence Society Newsletter*, July, pp. 5–10.

Botting, J.H. (1993b) 'The Facts about Thalidomide', *Research Defence Society Newsletter*, July, pp. 10–11.

Brown, D. (1995) 'Veal Review is Backed by Germany', the *Daily Telegraph*, 30 January.

Carruthers, P. (1992) *The Animals Issue*, Cambridge: Cambridge University Press.

Clark, A. (1993) *Diaries*, London: Phoenix.

Clarke, P.A.B. & Linzey, A. (1990) *Political Theory and Animal Rights*, London: Pluto Press.

Conservative Political Centre (1994) *Animal Welfare*, London.

de Beauvoir, S. (1983) *The Second Sex*, London: Penguin.

Donnelly, S. & Nolan, K. (eds) (1990) 'Animals, Science and Ethics', *Hastings Center Report*, May, 20, 3.

Elston, M.A. (1994) 'The Anti-Vivisectionist Movement and the Science of Medicine' in J. Gabe, D. Kelleher & G. Williams (eds) *Challenging Medicine*, London: Routledge.

Enders, J.F. Weller, T.H. & Robbins, F.C. (1949) 'Cultivation of the Lansing Strain of Poliomyelitis Virus in Cultures of Various Human Embryonic Tissues', *Science*, 109, pp. 85–7.

Erlichman, J. Vidal, J. & Keeble, J. (1995) 'A New Political Animal is Born', the *Guardian*, 7–8 January.

Everton, A. (1989) 'The Legal Protection of Farm Livestock: Avoidance of "Unnecessary Suffering" or the Positive Promotion of Welfare?' in D.E. Blackman, P.N. Humphreys & P. Todd (eds) *Animal Welfare and the Law*, Cambridge: Cambridge University Press.

Farm Animal Welfare Council (1990) *Report of the Enforcement Working Group.*

Finsen, L. & Finsen, S. (1994) *The Animal Rights Movement in America: From Compassion to Respect*, New York: Twayne.

Francione, G. (1994) 'Animals, Property and Legal Welfarism: "Unnecessary" Suffering and the "Humane" Treatment of Animals', *Rutgers Law Review*, 46.

Francione, G. (1995) *Animals, Property and the Law*, Philadelphia: Temple University Press.

Frey, R. (1980) *Interests and Rights: The Case Against Animals*, Oxford: Clarendon Press.

Frey, R. (1983) *Rights, Killing and Suffering*, Oxford: Blackwell.

Garner, R. (1993a) *Animals. Politics and Morality*, Manchester: Manchester University Press.

Garner, R. (1993b) 'A Strategy for Animal Rights', *The Vegan*, Summer, pp. 7–10.

Garner, R. (1994) 'Wildlife Conservation and the Moral Status of Animals', *Environmental Politics*, 3, 1, pp. 114–29.

Garner, R. (1995) 'The Politics of Animal Protection: A Research Agenda', *Society and Animals*, 3, 1, pp. 43–60.

Garner, R. (1996) *Environmental Politics: An Introduction*, Hemel Hempstead: Harvester Wheatsheaf.

Gilligan, C. (1982) *In a Different Voice*, Cambridge, Mass.: Harvard University Press.

Gitlin, T. (1980) *The Whole World is Watching: Mass Media in the Making and Unmaking of the New Left*, Berkeley: University of California Press.

Godlovitch, S., Godlovitch, R. & Harris, J. (eds) (1973) *Animals, Men and Morals*, New York: Taplinger.

Goodman, D. & Redclift, M. (1991) *Refashioning Nature: Food, Ecology and Culture*, London: Routledge.

Greanville, P. & Moss, D. (1985) 'The Emerging Face of the Movement', *The Animals' Agenda*, 5, March/April.

Harrison, R. (1964) *Animal Machines*, London: Vincent Stuart.

Hazard, H. & Amundson, S. (1994) 'Making Animal Rights a Political Issue', *The Animals' Agenda*, 14, 5, pp. 26–8.

Helm, S. (1995) 'Veal Row Divides Europe', the *Independent*, 30 January.

Hendriksen, C.F.M. (1988) *Laboratory Animals in Vaccine Production and Control: Replacement, Reduction and Refinement*, Dordrecht: Kluwer Academic Publishers.

HMSO (1965a) *Report of the Technical Committee to Enquire into the Welfare of Animals Kept Under Intensive Husbandry Systems* (the Brambell Committee), London: Cmnd. 2836.

HMSO (1965b) *Report of the Departmental Committee on Experiments on Animals* (the Littlewood Committee), London: Cmnd. 2641.

HMSO (1990) *Guidance on the Operation of the Animals (Scientific Procedures) Act 1986*, London: Home Office.

HMSO (1994) *Animal Health 1993: The Report of the Chief Veterinary Officer*, London, MAFF.

Hollands, C. (1980) *Compassion is the Bugler: The Struggle for Animal Rights*, Edinburgh: MacDonald.

Hospers, J. (ed.) (1987) *Monist* (special edition on animal rights), 70.

Jamison, W.V. & Lunch, W.M. (1992) 'Rights of Animals, Perceptions of Science, and Political Activism: Profile of American Animal Rights Activists', *Science, Technology and Human Values*, 17.

Jasper, J. (forthcoming) *The Art of Moral Protest: The Cultural Dimension of Social Movements*, Chicago: University of Chicago Press.

Jasper, J. & Nelkin, D. (1992) *The Animal Rights Crusade: The Growth of a Moral Protest*, New York: The Free Press.

Jasper, J. & Poulsen, J. (1993) 'Fighting Back: Vulnerabilities, Blunders and Countermobilization by the Targets in Three Animal Rights Campaigns', *Sociological Forum*, 8, 4.

Johnson, A. (1991) *Factory Farming*, Oxford: Blackwell.

Kaufman, S.R., Reines, B.P., Casele, H., Lawson, L. & Lurie, J. (1989) 'An Evaluation of Ten Randomly-Chosen Animal Models of Human Disease', *Perspectives on Animal Research*, 1, pp. 1–131.

Labour Party (1992) *Who Cares?*, London.

LaFollette, H. & Shanks, N. (1994) 'Animal Models in Animal Research: Some Epistemological Worries', *Public Affairs Quarterly*, 7, pp. 113–29.

Lawick-Goodall, J. (1971) *In the Shadow of Man*, London: Houghton Mifflin.

Leahy, M.P.T. (1991) *Against Liberation: Putting Animals in Perspective*, London: Routledge.

LeCornu, A. & Rowan, A.N. (1979) 'The Use of Non-Human Primates in the Development and Production of Poliomyelitis Vaccines', *Atla Abstracts*, 7, 1, pp. 10–19.

Liberal Democratic Party (1992) *A Matter of Conscience*, London.

Lifton, R.J. (1986) *The Nazi Doctors*, New York: Basic Books.

Lukes, S. (1985) *Marxism and Morality*, Oxford: Oxford University Press.

Lutherer, L.O. & Simon, M.S. (1992) *Targeted: The Anatomy of an Animal Rights Attack*, Norman: University of Oklahoma Press.

MacDonald, M. (1994) *Caught in the Act: The Feldberg Investigation*, Oxford: Jon Carpenter.

MAFF (1987) *Codes of Recommendations for the Welfare of Livestock: Domestic Fowls*.

MAFF (1991) *Action on Animal Welfare*.

Marsh, D. & Rhodes, R.A.W. (eds) (1992) *Policy Networks in British Government*, Oxford: Clarendon Press.

Marten, M. (1981) 'The Price of the Polio Vaccine', *Lab Animal*, 10, 7, pp. 20–5.

Mason, J. (1993) *An Unnatural Order*, New York: Simon & Schuster.

Mason, J. & Singer, P. (1990) *Animal Factories*, New York: Harmony.

McKeown, T. (1979) *The Role of Medicine*, Oxford: Blackwell.

Mclaughlin, R.M. (1990) 'Animal Rights vs Animal Welfare: Can Animal Use Meet the Needs of Science and Society?' in P.W. Concannon (ed.) *Animal Research,*

Animal Rights, Animal Legislation, Champaign, Ill.: Society for the Study of Reproduction.

Midgley, M. (1983) *Animals and Why They Matter*, Athens, Ga.: University of Georgia Press.

Miller, P. (1967) *The New England Mind*, Cambridge, Mass.: Harvard University Press.

Newkirk, I. (1992) 'Total Victory, Like Checkmate, Cannot Be Achieved in One Move', *The Animals' Agenda*, 12, pp. 43–4.

Norrby, S.R., O'Reilly, T. & Zak, O. (1993) 'Efficacy of Antimicrobial Agent Treatment in Relation to Treatment Regimen: Experimental Models and Clinical Evaluation', *Journal of Antimicrobial Chemotherapy*, 31, pp. 41–54.

Packaged Facts (1994) *The Pet Supplies Market*, New York.

Parliamentary Office of Science and Technology (1992) *The Use of Animals in Research, Development and Testing*.

Paton, W. (1993) *Man and Mouse*, Oxford: Oxford University Press.

Patterson, D. & Ryder, R. (eds) (1979) *Animals' Rights: A Symposium*, Fontwell: Centaur Press.

Paul, J.R. (1971) *History of Poliomyelitis*, New Haven: Yale University Press.

Phillips, M.T. (1993) 'The Researcher's Perception of Pain', *Animals in Society*, 1.

Phillips, M.T. & Sechzer, J.A. (1989) *Animal Research And Ethical Conflict: An Analysis of the Literature 1966–86*, New York: Springer-Verlag.

Regan, T. (1982) *All That Dwell Therein*, Berkeley: University of California Press.

Regan, T. (1983) *The Case for Animal Rights*, London: Routledge.

Regan, T. (1985) 'The Dog in the Lifeboat', *New York Review of Books*, 17 January.

Regan, T. & Francione, G. (1992) 'A Movement's Means Create its Ends', *The Animals' Agenda*, 12, 1, pp. 40–3.

Reines, B. (1990) 'The Relationship Between Laboratory and Clinical Studies in Psychopharmacologic Discovery', *Perspectives on Medical Research*, 2, pp. 13–26.

Reines, B. (undated) *The Truth Behind the Discovery of Insulin*, Jenkintown: The American Anti-Vivisection Society.

Robbins, J. (1987) *Diet for a New America*, Walpole, N.H.: Stillpoint.

Rowan, A.N. (1984) *Of Mice, Models and Men*, Albany: SUNY Press.

Rowan, A.N. (undated) 'Animal Rights versus Animal Welfare: A False Dichotomy?', *The Animal Policy Report*, Tufts University School of Veterinary Medicine, Center for Animals and Public Policy.

Rowan, A.N. (1989) 'Scientists Should Institute and Publicize Programs to Reduce the Use and Abuse of Animals in Research', *Chronicle of Higher Education*, 12 April, pp. B1–B3.

Rowan, A.N. & Loew, F.M. *et al.* (1994) *The Animal Research Controversy: Protest, Process & Public Policy*, North Grafton M.A.: Tufts University School of Veterinary Medicine.

Ryder, R. (1970) *Speciesism*, Oxford, leaflet.

Ryder, R. (1972) *The Extensive Use of Animals in Non Medical Research*, Edinburgh: Scottish Society for the Prevention of Vivisection.

Ryder, R. (1974a) *Speciesism: The Ethics of Vivisection*, Edinburgh: Scottish Society for the Prevention of Vivisection.

Ryder, R. (1974b) *Scientific Cruelty for Commercial Profit*, Edinburgh: Scottish Society for the Prevention of Vivisection.

Ryder, R. (1975) *Victims of Science*, London: Davis-Poynter.

Ryder, R. (1989) *Animal Revolution: Changing Attitudes Towards Speciesism*, Oxford: Basil Blackwell.

Sagan, L.A. (1987) *The Health of Nations: True Causes of Sickness and Well-being*, New York: Basic Books.

Shapiro, K. (1994) 'Towards Kinship: The Caring Sleuth', *The Animals' Agenda*, 14, 1, pp. 44–5.

Sharpe, R. (1988) *The Cruel Deception: The Use of Animals in Medical Research*, Wellingborough: Thorsons.

Sharpe, R. (1993) 'The Polio Files', *The AV Magazine*, 101, 5, pp. 8–13.

Shue, H. (1980) *Basic Rights*, Princeton N.J.: Princeton University Press.

Silverman, P.B. (1994) 'It's the "M" Word. Review of Animal Models in Psychiatry, Volumes I & II', *Contemporary Psychology*, 39, pp. 659–60.

Singer, P. (1975) *Animal Liberation*, London: Jonathon Cape (2nd edn published in 1990).

Singer, P. (1985) 'Ten Years of Animal Liberation', *New York Review of Books*, 17 January.

Singer, P. (1993) *Practical Ethics*, Cambridge: Cambridge University Press.

Smith, J.A. & Boyd, K.M. (eds) (1991) *Lives in the Balance: The Ethics of Using Animals in Biomedical Research*, Oxford: Oxford University Press.

Smith, M.J. (1990) *The Politics of Agricultural Support in Britain: The Development of the Agricultural Policy Community*, Aldershot: Dartmouth.

Spiegel, M. (1988) *The Dreaded Comparison: Humans and Animal Slavery*, New York: Mirror Books.

Steinmetz, P.N. & Tillery, S.I.H. (1994) 'Animal Models: Some Empirical Worries', *Public Affairs Quarterly*, 8, pp. 287–98.

Stephens, M.L. (1994) 'Animal Use in US Labs: A 50% Drop?', *The Animals' Agenda*, 14, 4, pp. 12–13.

Stevenson, P. (1994) *A Far Cry from Noah*, London: Green Print.

Strand, R. & Strand, P. (1993) *The Hijacking of the Humane Movement*, Doral: Wilsonville.

Verhetsel, E. (1986) *They Threaten Your Health*, Tucson: People for the Ethical Treatment of Animals.

Vines, G. (1994) 'Lobby Groups Pile on the Pressure', the *Observer*, 10 July.

Walsh, E.J. (1981) 'Resource Mobilization and Citizen Protest in Communities Around Three Mile Island', *Social Problems*, 29.

Willis, L.R. & Hulsey, M.G. (1994) 'Worries About Animal Models in Biomedical Research: A Response to LaFollette and Shanks', *Public Affairs Quarterly*, 8: pp. 205–18.

Wolfe, A. (1990) 'Social Theory and the Second Biological Revolution', *Social Research*, 57.

Wynne-Tyson, J. (1975) *Food for a Future: The Complete Case for Vegetarianism*, New York: Universe Books.

Wynne-Tyson, J. (ed.) (1985) *The Extended Circle*, Fontwell: Centaur Press.

Index

abortion, 134, 138
AHA, *see* American Humane
    Association
Agriculture (Miscellaneous Provisions)
    Act 1968, 73, 74, 77, 85, 86, 125
Alcohol, Drug Abuse, and Mental
    Health Administration, 43
ALF, *see* Animal Liberation Front
Allen, F., 115–16, 118
Americans for Medical Progress
    (AMP), 43, 59–60
American Humane Association (AHA),
    194, 205
American Society for the Protection of
    Animals, 130
Amnesty International, 134
AMP, *see* Americans for Medical
    Progress
AMRIC, *see* Animals in Medical
    Research Information Centre
Amundson, S., 203
Animal Aid, xiii
animal experimentation, xiii, 12–15,
    44–5, 46, 51, 55–6, 63–5, 76–81
    alternatives to, 110–11
    and the animal protection
        movement, 139, 171–4, 175
    and the European Union, 150–1,
        161–2
    at American Museum of Natural
        History, 132
    cosmetics testing, 135, 139, 182,
        183, 184, 196
    fall in the use of animals, 104,
        110–11
    insulin case study, 114–19
    moral arguments about, 105, 137
    necessity of, 106–11
    policy making, 124–5
    polio case study, 119–22
    primate research, 121, 122, 150, 162
    suffering inflicted, 111–13
Animal Health Act 1981, 74
Animal Legal Defense Fund, 132

Animal Liberation Front (ALF), 133
Animal Procedures Committee (APC),
    64, 77, 79, 80, 125
Animals' Agenda, 133, 140, 199, 206
Animals in Medical Research
    Information Centre (AMRIC),
    174
Animals (Scientific Procedures) Act
    1986, xiii, 61–2, 77–81, 82, 86–7,
    88, 113, 125, 171, 175, 181, 182
Animal Welfare Act, xiii, 5, 45, 46,
    48–9, 58, 125, 139
APC, *see* Animal Procedures
    Committee
argument from marginal cases, 2–3, 11,
    14–15, 25–6, 167
Ashdown, P., 180

Banks, T., 170
Bardot, B., 191
Barnes, D., 45
Bashevis Singer, I., 194
battery cages, 5, 16, 57, 85–6, 90, 176,
    203
Beauty Without Cruelty, 7, 170
Bentham, J., 1, 8–9, 10, 22, 167
Benton, T., xiv, xv, 2–4
Best, C., 115, 118
Bethke Elshtain, J., 135
Bliss, M., 115, 117, 118
Body, R., 170, 178, 189
Bovine Spongiform Encephalopathy
    (BSE), 66, 90, 95
Bowden, A., 170
Brambell Committee, 61, 70–4, 169
British Union for the Abolition of
    Vivisection (BUAV), xiii, 161,
    178, 185
British Veterinary Association (BVA),
    xiii
Brittan, L., 188
Brophy, B., 7, 168, 195
BSE, *see* Bovine Spongiform
    Encephalopathy

BUAV, *see* British Union for the Abolition of Vivisection
Buxton, F., 190
BVA, *see* British Veterinary Association

Callaghan, J., 175
Carruthers, P., 19, 20, 25
Chickens Lib, 178
Clark, A., 170, 190, 191
Coe, S., 135
Committee for the Reform Animal Experimentation (CRAE), xiii, 173
Compassion in World Farming, 74, 75, 162, 185, 187, 188, 189, 191, 203
Conservative Party, 175, 176, 179, 182–3, 184, 186, 187, 191
Convention on International Trade in Endangered Species, 163
Corbett, P., 7
Council of Europe, 156, 157, 191
CRAE, *see* Committee to Reform Animal Experimentation
Crawley, T., 116
Creamer, J., 188
Crossman, R., 126
Cruelty to Animals Act 1876, 77, 80–1, 169, 170, 171

Darwin, C., 21, 25
Davies, B., 177, 179, 185, 186
Davies, R., 187
de Beauvoir, S., 195
Delors, J., 186
Denmark, 144, 157
Department of Health and Human Services, 43
Department of the Environment, 82, 124, 181
Department of Trade and Industry, 181
Descartes, R., 21
Doris Day Animal League, 203
Dowding, M., 7, 170
Druce, C., 178
D'Silva, J., 178, 185
Duffy, M., 7

ECVAM, *see* European Centre for the Validation of Alternative Methods

Einstein, A., 102
elections, xii, 126, 171, 175–6, 179, 183, 184, 203–4
Elston, M.A., 125
enforcement of animal welfare laws, 83–7
environmentalism, 35, 181
and animal rights, xv, 141
and the animal protection movement, 66, 126, 129, 131, 132, 134, 135, 140
and the European Union, 147, 163
environmental effects of factory farming, 20, 66, 93–4, 95, 97, 99
environmental movement, 124, 131, 132, 138, 154
Eurogroup for Animal Welfare, 89, 157–8, 159, 160–1, 162, 163, 176–7, 187
European Centre for the Validation of Alternative Methods (ECVAM), 150, 154
European Federation of Veterinarians (FVE), 162
European Union, 87–9, 127, 143–65, 176–7
and animal experimentation, 161–2
and animal transportation, 74–5, 84–5, 88, 150, 153, 155, 157, 163, 191
and bullfighting, 146
and farm animal welfare, 149, 159, 163, 185
and subsidiarity, 144, 145, 185
and the legal status of animals, 82, 88, 164–5, 176, 185, 187
export of live animals, 19, 67, 74–5, 90, 127, 169, 175, 183, 188–91, 204

factory farming *see also* battery cages, veal calves and sow stalls, xiv, xv, 15–17, 20, 30, 32, 38, 46, 65, 66, 70–2, 92–4, 96, 101, 131
Farm Animal Welfare Council (FAWC), 74, 85, 125, 183
Fascell, D.B., 43
FAWC, *see* Farm Animal Welfare Council

feminism, *see* women
Feminists for Animal Rights, 140
Federal Bureau of Investigation, 130
Feldberg, W., 13, 18, 87
Fischler, F., 149
Fisher, C., 188
Fookes, J., 170
Fox, M., 62, 65–6
FRAME, *see* Fund for the Replacement
    of Animals in Scientific
    Experiments
Francione, G.L., xiii, xiv, 4–6, 62, 196
Frey, R.G., 24,
Fund for the Replacement of Animals
    in Scientific Experiments
    (FRAME), xiii
fur,
    and public opinion, 183
    and the European Union, 148, 153,
        159, 163
    animal suffering in its production,
        17
    campaign against, 7, 46, 138, 178,
        196, 200
    consumers, 135
    decline in sales, xii, 139
    media coverage, 130
FVE, *see* European Federation of
    Veterinarians

Gale, R., 187, 191
GATT, *see* General Agreement on
    Tariffs and Trade
GECCAP, *see* General Election Co-
    ordinating Committee for Animal
    Protection
General Agreement on Tariffs and
    Trade (GATT), 89, 93, 94, 127,
    163, 187–8, 191
General Election Co-ordinating
    Committee for Animal Protection
    (GECCAP), 175–6, 203–4
Gennarelli, T., 133
Germany, 144, 148, 155, 164, 189,
    190, 191
Gilligan, C., 137
Glover, M., 178, 189
Godlovitch, R., 17
Goodall, J., 10

Goodwin, F.K., 43–4
Greece, 127
Green, P., 188
Gummer, J., 183, 186

Hammond, C., 189
Harrison, R., 7, 15, 70
Hazard, H., 203
Hollands, C., 171, 172, 173, 175
Home Office, 62, 64, 78, 80, 82, 87,
    125, 170, 171, 179, 181, 182
Houghton, D., 67, 170–71, 172, 173,
    175
HSUS, *see* Humane Society of the
    United States
Hughes, E., 115–16
Humane Society of the United States
    (HSUS), 101, 162
hunting, 67, 139, 141, 168, 176, 182,
    183, 184, 196, 203, 204

IFAW, *see* International Fund for
    Animal Welfare
International Fund for Animal Welfare
    (IFAW), 124, 161, 162, 175, 177,
    179, 183, 184, 185, 186, 187,
    188, 191
ivory, 131

Jasper, J., 126
Johnson, S., 191
Jordan, B., 171, 173

Kant, E., 23
Kinnock, N., 180

Labour Party, 170, 171, 175, 176, 179,
    182–3, 184, 186, 187, 190
LACS, *see* League Against Cruel
    Sports
Lane, C., 189
League Against Cruel Sports, 170, 184,
    203
Leahy, M.P.T., 18, 25
Lewis, P., 178, 189
Liberal Democratic Party, 176, 179,
    182–3, 184, 185, 186, 187, 190
Liberal Party, 175
Linzey, A.,xi,

Littlewood Report, 169
Locke, J., 47–8, 49
Lukes, S., 33, 36
Lumley, J., 189
Lynx, 178

MAFF, *see* Ministry of Agriculture,
    Fisheries and Food
Major, J., 180, 187
Martin's Act 1822, 69
Martlew, E., 190
Mason, J., 195
Marx, K., 33, 35, 135
McKenna, V., 178
media, 189, 197–201, 204, 206
Mellor, D., 174
Midgley, M., 66, 137–8
Milburn, C., 188
Ministry of Agriculture, Fisheries and
    Food (MAFF), 75, 82, 124, 170,
    181, 182, 183
Minkowski, O., 117
Morley, E., 187, 190

National Anti-Vivisection Society
    (American), 45
National Anti-Vivisection Society
    (British) (NAVS), xiii, 170, 188
National Farmers Union, 124
National Institutes of Health, 139
NAVS, *see* National Anti-Vivisection
    Society
NFU, *see* National Farmers Union
Nelson, L., 7
Netherlands, 144, 158, 190
Newkirk, I., 45

Ormrod, S., 178

Pacheco, A., 132
PAL, *see* Political Animal Lobby
Paton, W., 107
Patten, C., 180
Paul, J.R., 119, 120
Pedler, K., 171, 173
People for the Ethical Treatment of
    Animals, 45, 132, 133
Phipps, J., 189
Plant, R., 168

policy communities, 124–5
Political Animal Lobby (PAL), 124,
    179–80, 185, 186–7, 188, 191,
    192
property status of animals, 4, 5, 47–51,
    56, 57, 58, 62, 68, 69, 81, 196
Protection of Animals Act 1911, 68–9,
    70, 72, 73, 77, 169, 181

Radford, M., 61–2
RDS, *see* Research Defence Society
Rees, M., 171, 174
Regan, T. xi, xiii, xiv, 1–2, 3, 23–6, 27,
    28, 30, 31, 32, 38, 40, 42, 45,
    51–3, 55, 63, 136, 138, 197
Reines, B., 108–9,114–15, 116, 117
Research Defence Society (RDS), 174
Respect for Animals, 189
Roberts, P., 178, 185
Rowan, A., 45, 62, 63–4, 65, 66
Royal Society for the Prevention of
    Cruelty to Animals (RSPCA),
    and Eurogroup, 158, 160, 176, 185,
        187
    and GATT, 188
    and the Animal Experimentation
        Committee, 171, 173
    and the export of live animals, 74,
        191
    and the High Court, 75
    and the Scottish Seals issue, 175
    historical development, 169, 170,
        178, 190
    policing role, 73, 84
Royal Society for the Protection of
    Birds (RSPB), 161
RSPB, *see* Royal Society for the
    Protection of Birds
RSPCA, *see* Royal Society for the
    Prevention of Cruelty to Animals
Ryder, R. xi, 2, 11, 13, 124

Salt, H. 1
Schweitzer, A. 1
sexism, *see* women
Seymour-Rouse, E., 177
Shapiro, K., 206
Sharpe, R., 106, 112, 115
Shue, H., 53–5, 57

Singer, P. xi, 1–2, 3, 21–2, 25, 50, 51,
    64, 111, 131–2, 196, 197
Smith, J., 186
socialism, xiv, 19, 27, 32, 35, 36, 140,
    141, 152, 167
sow stalls, 16, 72, 159, 163, 170, 204
Spain, 127
speciesism, 2, 11, 12, 14, 29, 166, 167,
    193, 196, 201
Spira, H., 64, 132
State Veterinary Service (SVS), 73, 84
Stevenson, P., 178, 185
Summerskill, S., 171
Summit for the Animals, 202
SVS, *see* State Veterinary Service

Taub, E., 132
Taylor, M., 187
Taylor, T., 190
Thatcher, M., 191
Tischler, J., 132
Travers, W., 178
Tyler, P., 190

United States Department of
    Agriculture (USDA), 49, 98, 113,
    129
USDA, *see* United States Department
    of Agriculture
utilitarianism, 22–3, 24, 26, 39, 41, 51,
    166

veal calves, 5, 16, 72, 74, 144, 159,
    163, 170, 190, 204
vegetarianism, xii, 12, 18, 39, 98, 100,
    101, 123, 196, 201, 207
vivisection, *see* animal experimentation

Waldegrave, W., 191
whales, 131, 163, 184, 186
Whitelaw, W., 171, 175
Wilberforce, W., 190
wild animals (*see also*, hunting, ivory
    and whales), 39, 40, 96, 102, 138,
    146, 149, 151, 153, 159, 161,
    162, 175, 183
Wild Mammals (Protection) Act 1996,
    69, 183, 204
Wilkins, D., 161
Wittgenstein, L., 10, 18, 25
women, 2, 8, 55, 140, 181
    and enfranchisment, xv,
    and feminism, xiv, 7, 19, 27, 28, 32,
        36, 129, 131, 132, 138, 141, 200
    and sexism, 14, 18, 132, 140, 192
    and the animal protection
        movement, 133, 134, 140, 169,
        184, 195, 196
World Society for the Protection of
    Animals, 157, 185, 188
World Trade Organization (WTO), 94,
    163, 184, 187–8, 191
WTO, *see* World Trade Organization